RUBÁIYÁT OF

Omar Khayyám

ii
M.Sayah

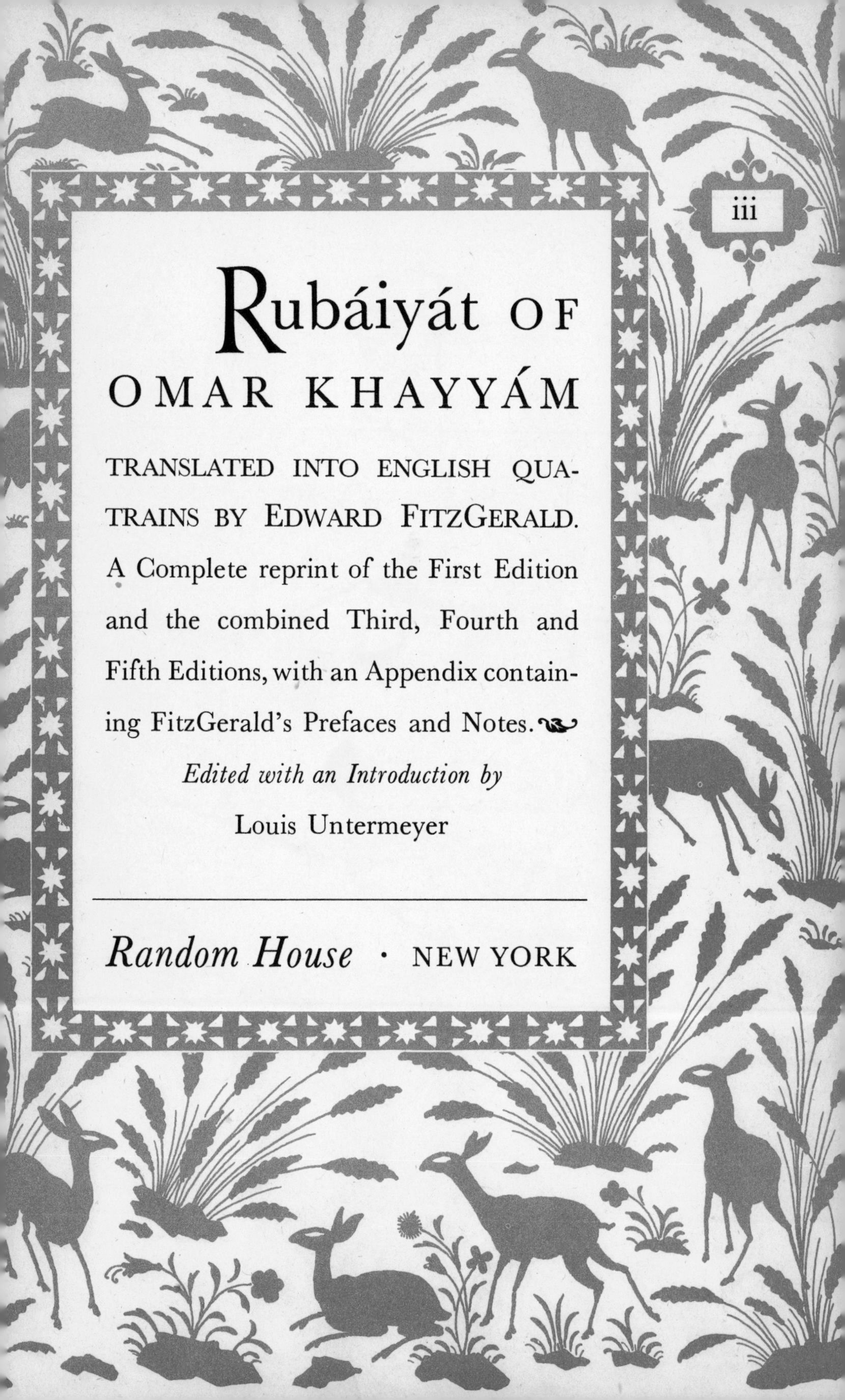

Rubáiyát OF OMAR KHAYYÁM

TRANSLATED INTO ENGLISH QUATRAINS BY EDWARD FITZGERALD. A Complete reprint of the First Edition and the combined Third, Fourth and Fifth Editions, with an Appendix containing FitzGerald's Prefaces and Notes.

Edited with an Introduction by

Louis Untermeyer

Random House · NEW YORK

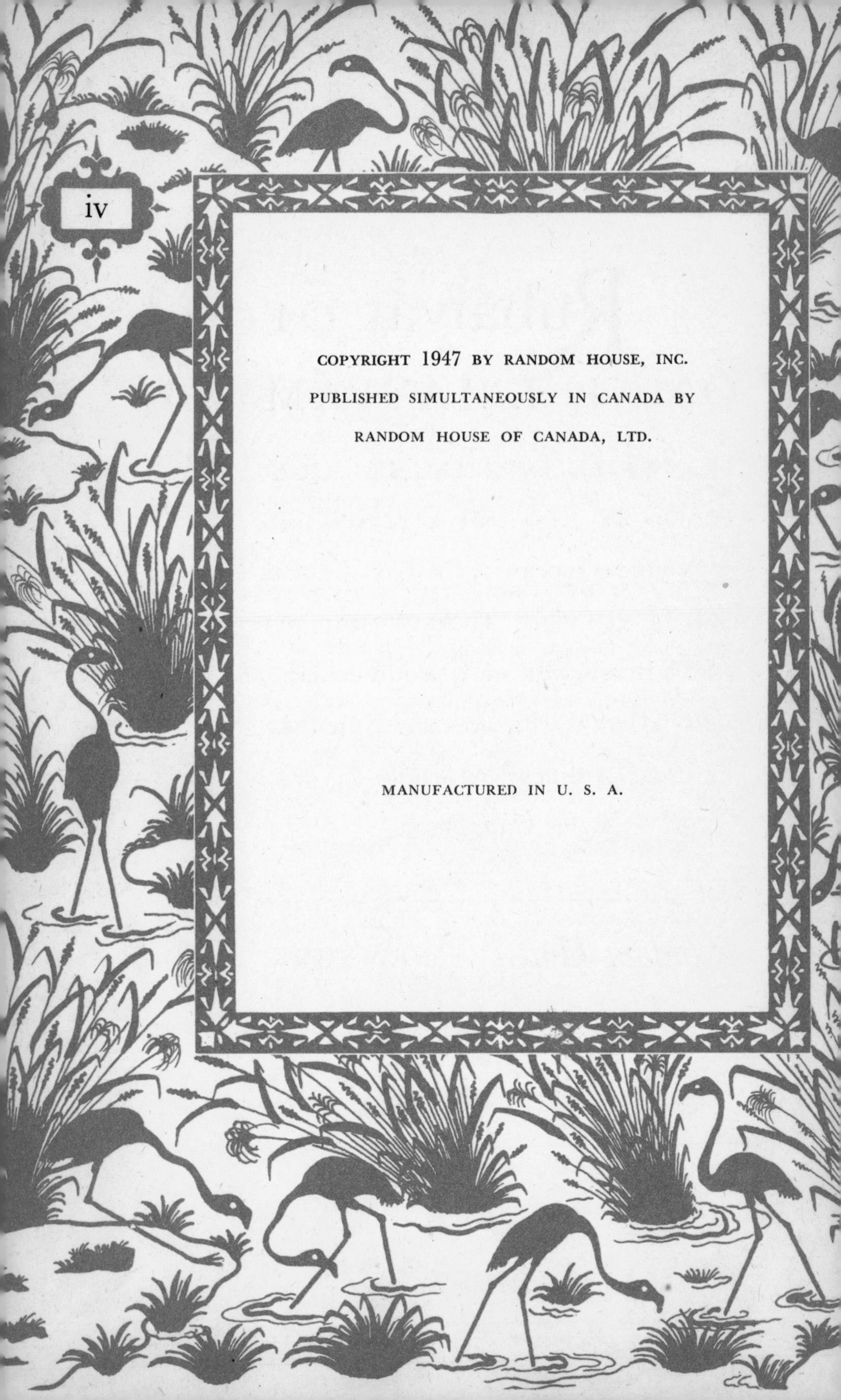

PUBLISHED SIMULTANEOUSLY IN CANADA BY

RANDOM HOUSE OF CANADA, LTD.

MANUFACTURED IN U. S. A.

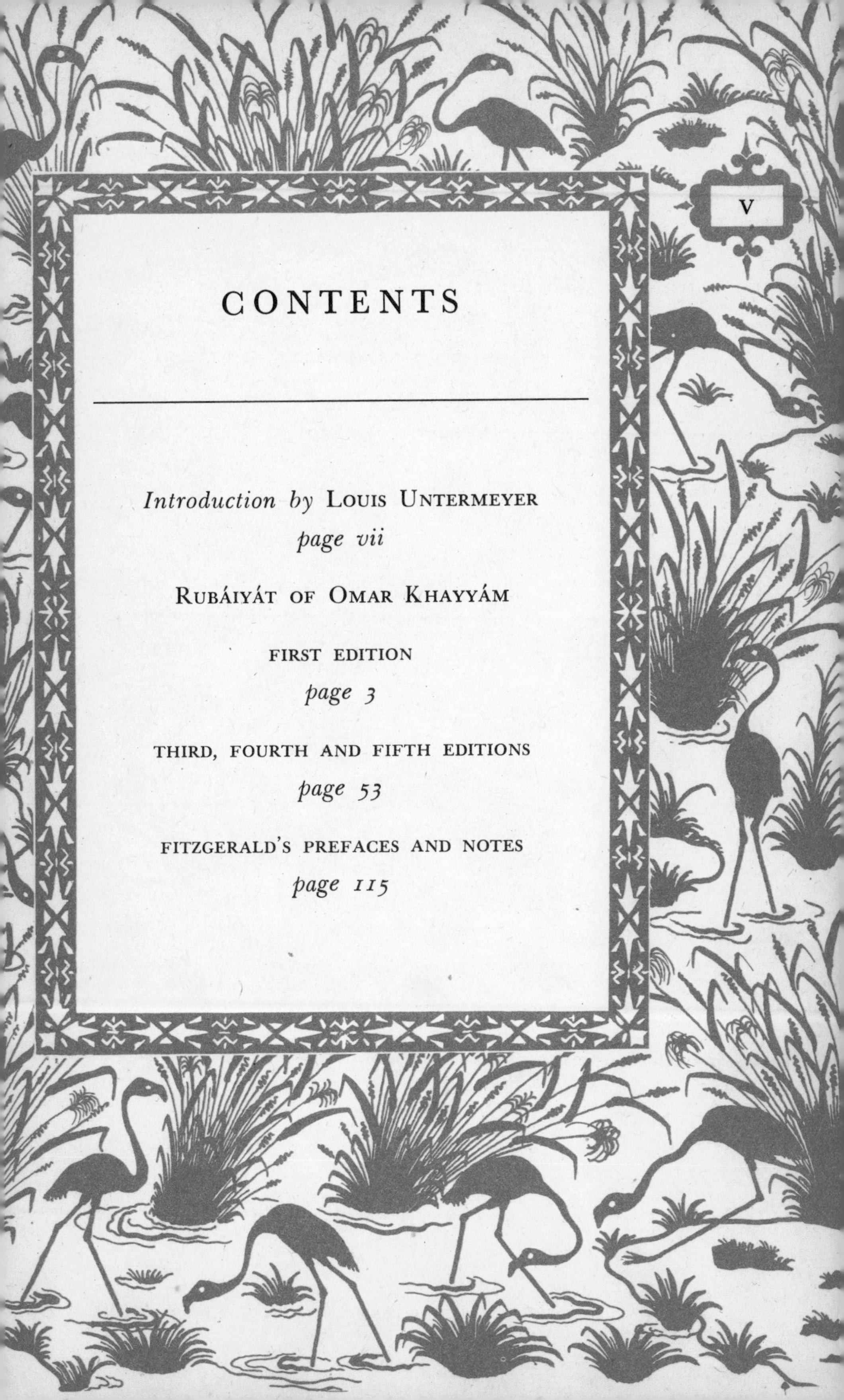

CONTENTS

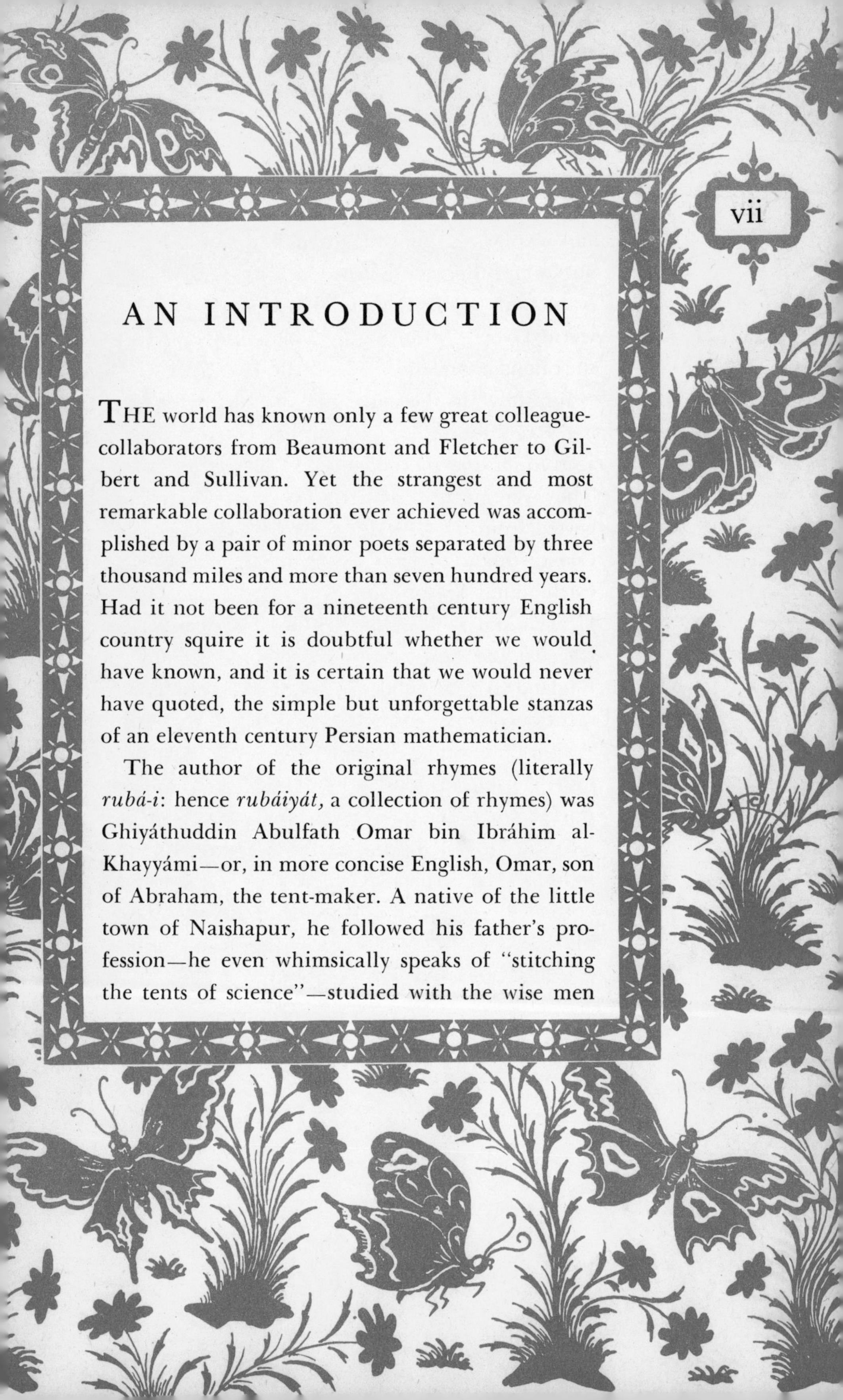

AN INTRODUCTION

THE world has known only a few great colleague-collaborators from Beaumont and Fletcher to Gilbert and Sullivan. Yet the strangest and most remarkable collaboration ever achieved was accomplished by a pair of minor poets separated by three thousand miles and more than seven hundred years. Had it not been for a nineteenth century English country squire it is doubtful whether we would have known, and it is certain that we would never have quoted, the simple but unforgettable stanzas of an eleventh century Persian mathematician.

The author of the original rhymes (literally *rubá-i*: hence *rubáiyát,* a collection of rhymes) was Ghiyáthuddin Abulfath Omar bin Ibráhim al-Khayyámi—or, in more concise English, Omar, son of Abraham, the tent-maker. A native of the little town of Naishapur, he followed his father's profession—he even whimsically speaks of "stitching the tents of science"—studied with the wise men

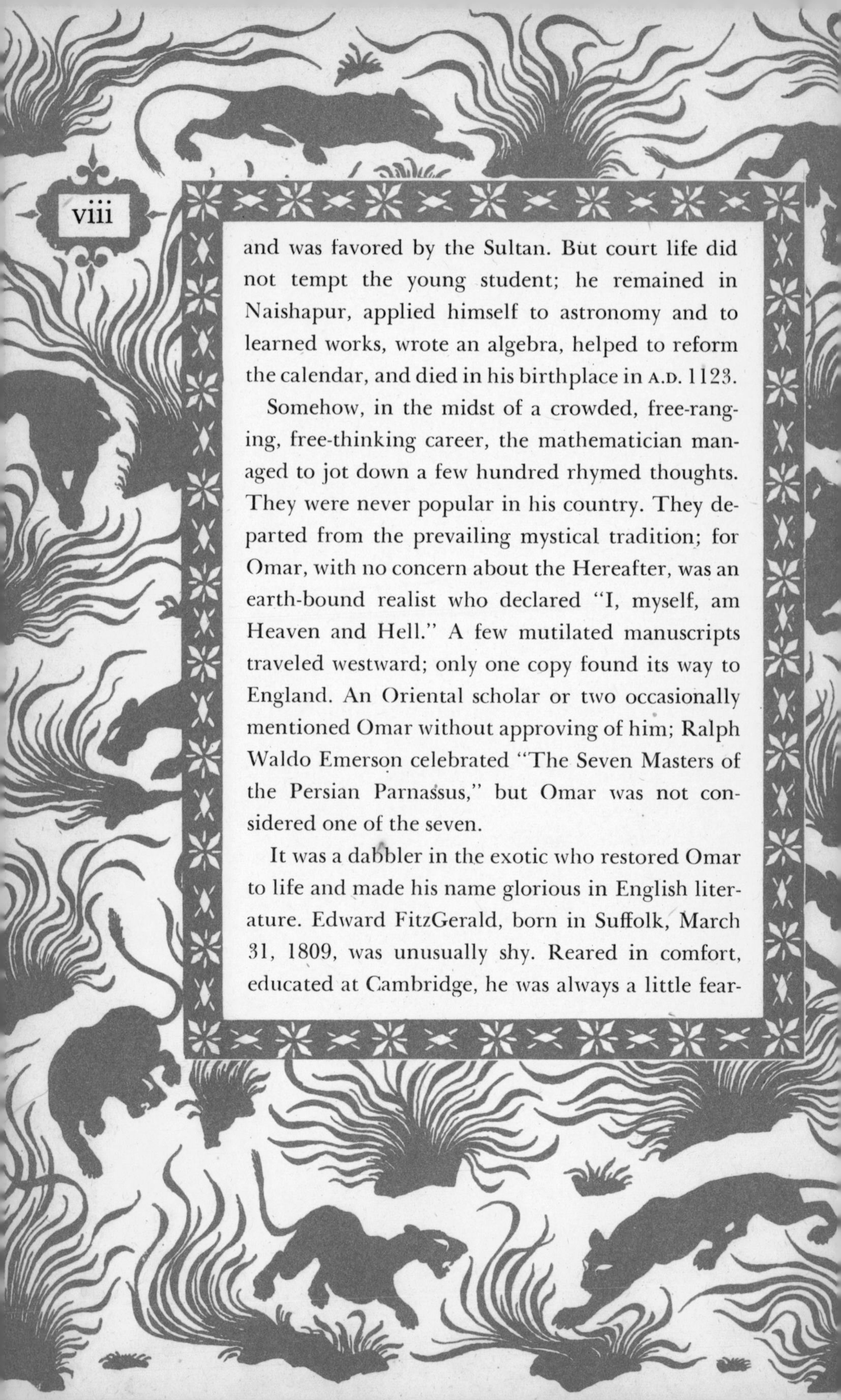

and was favored by the Sultan. But court life did not tempt the young student; he remained in Naishapur, applied himself to astronomy and to learned works, wrote an algebra, helped to reform the calendar, and died in his birthplace in A.D. 1123.

Somehow, in the midst of a crowded, free-ranging, free-thinking career, the mathematician managed to jot down a few hundred rhymed thoughts. They were never popular in his country. They departed from the prevailing mystical tradition; for Omar, with no concern about the Hereafter, was an earth-bound realist who declared "I, myself, am Heaven and Hell." A few mutilated manuscripts traveled westward; only one copy found its way to England. An Oriental scholar or two occasionally mentioned Omar without approving of him; Ralph Waldo Emerson celebrated "The Seven Masters of the Persian Parnassus," but Omar was not considered one of the seven.

It was a dabbler in the exotic who restored Omar to life and made his name glorious in English literature. Edward FitzGerald, born in Suffolk, March 31, 1809, was unusually shy. Reared in comfort, educated at Cambridge, he was always a little fear-

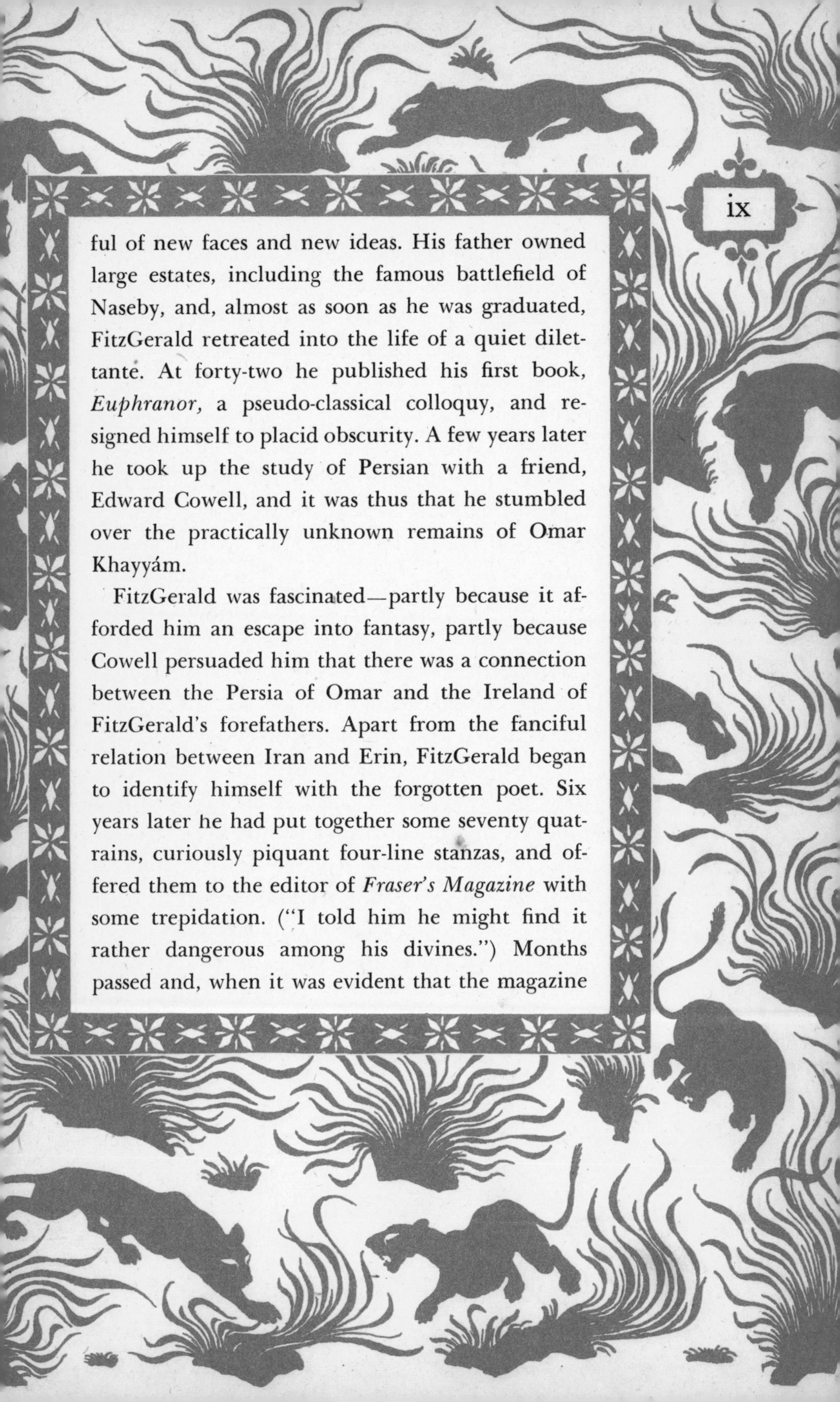

ful of new faces and new ideas. His father owned large estates, including the famous battlefield of Naseby, and, almost as soon as he was graduated, FitzGerald retreated into the life of a quiet dilettante. At forty-two he published his first book, *Euphranor,* a pseudo-classical colloquy, and resigned himself to placid obscurity. A few years later he took up the study of Persian with a friend, Edward Cowell, and it was thus that he stumbled over the practically unknown remains of Omar Khayyám.

FitzGerald was fascinated—partly because it afforded him an escape into fantasy, partly because Cowell persuaded him that there was a connection between the Persia of Omar and the Ireland of FitzGerald's forefathers. Apart from the fanciful relation between Iran and Erin, FitzGerald began to identify himself with the forgotten poet. Six years later he had put together some seventy quatrains, curiously piquant four-line stanzas, and offered them to the editor of *Fraser's Magazine* with some trepidation. ("I told him he might find it rather dangerous among his divines.") Months passed and, when it was evident that the magazine

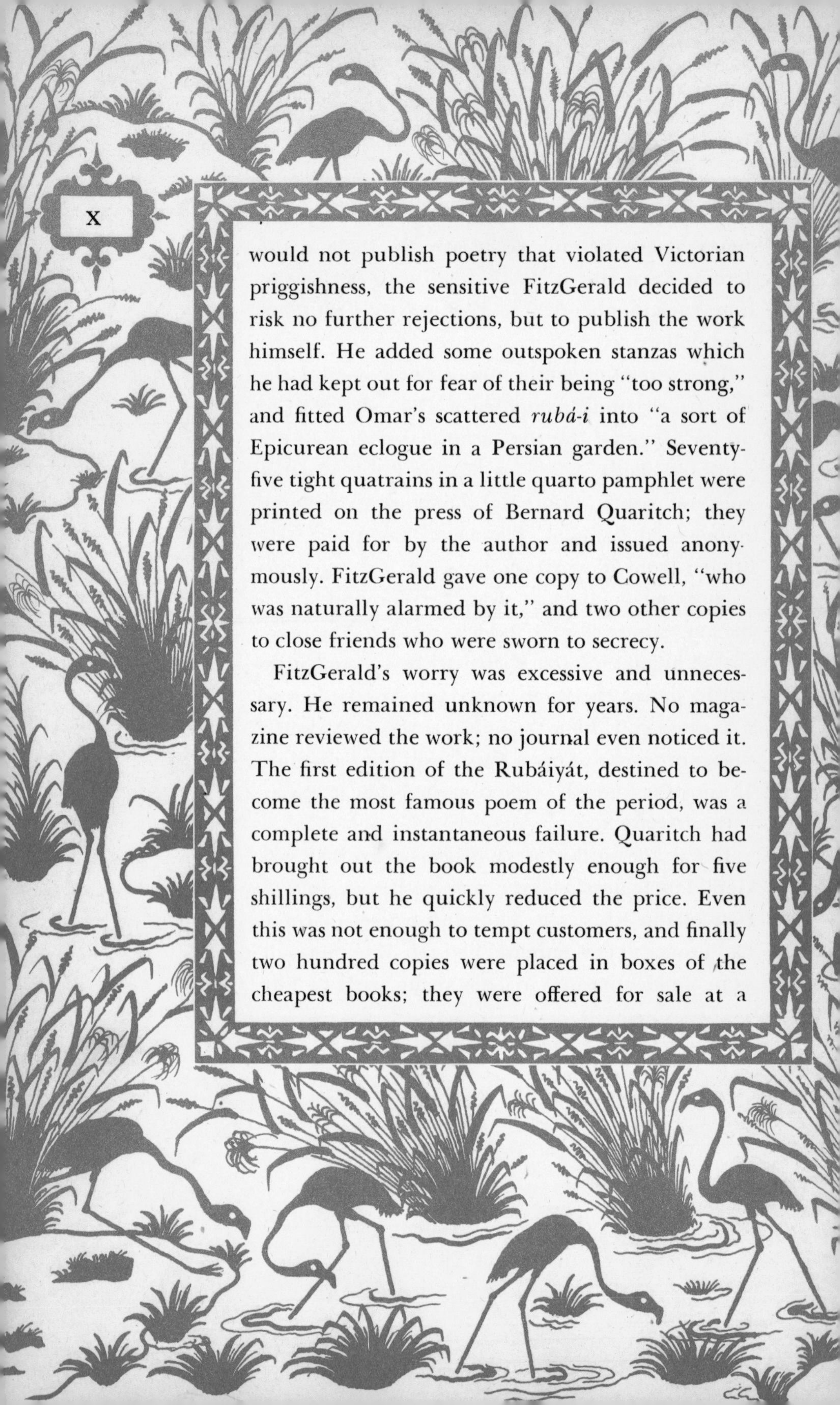

would not publish poetry that violated Victorian priggishness, the sensitive FitzGerald decided to risk no further rejections, but to publish the work himself. He added some outspoken stanzas which he had kept out for fear of their being "too strong," and fitted Omar's scattered *rubá-i* into "a sort of Epicurean eclogue in a Persian garden." Seventy-five tight quatrains in a little quarto pamphlet were printed on the press of Bernard Quaritch; they were paid for by the author and issued anonymously. FitzGerald gave one copy to Cowell, "who was naturally alarmed by it," and two other copies to close friends who were sworn to secrecy.

FitzGerald's worry was excessive and unnecessary. He remained unknown for years. No magazine reviewed the work; no journal even noticed it. The first edition of the Rubáiyát, destined to become the most famous poem of the period, was a complete and instantaneous failure. Quaritch had brought out the book modestly enough for five shillings, but he quickly reduced the price. Even this was not enough to tempt customers, and finally two hundred copies were placed in boxes of the cheapest books; they were offered for sale at a

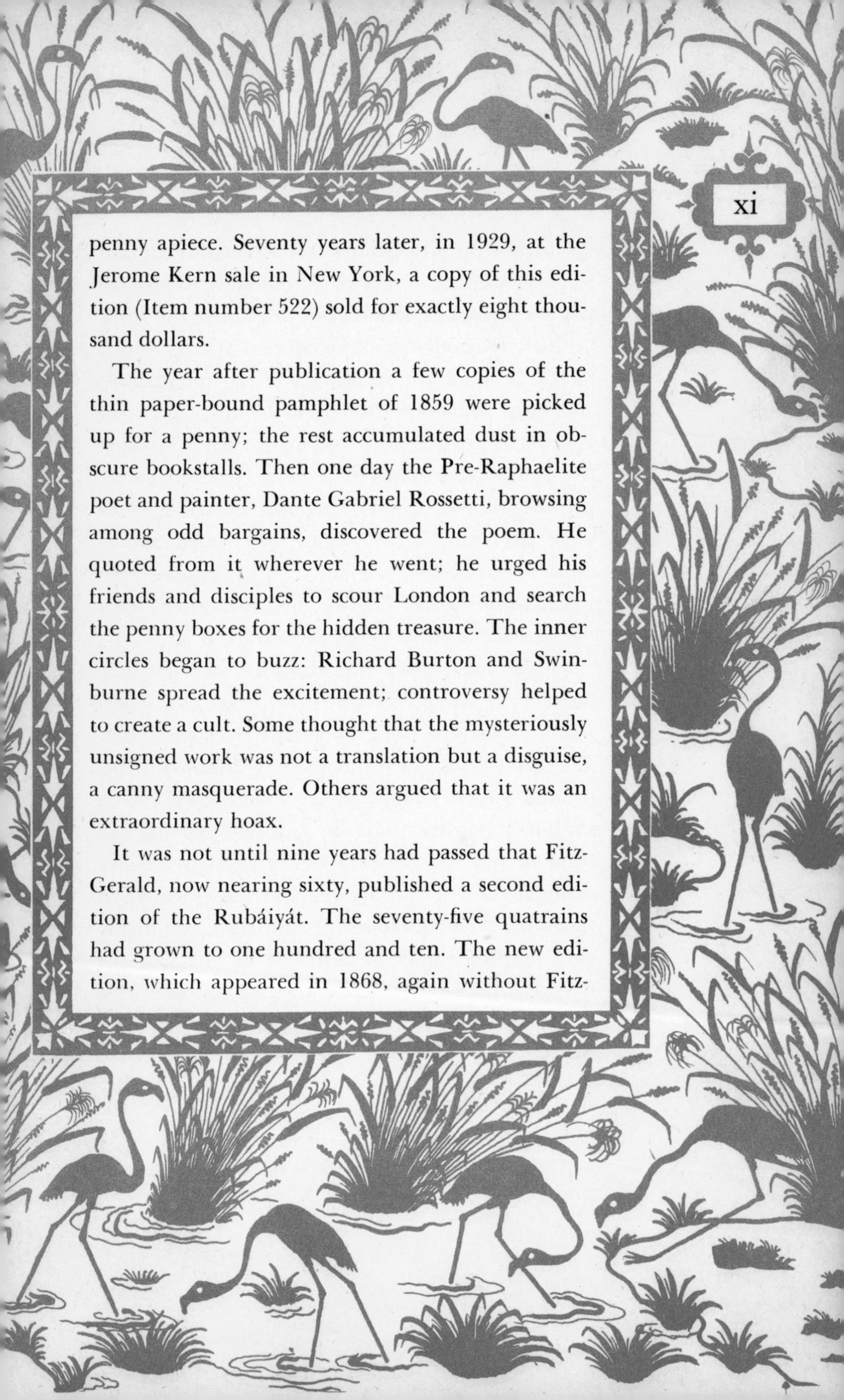

penny apiece. Seventy years later, in 1929, at the Jerome Kern sale in New York, a copy of this edition (Item number 522) sold for exactly eight thousand dollars.

The year after publication a few copies of the thin paper-bound pamphlet of 1859 were picked up for a penny; the rest accumulated dust in obscure bookstalls. Then one day the Pre-Raphaelite poet and painter, Dante Gabriel Rossetti, browsing among odd bargains, discovered the poem. He quoted from it wherever he went; he urged his friends and disciples to scour London and search the penny boxes for the hidden treasure. The inner circles began to buzz: Richard Burton and Swinburne spread the excitement; controversy helped to create a cult. Some thought that the mysteriously unsigned work was not a translation but a disguise, a canny masquerade. Others argued that it was an extraordinary hoax.

It was not until nine years had passed that FitzGerald, now nearing sixty, published a second edition of the Rubáiyát. The seventy-five quatrains had grown to one hundred and ten. The new edition, which appeared in 1868, again without Fitz-

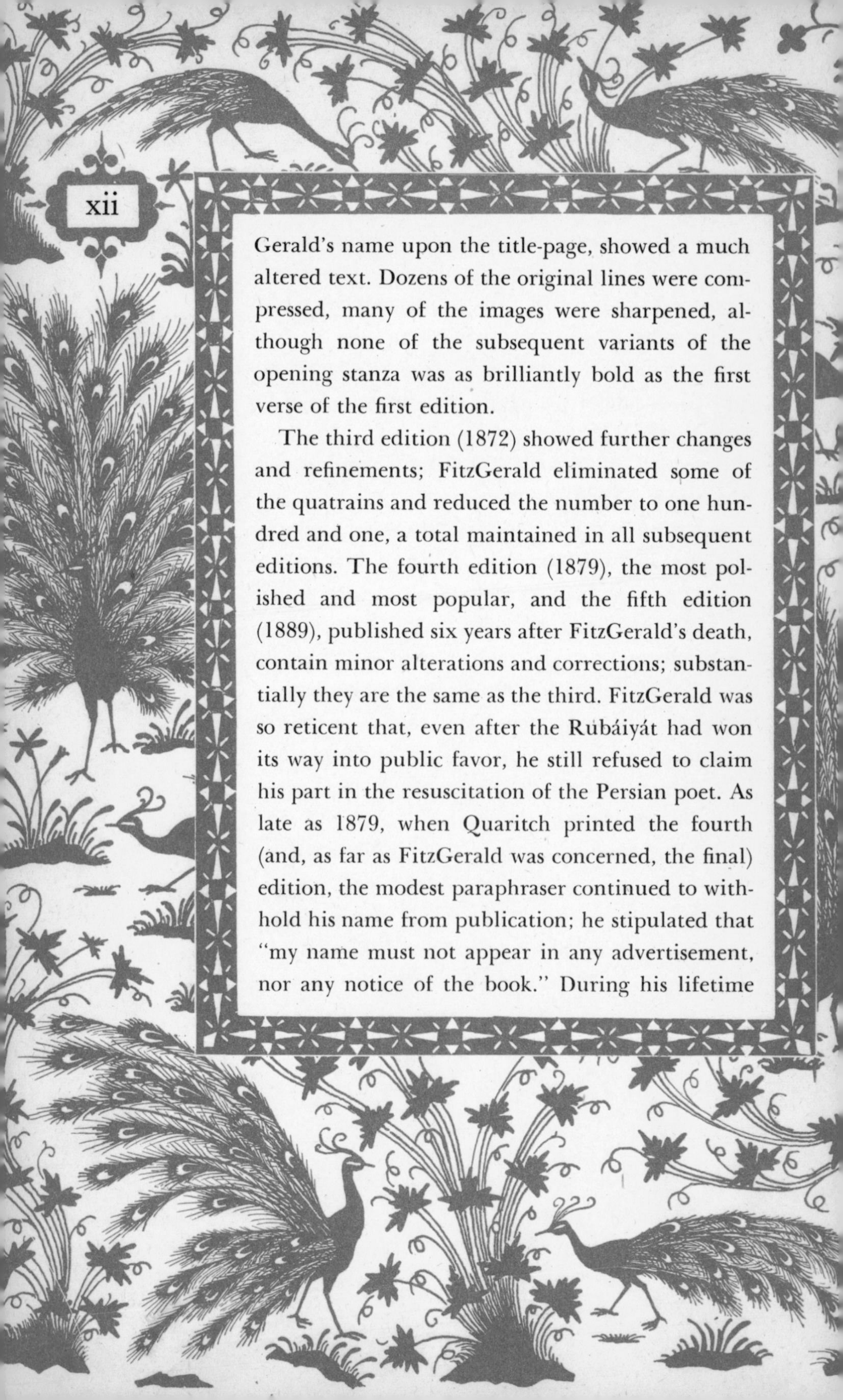

Gerald's name upon the title-page, showed a much altered text. Dozens of the original lines were compressed, many of the images were sharpened, although none of the subsequent variants of the opening stanza was as brilliantly bold as the first verse of the first edition.

The third edition (1872) showed further changes and refinements; FitzGerald eliminated some of the quatrains and reduced the number to one hundred and one, a total maintained in all subsequent editions. The fourth edition (1879), the most polished and most popular, and the fifth edition (1889), published six years after FitzGerald's death, contain minor alterations and corrections; substantially they are the same as the third. FitzGerald was so reticent that, even after the Rubáiyát had won its way into public favor, he still refused to claim his part in the resuscitation of the Persian poet. As late as 1879, when Quaritch printed the fourth (and, as far as FitzGerald was concerned, the final) edition, the modest paraphraser continued to withhold his name from publication; he stipulated that "my name must not appear in any advertisement, nor any notice of the book." During his lifetime

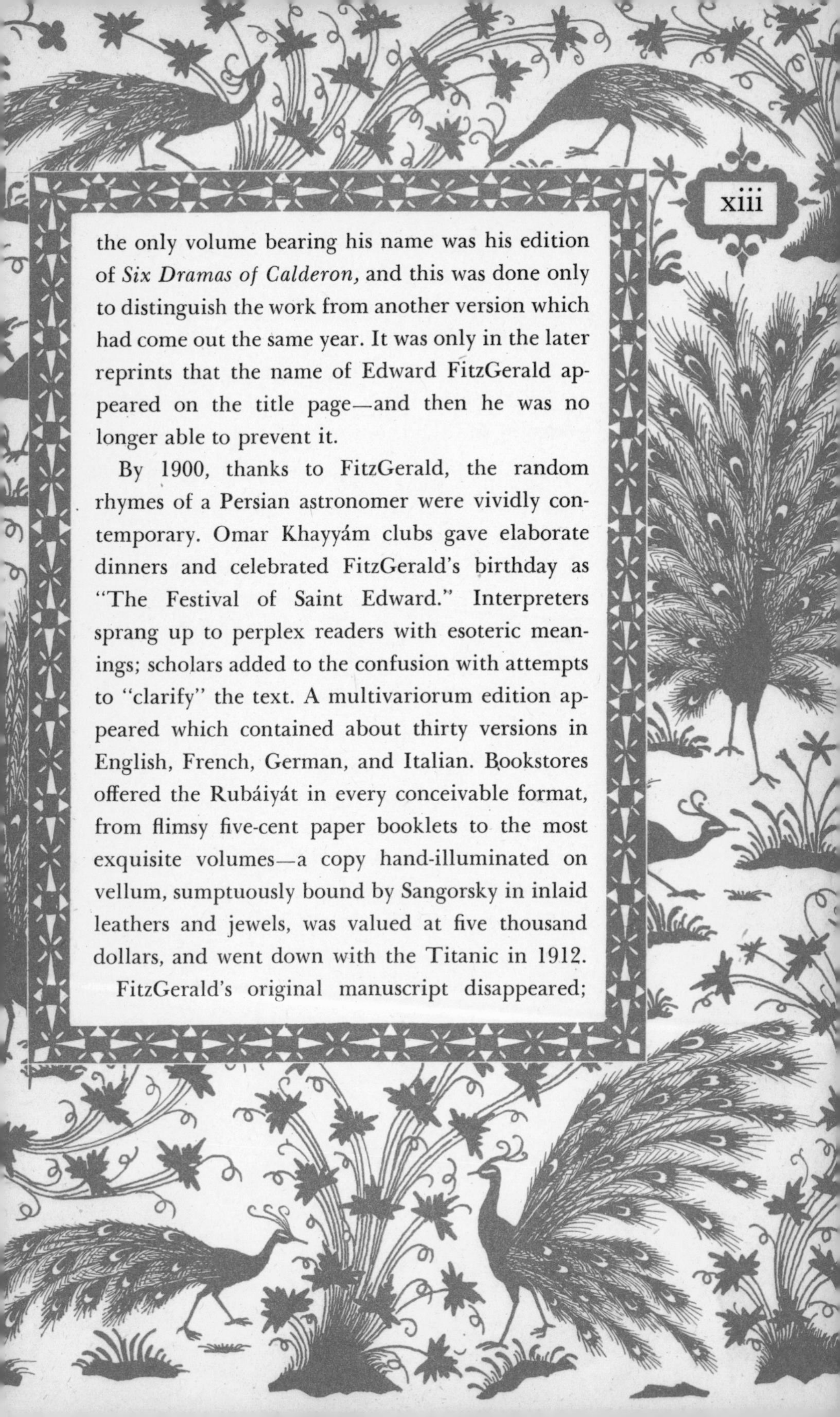

the only volume bearing his name was his edition of *Six Dramas of Calderon,* and this was done only to distinguish the work from another version which had come out the same year. It was only in the later reprints that the name of Edward FitzGerald appeared on the title page—and then he was no longer able to prevent it.

By 1900, thanks to FitzGerald, the random rhymes of a Persian astronomer were vividly contemporary. Omar Khayyám clubs gave elaborate dinners and celebrated FitzGerald's birthday as "The Festival of Saint Edward." Interpreters sprang up to perplex readers with esoteric meanings; scholars added to the confusion with attempts to "clarify" the text. A multivariorum edition appeared which contained about thirty versions in English, French, German, and Italian. Bookstores offered the Rubáiyát in every conceivable format, from flimsy five-cent paper booklets to the most exquisite volumes—a copy hand-illuminated on vellum, sumptuously bound by Sangorsky in inlaid leathers and jewels, was valued at five thousand dollars, and went down with the Titanic in 1912.

FitzGerald's original manuscript disappeared;

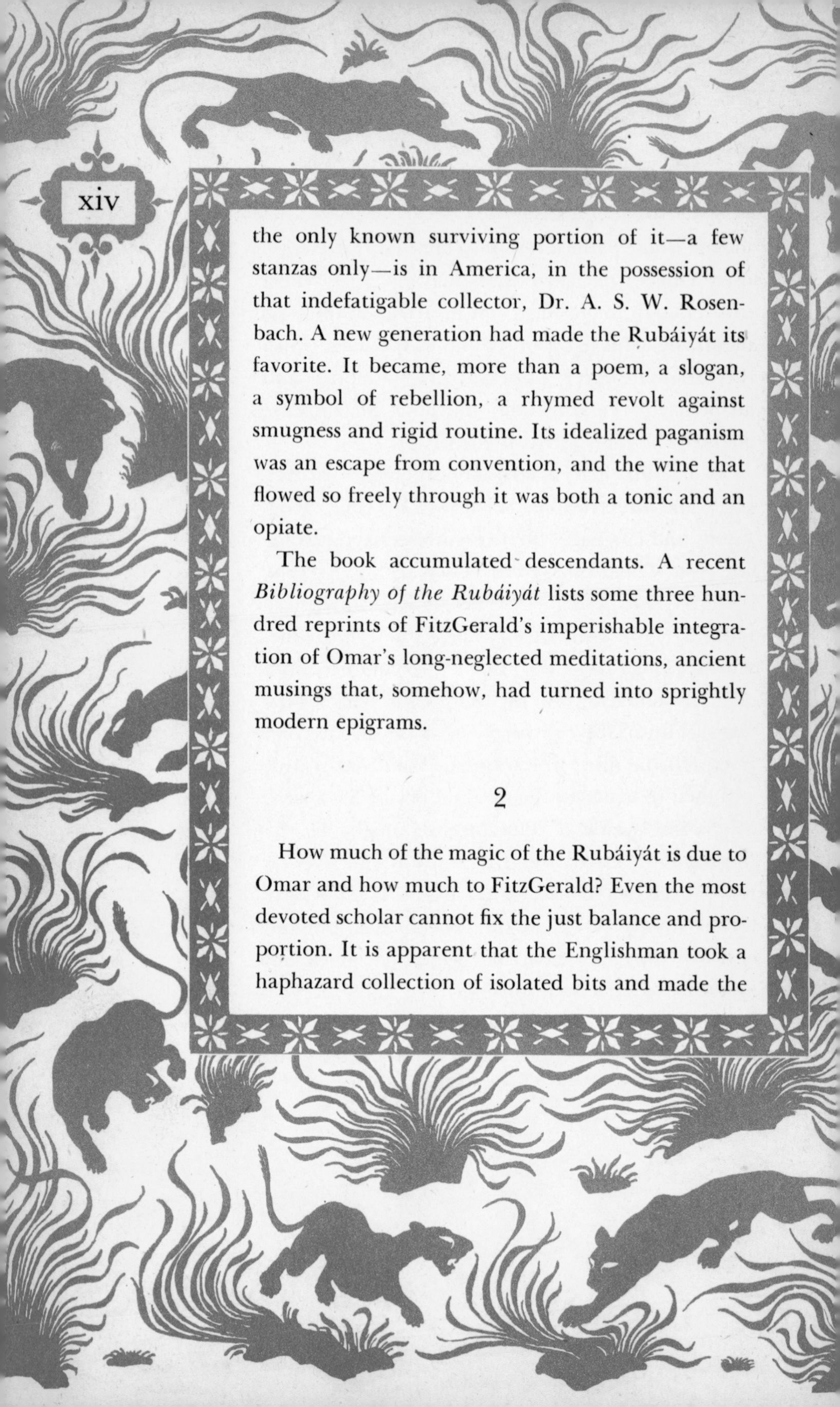

the only known surviving portion of it—a few stanzas only—is in America, in the possession of that indefatigable collector, Dr. A. S. W. Rosenbach. A new generation had made the Rubáiyát its favorite. It became, more than a poem, a slogan, a symbol of rebellion, a rhymed revolt against smugness and rigid routine. Its idealized paganism was an escape from convention, and the wine that flowed so freely through it was both a tonic and an opiate.

The book accumulated descendants. A recent *Bibliography of the Rubáiyát* lists some three hundred reprints of FitzGerald's imperishable integration of Omar's long-neglected meditations, ancient musings that, somehow, had turned into sprightly modern epigrams.

2

How much of the magic of the Rubáiyát is due to Omar and how much to FitzGerald? Even the most devoted scholar cannot fix the just balance and proportion. It is apparent that the Englishman took a haphazard collection of isolated bits and made the

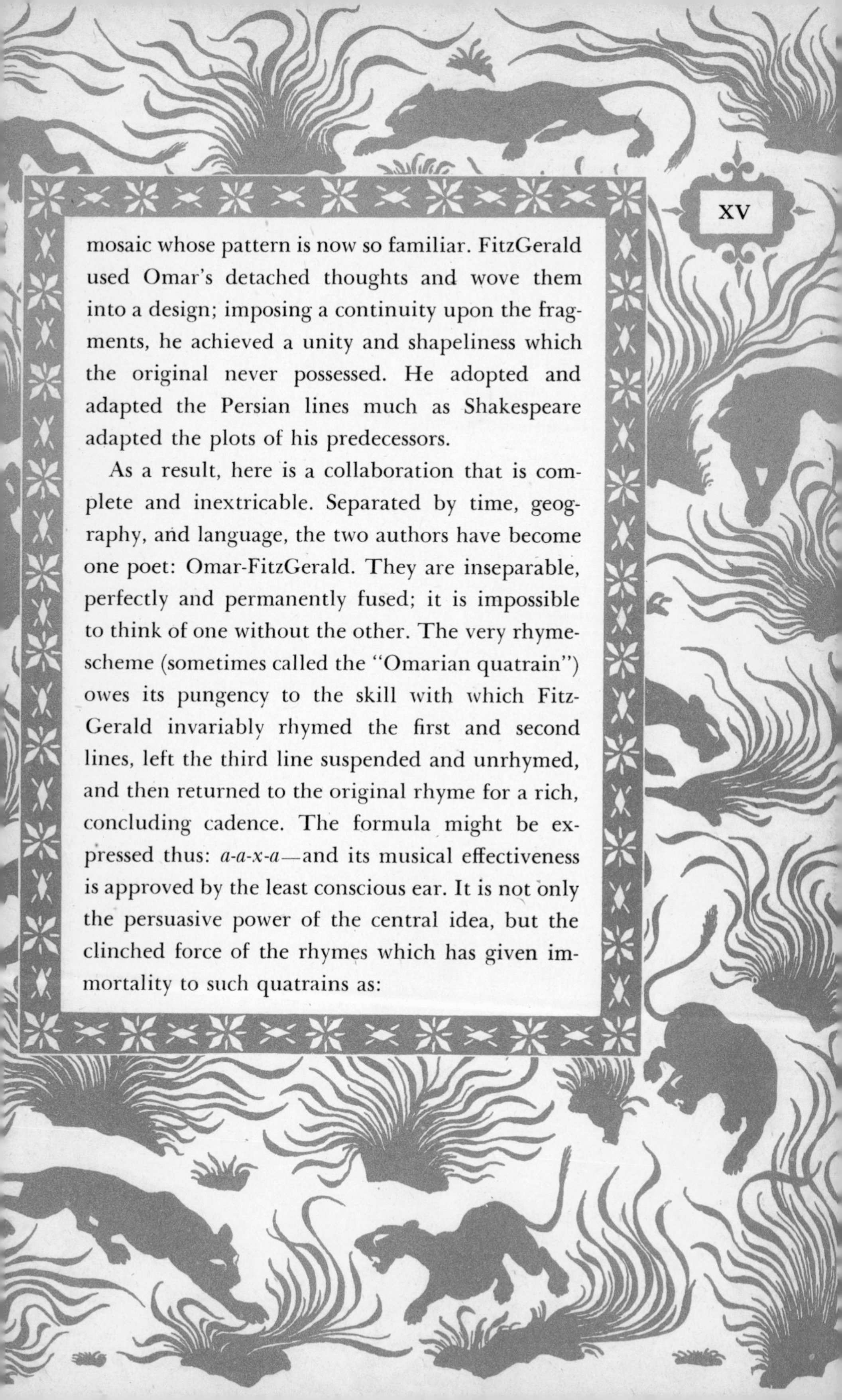

mosaic whose pattern is now so familiar. FitzGerald used Omar's detached thoughts and wove them into a design; imposing a continuity upon the fragments, he achieved a unity and shapeliness which the original never possessed. He adopted and adapted the Persian lines much as Shakespeare adapted the plots of his predecessors.

As a result, here is a collaboration that is complete and inextricable. Separated by time, geography, and language, the two authors have become one poet: Omar-FitzGerald. They are inseparable, perfectly and permanently fused; it is impossible to think of one without the other. The very rhymescheme (sometimes called the "Omarian quatrain") owes its pungency to the skill with which FitzGerald invariably rhymed the first and second lines, left the third line suspended and unrhymed, and then returned to the original rhyme for a rich, concluding cadence. The formula might be expressed thus: *a-a-x-a*—and its musical effectiveness is approved by the least conscious ear. It is not only the persuasive power of the central idea, but the clinched force of the rhymes which has given immortality to such quatrains as:

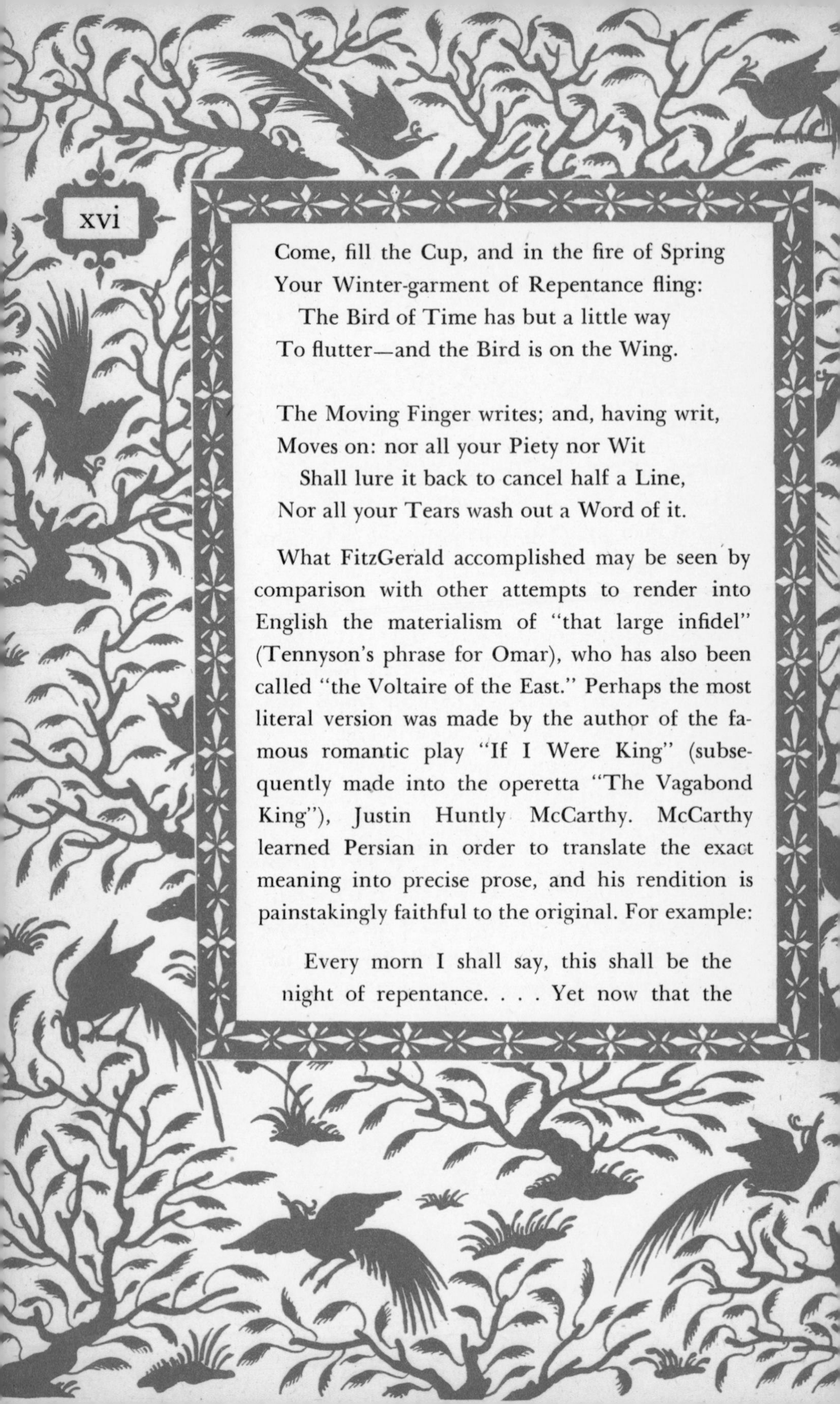

Come, fill the Cup, and in the fire of Spring
Your Winter-garment of Repentance fling:
The Bird of Time has but a little way
To flutter—and the Bird is on the Wing.

The Moving Finger writes; and, having writ,
Moves on: nor all your Piety nor Wit
Shall lure it back to cancel half a Line,
Nor all your Tears wash out a Word of it.

What FitzGerald accomplished may be seen by comparison with other attempts to render into English the materialism of "that large infidel" (Tennyson's phrase for Omar), who has also been called "the Voltaire of the East." Perhaps the most literal version was made by the author of the famous romantic play "If I Were King" (subsequently made into the operetta "The Vagabond King"), Justin Huntly McCarthy. McCarthy learned Persian in order to translate the exact meaning into precise prose, and his rendition is painstakingly faithful to the original. For example:

Every morn I shall say, this shall be the night of repentance. . . . Yet now that the

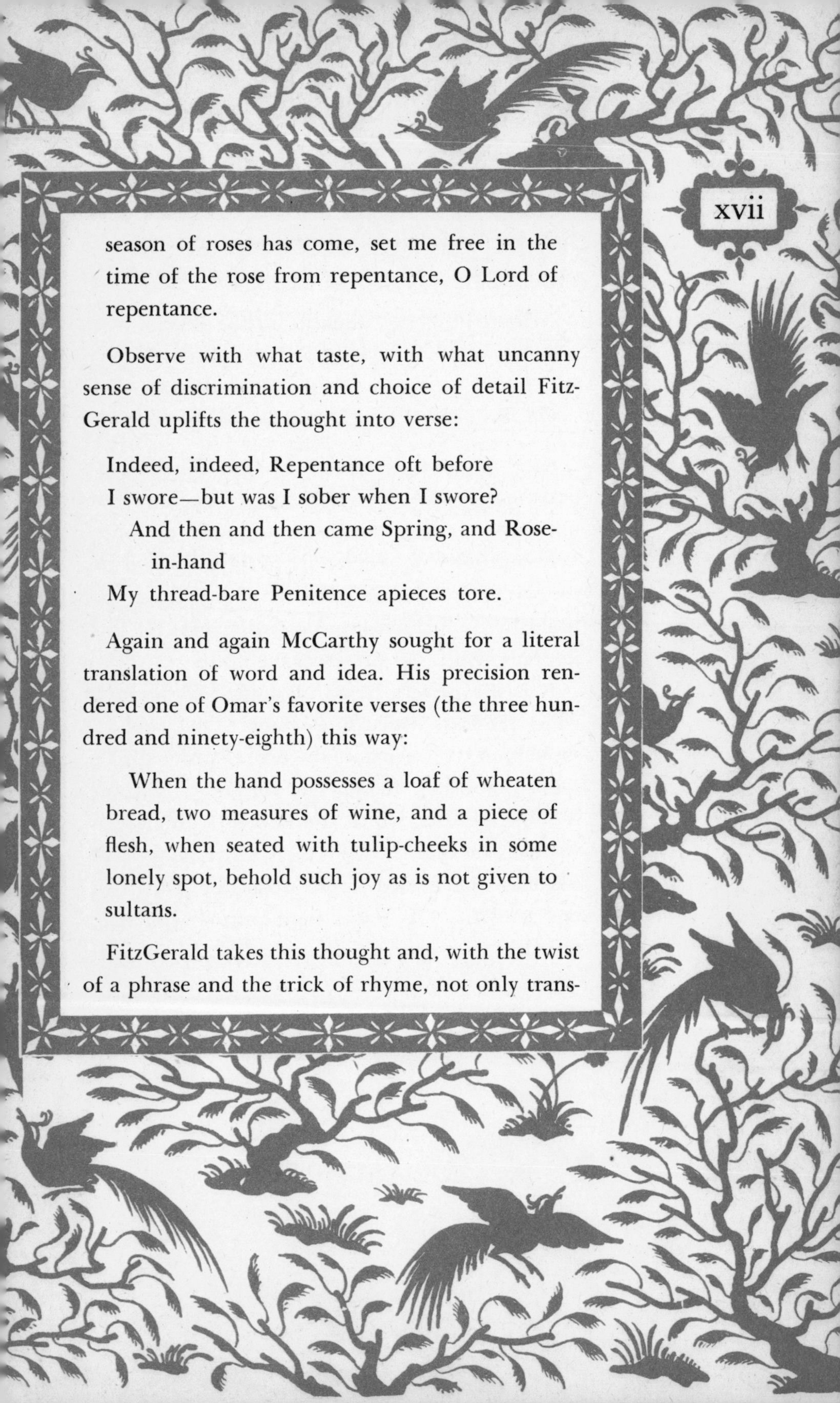

season of roses has come, set me free in the time of the rose from repentance, O Lord of repentance.

Observe with what taste, with what uncanny sense of discrimination and choice of detail FitzGerald uplifts the thought into verse:

Indeed, indeed, Repentance oft before
I swore—but was I sober when I swore?
And then and then came Spring, and Rose-in-hand
My thread-bare Penitence apieces tore.

Again and again McCarthy sought for a literal translation of word and idea. His precision rendered one of Omar's favorite verses (the three hundred and ninety-eighth) this way:

When the hand possesses a loaf of wheaten bread, two measures of wine, and a piece of flesh, when seated with tulip-cheeks in some lonely spot, behold such joy as is not given to sultans.

FitzGerald takes this thought and, with the twist of a phrase and the trick of rhyme, not only trans-

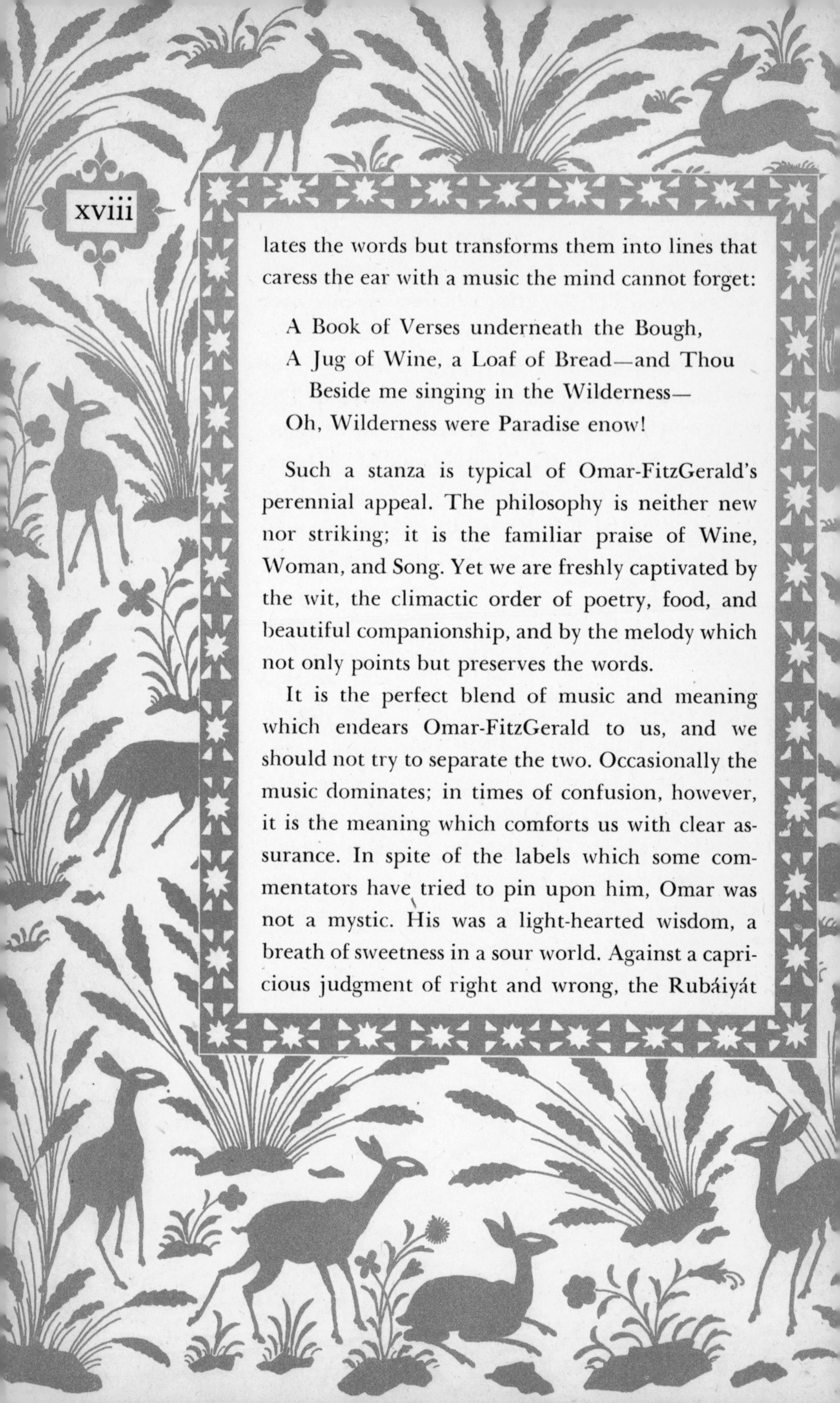

lates the words but transforms them into lines that caress the ear with a music the mind cannot forget:

A Book of Verses underneath the Bough,
A Jug of Wine, a Loaf of Bread—and Thou
  Beside me singing in the Wilderness—
Oh, Wilderness were Paradise enow!

Such a stanza is typical of Omar-FitzGerald's perennial appeal. The philosophy is neither new nor striking; it is the familiar praise of Wine, Woman, and Song. Yet we are freshly captivated by the wit, the climactic order of poetry, food, and beautiful companionship, and by the melody which not only points but preserves the words.

It is the perfect blend of music and meaning which endears Omar-FitzGerald to us, and we should not try to separate the two. Occasionally the music dominates; in times of confusion, however, it is the meaning which comforts us with clear assurance. In spite of the labels which some commentators have tried to pin upon him, Omar was not a mystic. His was a light-hearted wisdom, a breath of sweetness in a sour world. Against a capricious judgment of right and wrong, the Rubáiyát

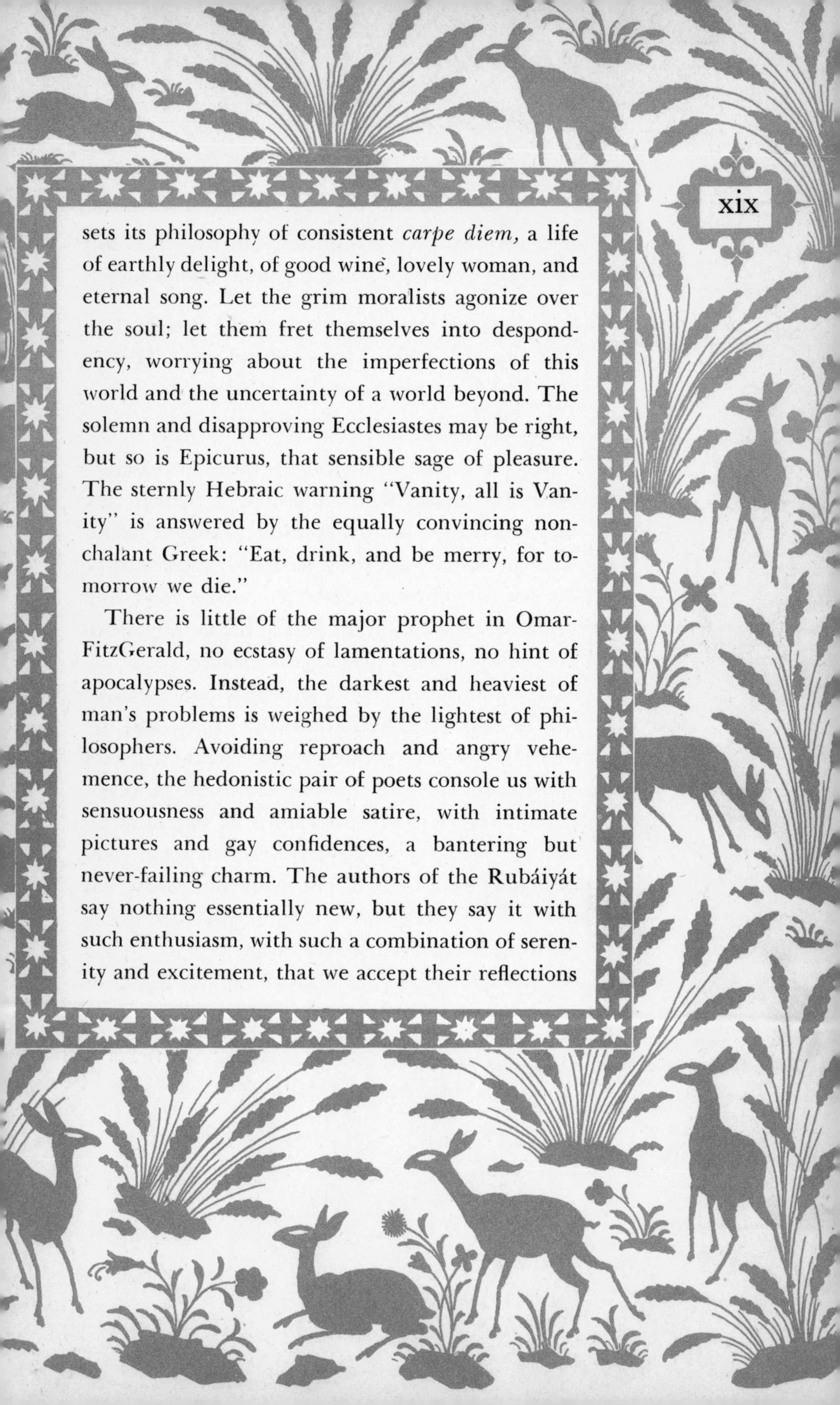

sets its philosophy of consistent *carpe diem,* a life of earthly delight, of good wine, lovely woman, and eternal song. Let the grim moralists agonize over the soul; let them fret themselves into despondency, worrying about the imperfections of this world and the uncertainty of a world beyond. The solemn and disapproving Ecclesiastes may be right, but so is Epicurus, that sensible sage of pleasure. The sternly Hebraic warning "Vanity, all is Vanity" is answered by the equally convincing nonchalant Greek: "Eat, drink, and be merry, for tomorrow we die."

There is little of the major prophet in Omar-FitzGerald, no ecstasy of lamentations, no hint of apocalypses. Instead, the darkest and heaviest of man's problems is weighed by the lightest of philosophers. Avoiding reproach and angry vehemence, the hedonistic pair of poets console us with sensuousness and amiable satire, with intimate pictures and gay confidences, a bantering but never-failing charm. The authors of the Rubáiyát say nothing essentially new, but they say it with such enthusiasm, with such a combination of serenity and excitement, that we accept their reflections

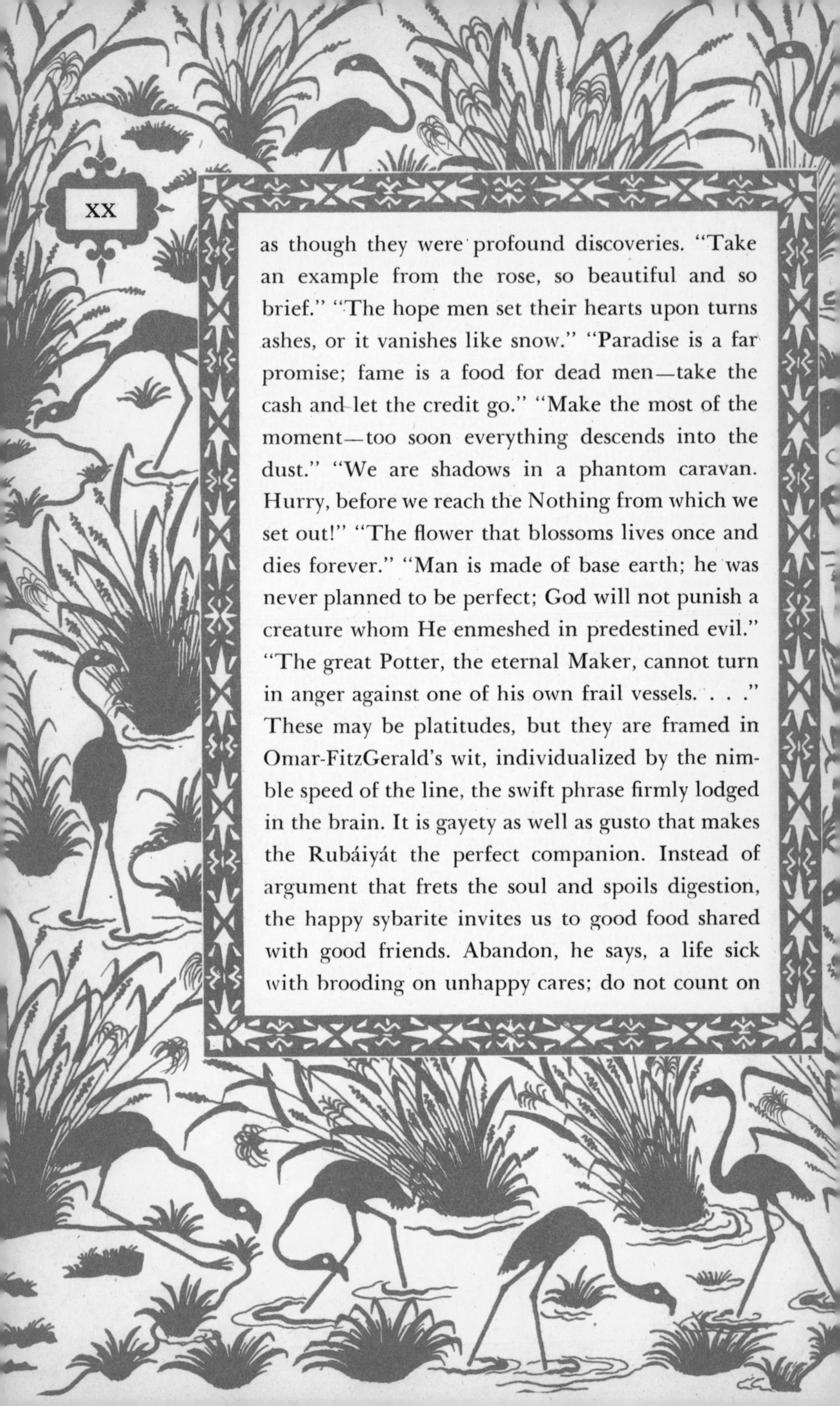

as though they were profound discoveries. "Take an example from the rose, so beautiful and so brief." "The hope men set their hearts upon turns ashes, or it vanishes like snow." "Paradise is a far promise; fame is a food for dead men—take the cash and let the credit go." "Make the most of the moment—too soon everything descends into the dust." "We are shadows in a phantom caravan. Hurry, before we reach the Nothing from which we set out!" "The flower that blossoms lives once and dies forever." "Man is made of base earth; he was never planned to be perfect; God will not punish a creature whom He enmeshed in predestined evil." "The great Potter, the eternal Maker, cannot turn in anger against one of his own frail vessels. . . ." These may be platitudes, but they are framed in Omar-FitzGerald's wit, individualized by the nimble speed of the line, the swift phrase firmly lodged in the brain. It is gayety as well as gusto that makes the Rubáiyát the perfect companion. Instead of argument that frets the soul and spoils digestion, the happy sybarite invites us to good food shared with good friends. Abandon, he says, a life sick with brooding on unhappy cares; do not count on

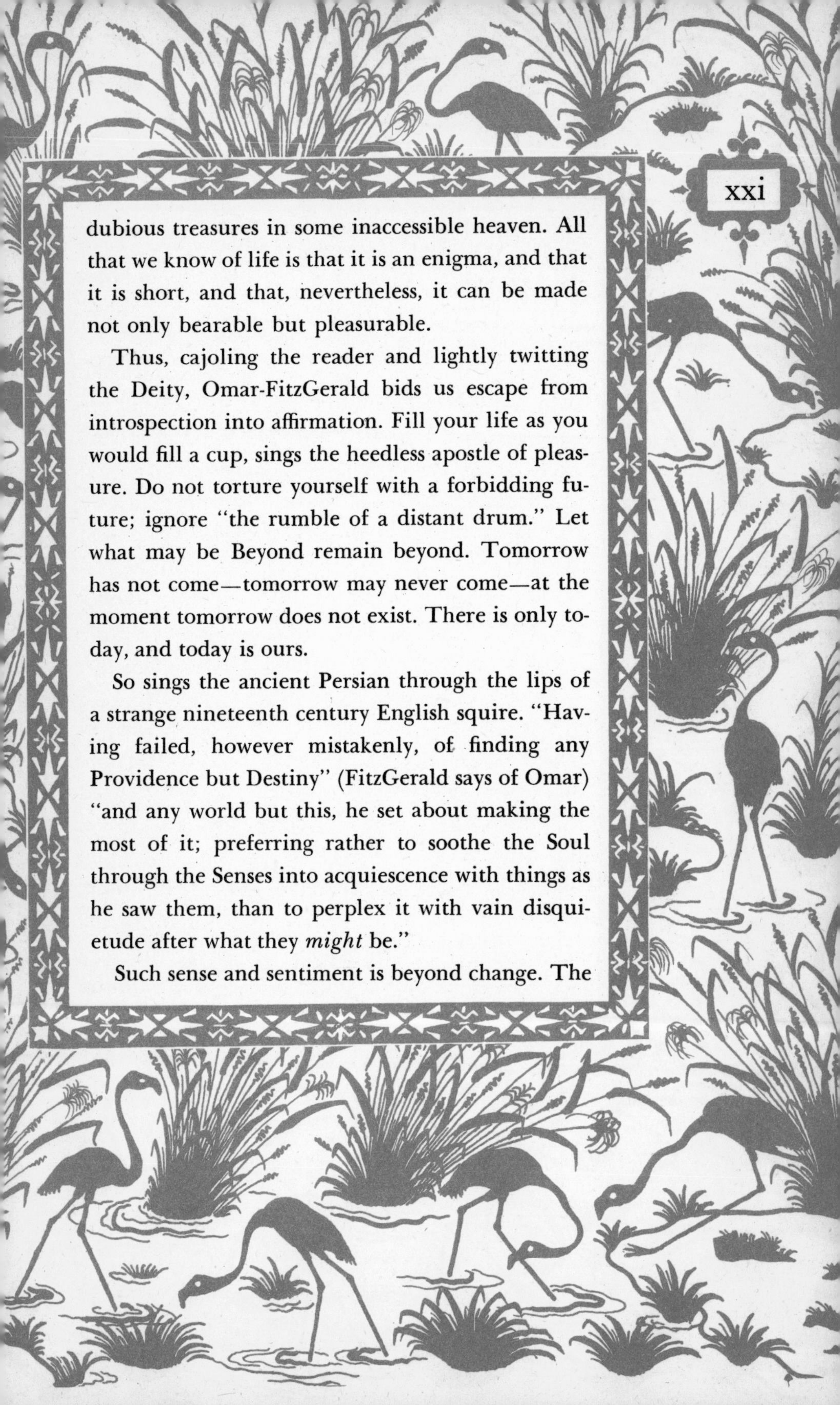

dubious treasures in some inaccessible heaven. All that we know of life is that it is an enigma, and that it is short, and that, nevertheless, it can be made not only bearable but pleasurable.

Thus, cajoling the reader and lightly twitting the Deity, Omar-FitzGerald bids us escape from introspection into affirmation. Fill your life as you would fill a cup, sings the heedless apostle of pleasure. Do not torture yourself with a forbidding future; ignore "the rumble of a distant drum." Let what may be Beyond remain beyond. Tomorrow has not come—tomorrow may never come—at the moment tomorrow does not exist. There is only today, and today is ours.

So sings the ancient Persian through the lips of a strange nineteenth century English squire. "Having failed, however mistakenly, of finding any Providence but Destiny" (FitzGerald says of Omar) "and any world but this, he set about making the most of it; preferring rather to soothe the Soul through the Senses into acquiescence with things as he saw them, than to perplex it with vain disquietude after what they *might* be."

Such sense and sentiment is beyond change. The

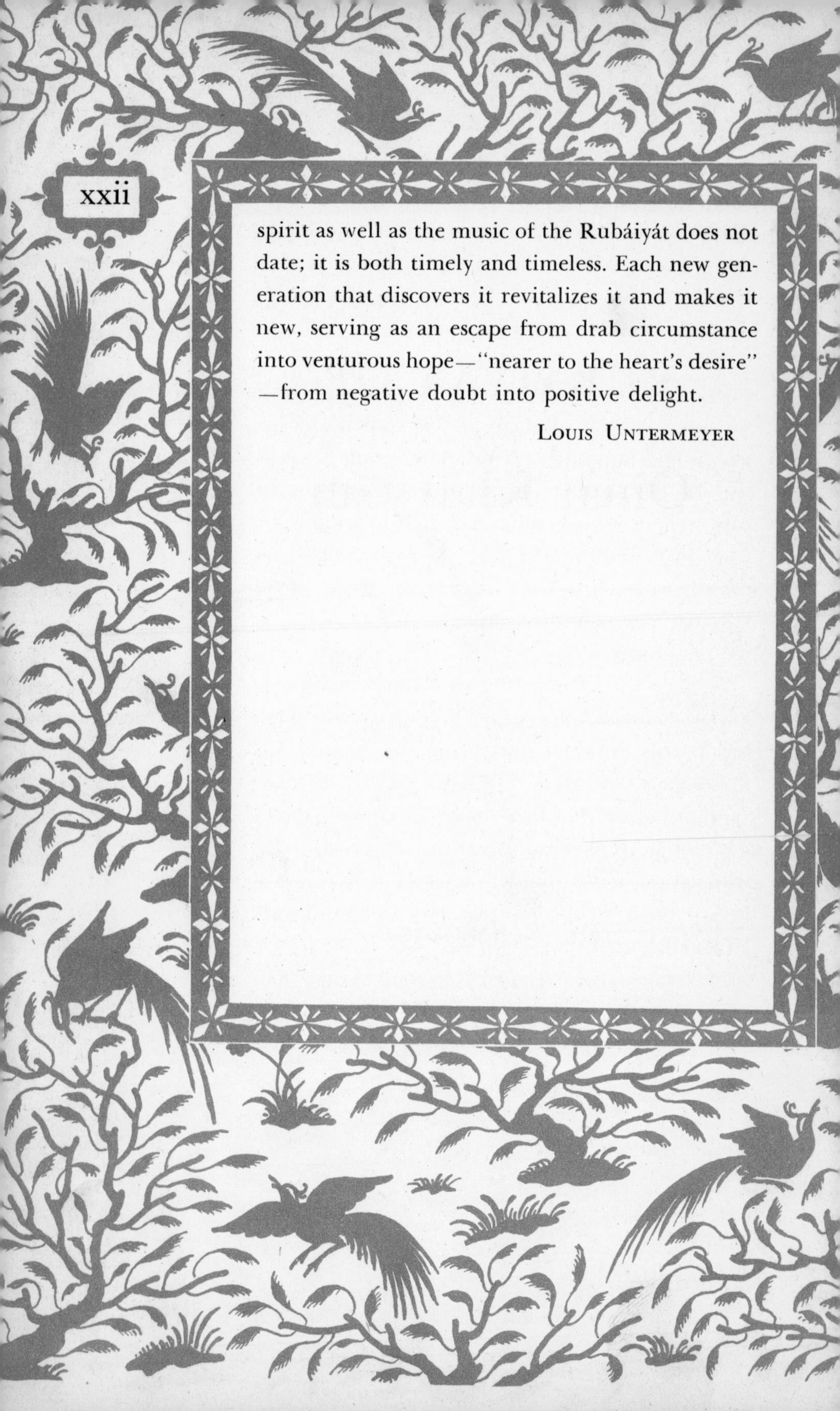

spirit as well as the music of the Rubáiyát does not date; it is both timely and timeless. Each new generation that discovers it revitalizes it and makes it new, serving as an escape from drab circumstance into venturous hope—"nearer to the heart's desire"—from negative doubt into positive delight.

LOUIS UNTERMEYER

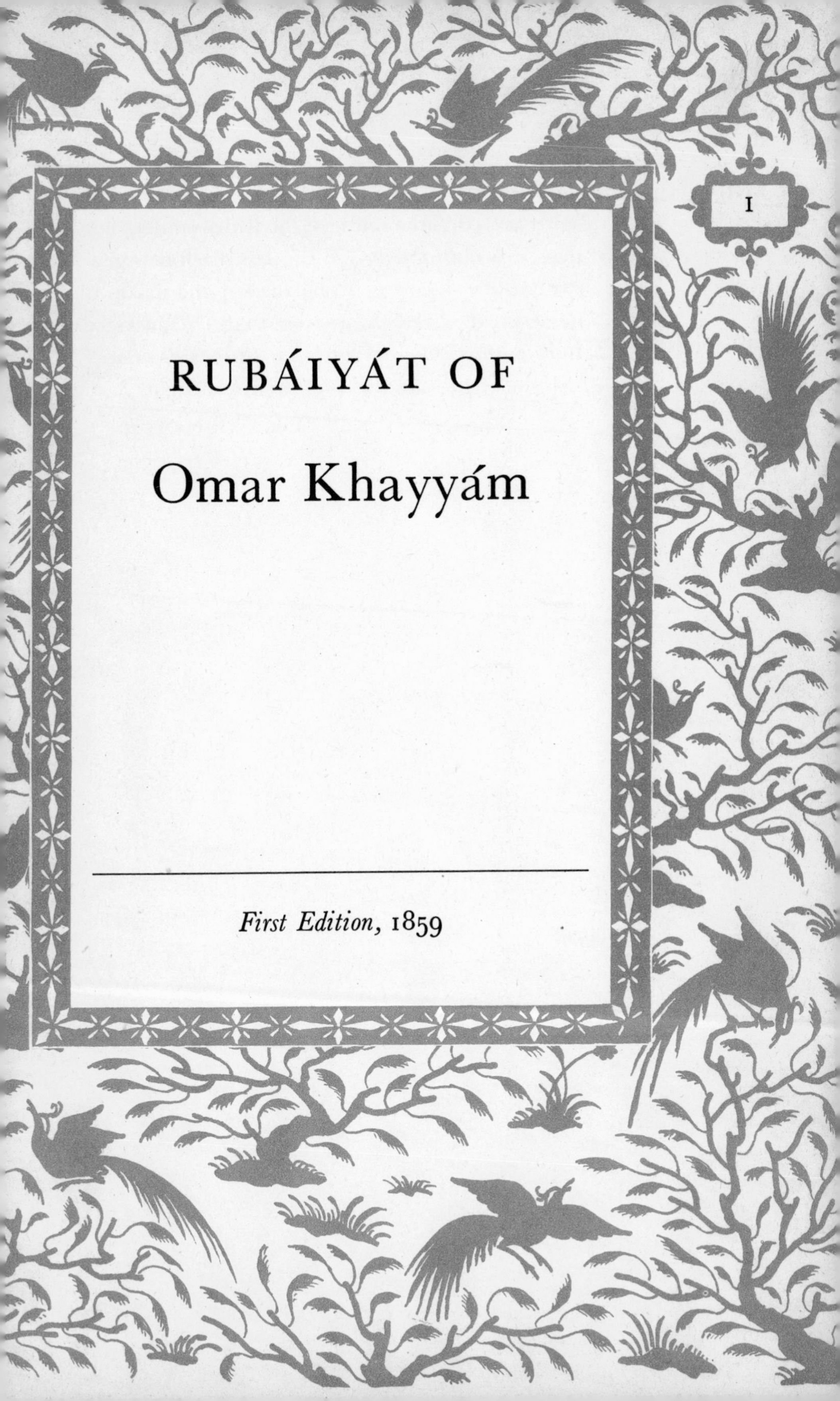

RUBÁIYÁT OF

Omar Khayyám

First Edition, 1859

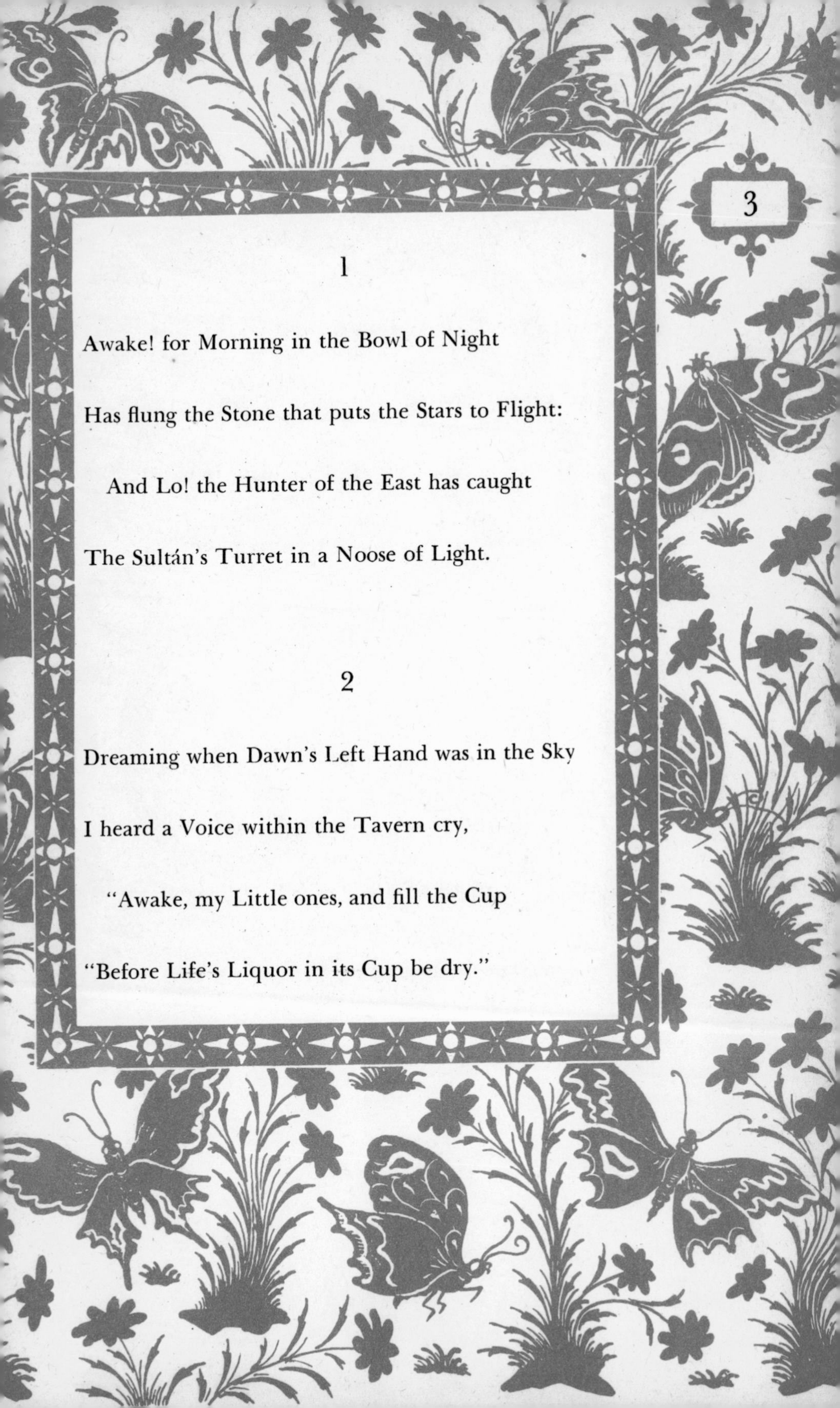

1

Awake! for Morning in the Bowl of Night
Has flung the Stone that puts the Stars to Flight:
And Lo! the Hunter of the East has caught
The Sultán's Turret in a Noose of Light.

2

Dreaming when Dawn's Left Hand was in the Sky
I heard a Voice within the Tavern cry,
"Awake, my Little ones, and fill the Cup
"Before Life's Liquor in its Cup be dry."

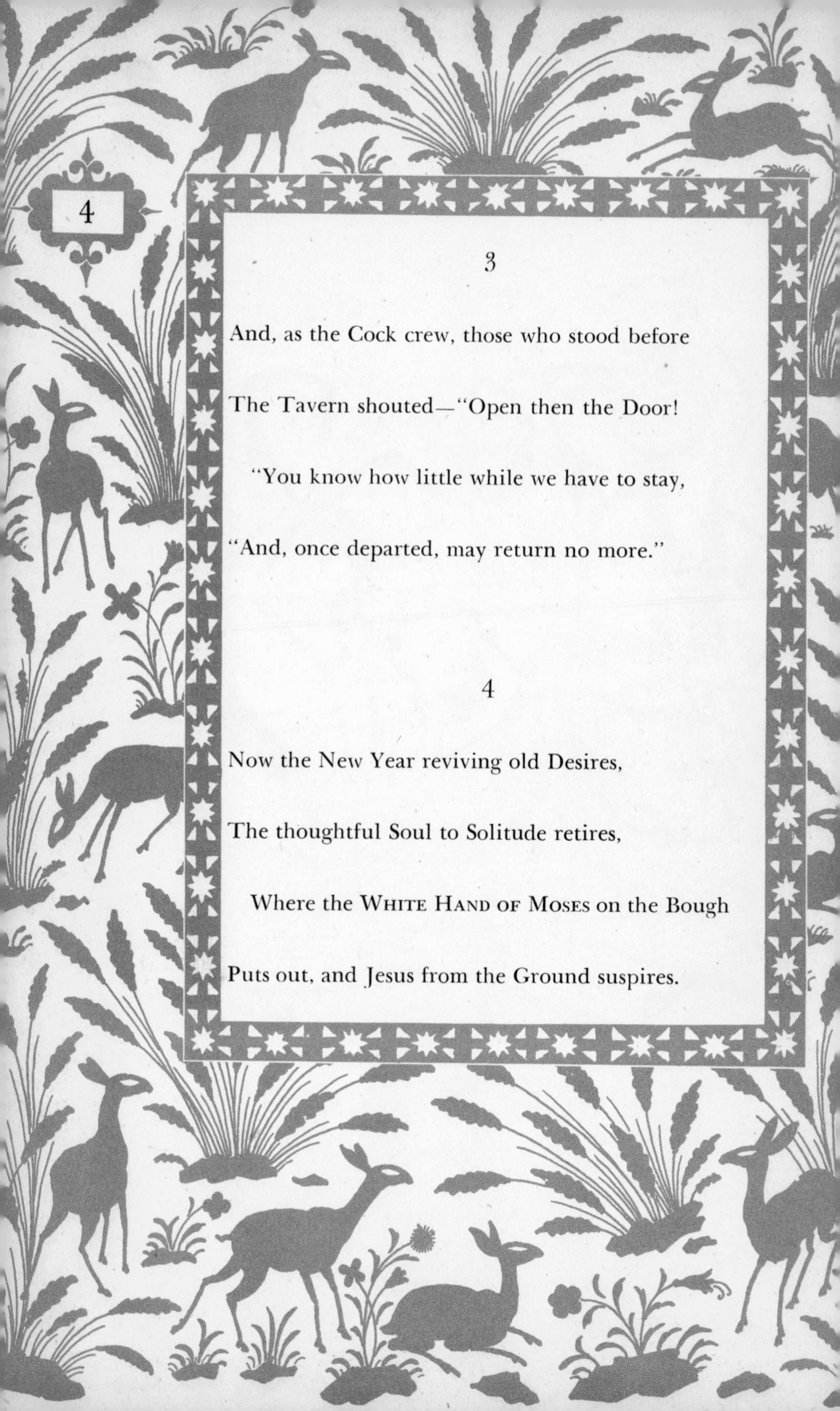

3

And, as the Cock crew, those who stood before
The Tavern shouted—"Open then the Door!
"You know how little while we have to stay,
"And, once departed, may return no more."

4

Now the New Year reviving old Desires,
The thoughtful Soul to Solitude retires,
Where the WHITE HAND OF MOSES on the Bough
Puts out, and Jesus from the Ground suspires.

5
M. Sayah

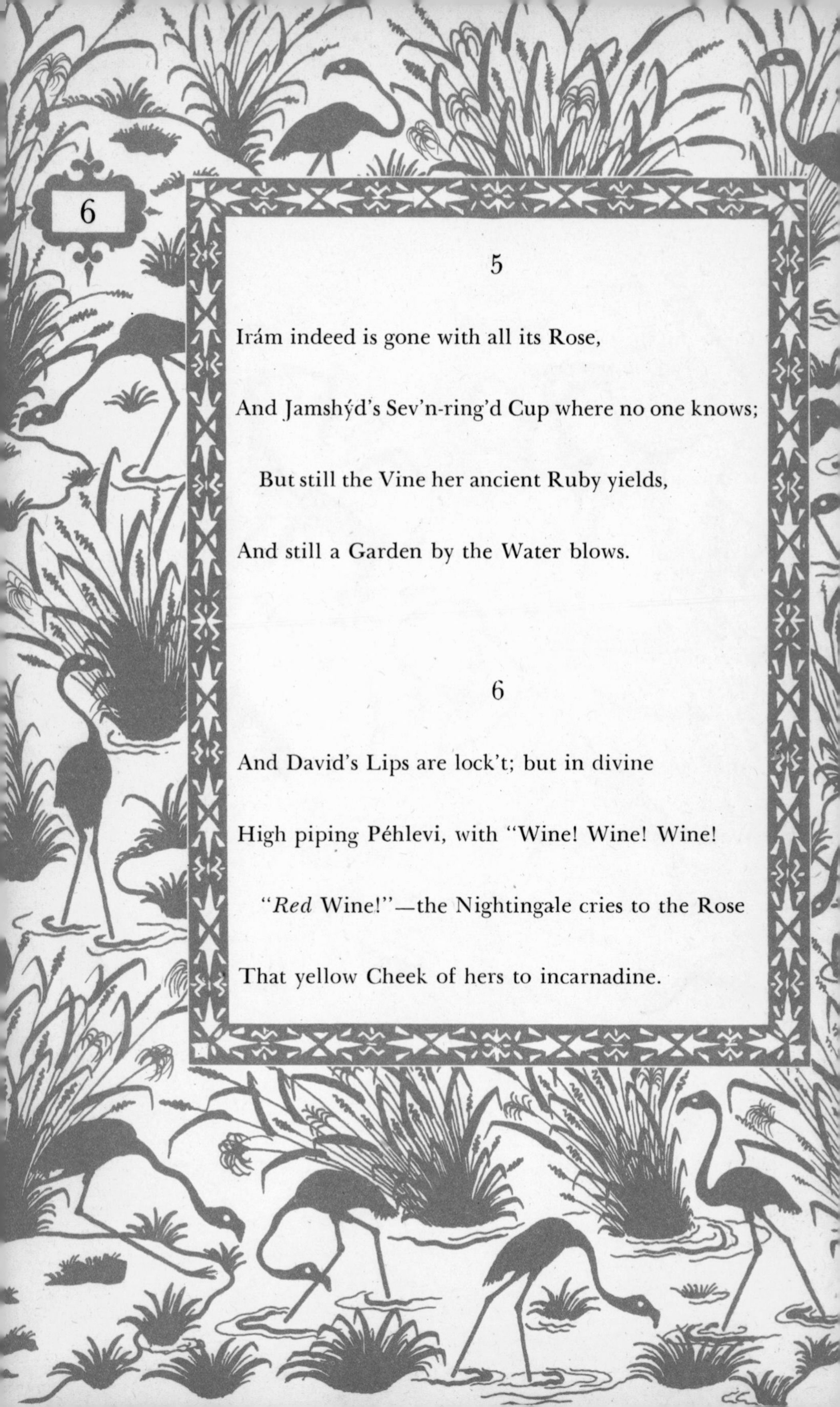

5

Irám indeed is gone with all its Rose,
And Jamshýd's Sev'n-ring'd Cup where no one knows;
    But still the Vine her ancient Ruby yields,
And still a Garden by the Water blows.

6

And David's Lips are lock't; but in divine
High piping Péhlevi, with "Wine! Wine! Wine!
    "*Red* Wine!"—the Nightingale cries to the Rose
That yellow Cheek of hers to incarnadine.

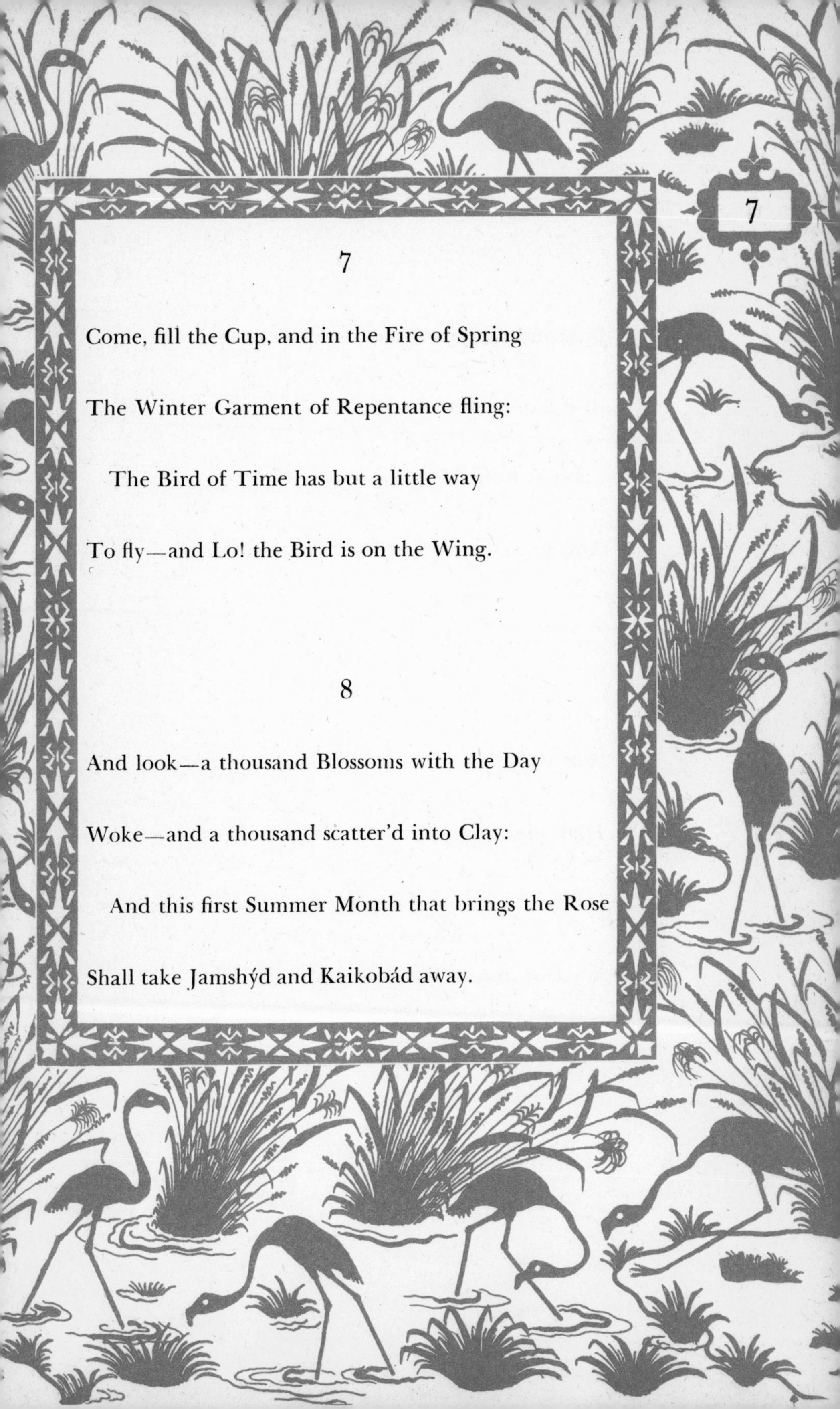

7

Come, fill the Cup, and in the Fire of Spring
The Winter Garment of Repentance fling:
  The Bird of Time has but a little way
To fly—and Lo! the Bird is on the Wing.

8

And look—a thousand Blossoms with the Day
Woke—and a thousand scatter'd into Clay:
  And this first Summer Month that brings the Rose
Shall take Jamshýd and Kaikobád away.

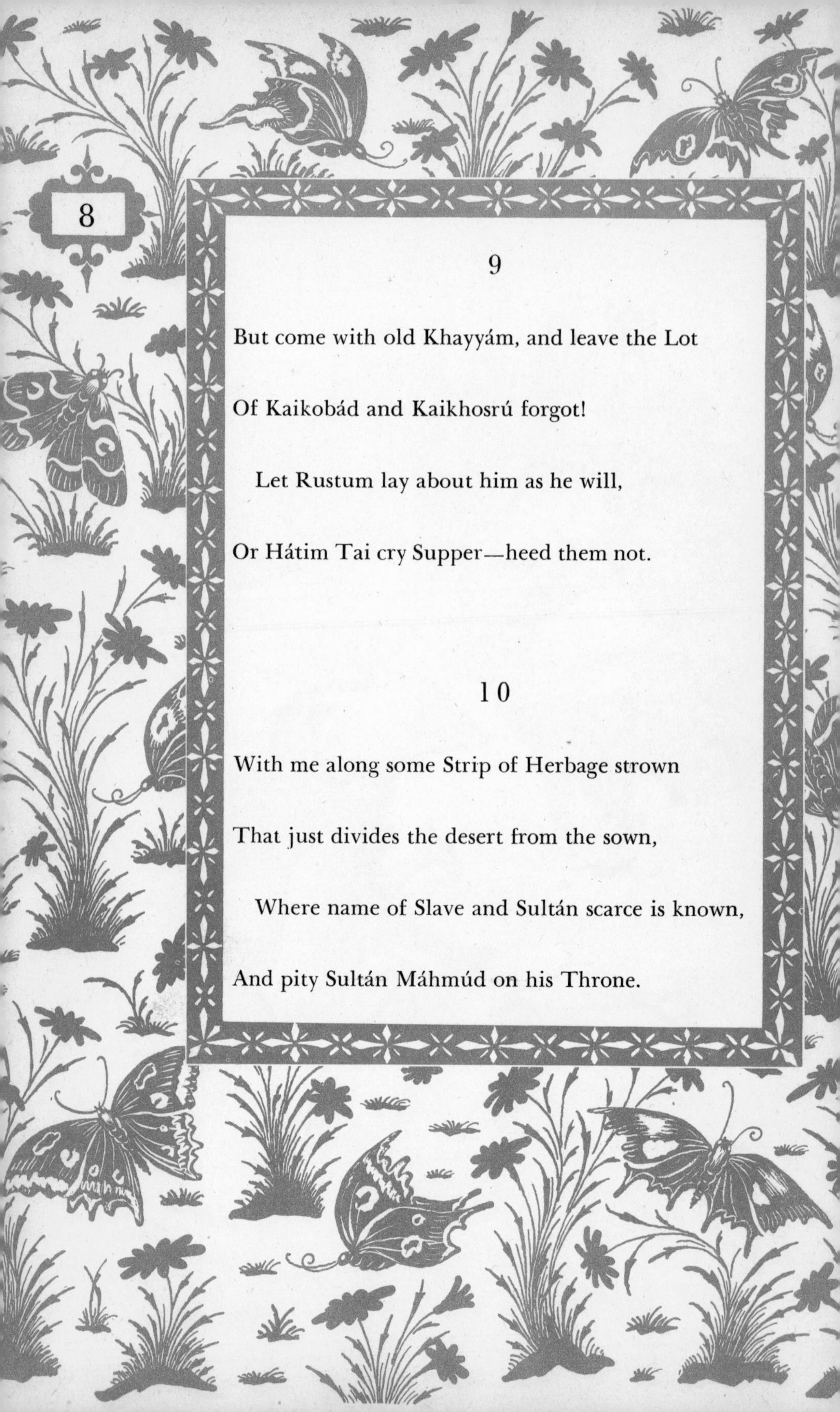

9

But come with old Khayyám, and leave the Lot
Of Kaikobád and Kaikhosrú forgot!
  Let Rustum lay about him as he will,
Or Hátim Tai cry Supper—heed them not.

10

With me along some Strip of Herbage strown
That just divides the desert from the sown,
  Where name of Slave and Sultán scarce is known,
And pity Sultán Máhmúd on his Throne.

9

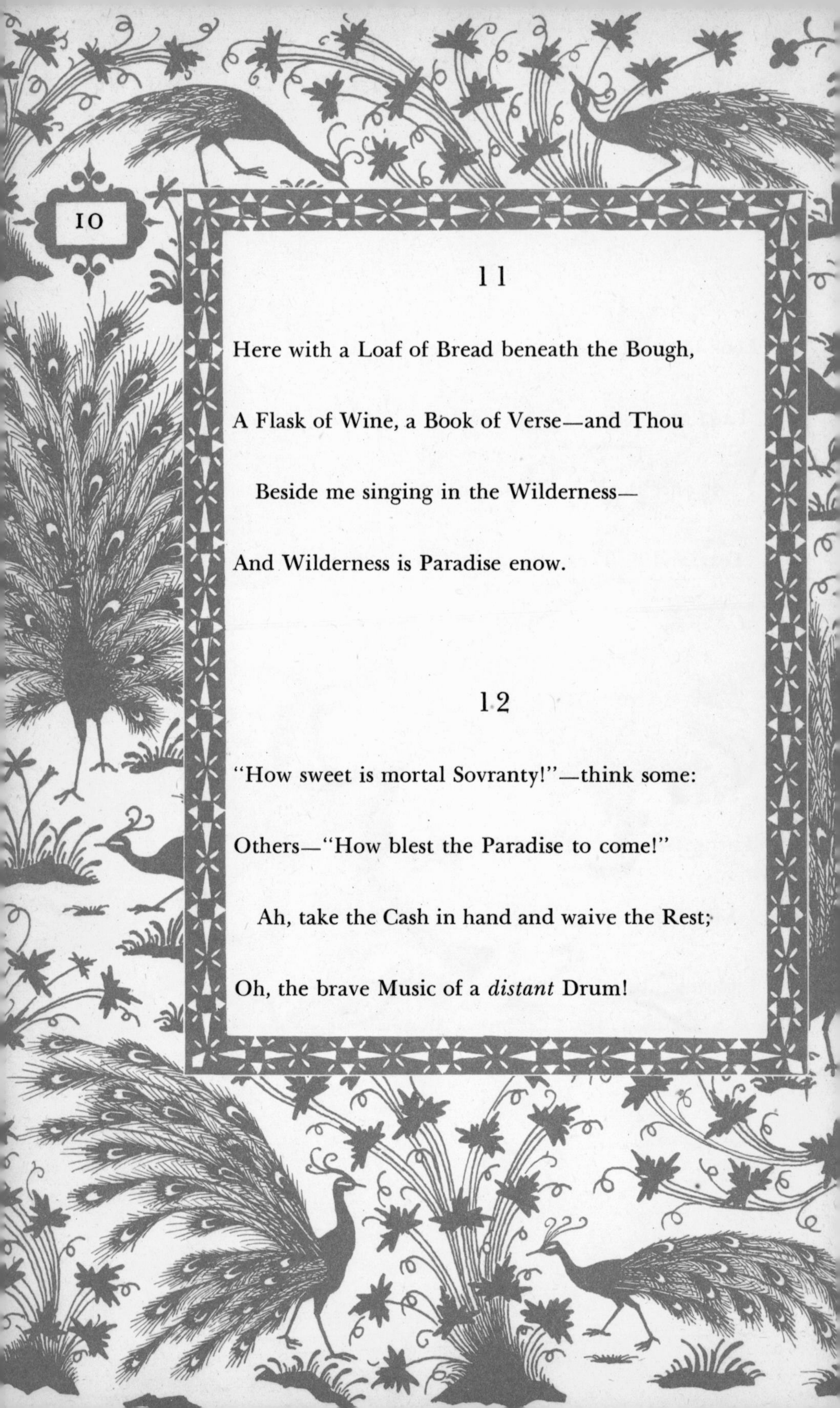

11

Here with a Loaf of Bread beneath the Bough,
A Flask of Wine, a Book of Verse—and Thou
  Beside me singing in the Wilderness—
And Wilderness is Paradise enow.

12

"How sweet is mortal Sovranty!"—think some:
Others—"How blest the Paradise to come!"
  Ah, take the Cash in hand and waive the Rest;
Oh, the brave Music of a *distant* Drum!

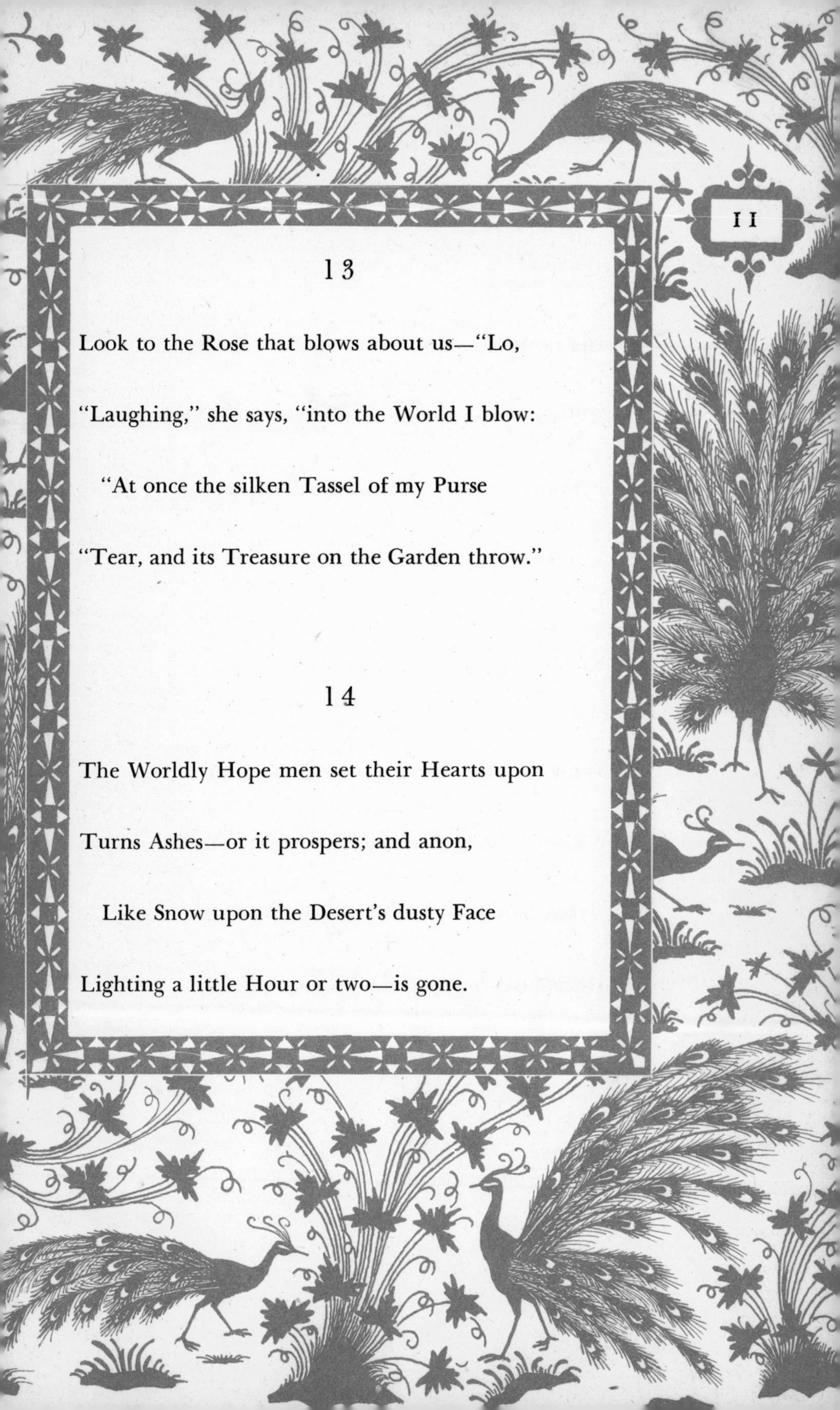

13

Look to the Rose that blows about us—"Lo,
"Laughing," she says, "into the World I blow:
"At once the silken Tassel of my Purse
"Tear, and its Treasure on the Garden throw."

14

The Worldly Hope men set their Hearts upon
Turns Ashes—or it prospers; and anon,
Like Snow upon the Desert's dusty Face
Lighting a little Hour or two—is gone.

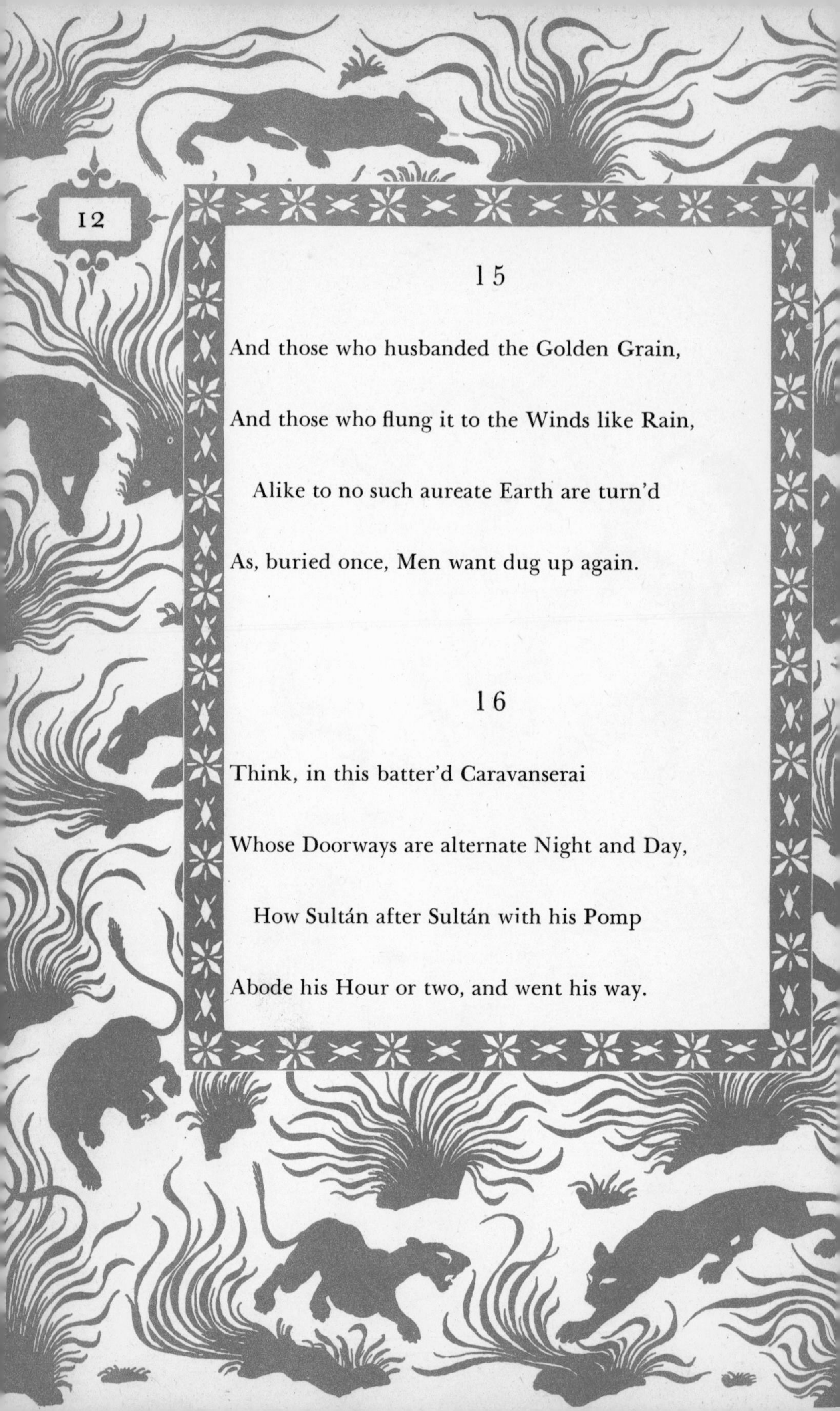

15

And those who husbanded the Golden Grain,
And those who flung it to the Winds like Rain,
Alike to no such aureate Earth are turn'd
As, buried once, Men want dug up again.

16

Think, in this batter'd Caravanserai
Whose Doorways are alternate Night and Day,
How Sultán after Sultán with his Pomp
Abode his Hour or two, and went his way.

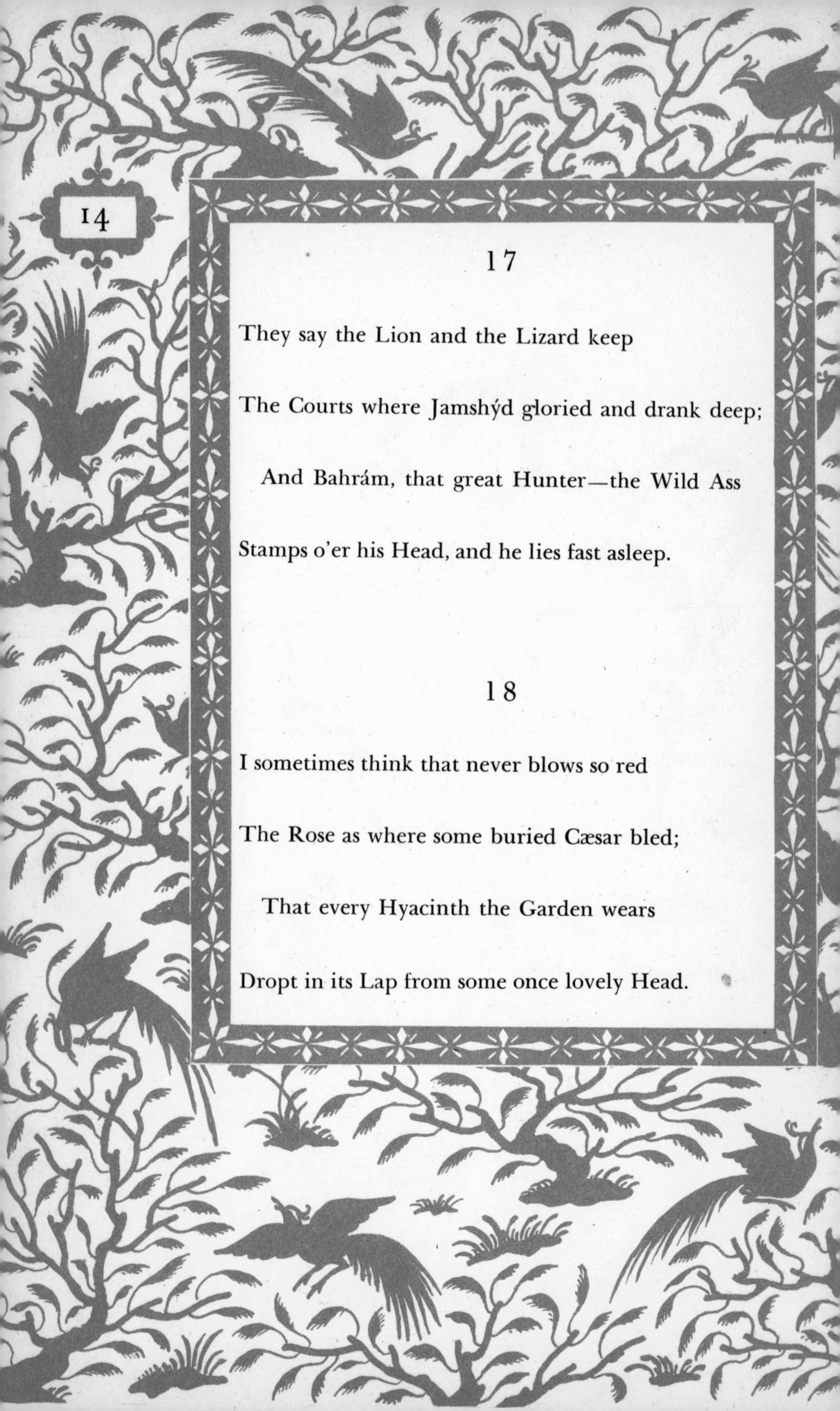

17

They say the Lion and the Lizard keep
The Courts where Jamshýd gloried and drank deep;
  And Bahrám, that great Hunter—the Wild Ass
Stamps o'er his Head, and he lies fast asleep.

18

I sometimes think that never blows so red
The Rose as where some buried Cæsar bled;
  That every Hyacinth the Garden wears
Dropt in its Lap from some once lovely Head.

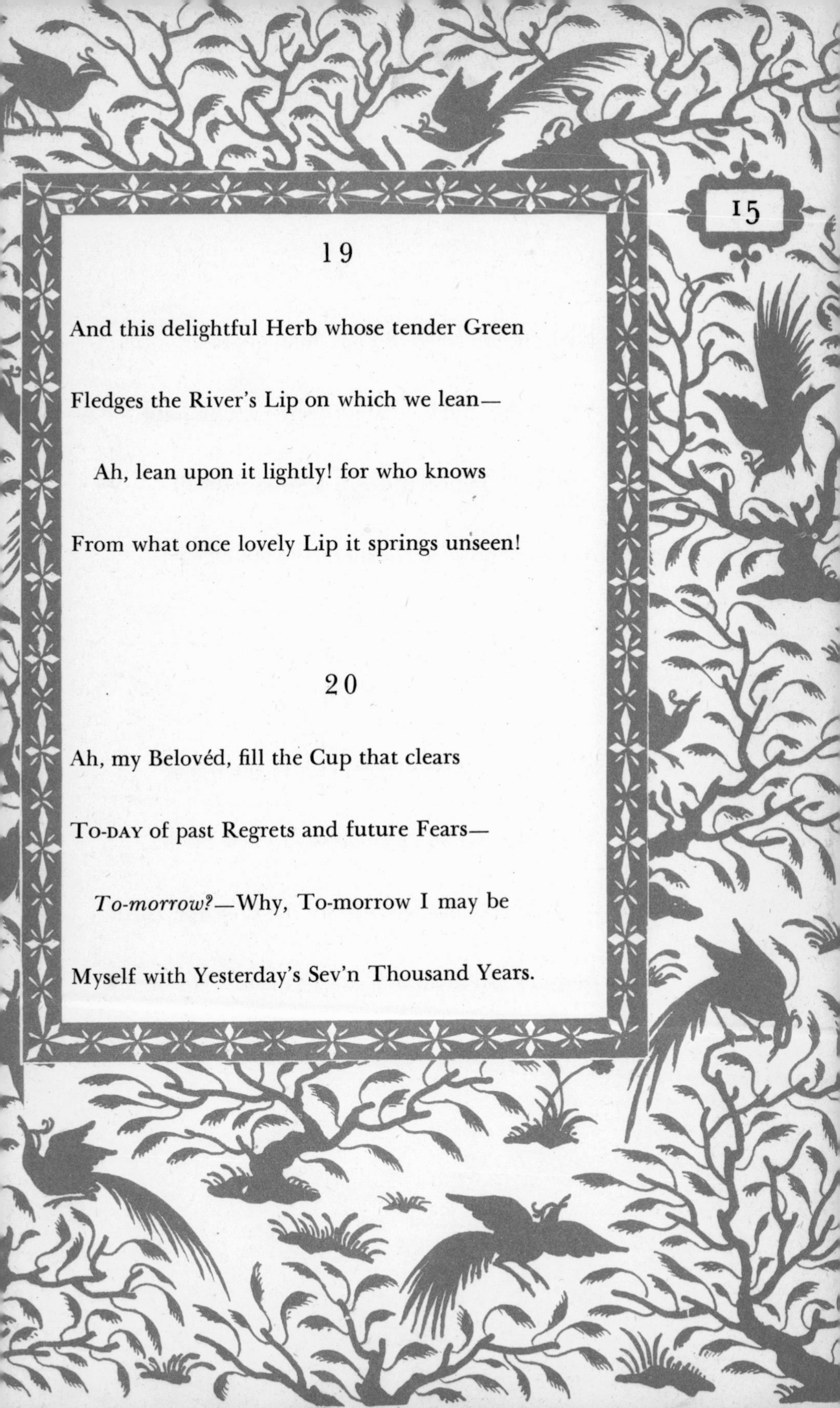

19

And this delightful Herb whose tender Green
Fledges the River's Lip on which we lean—
   Ah, lean upon it lightly! for who knows
From what once lovely Lip it springs unseen!

20

Ah, my Belovéd, fill the Cup that clears
TO-DAY of past Regrets and future Fears—
   To-morrow?—Why, To-morrow I may be
Myself with Yesterday's Sev'n Thousand Years.

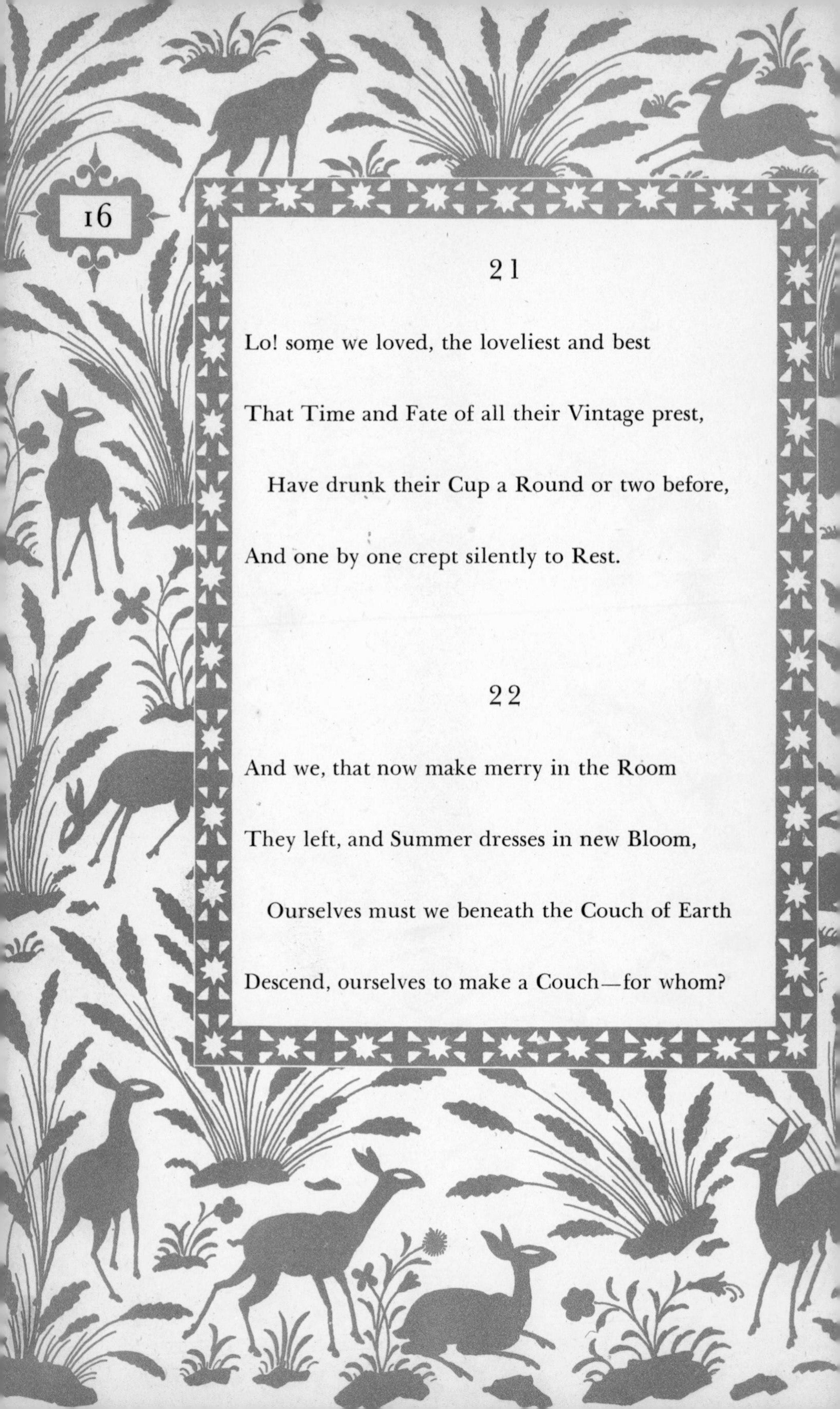

21

Lo! some we loved, the loveliest and best
That Time and Fate of all their Vintage prest,
    Have drunk their Cup a Round or two before,
And one by one crept silently to Rest.

22

And we, that now make merry in the Room
They left, and Summer dresses in new Bloom,
    Ourselves must we beneath the Couch of Earth
Descend, ourselves to make a Couch—for whom?

17
M. Sayah

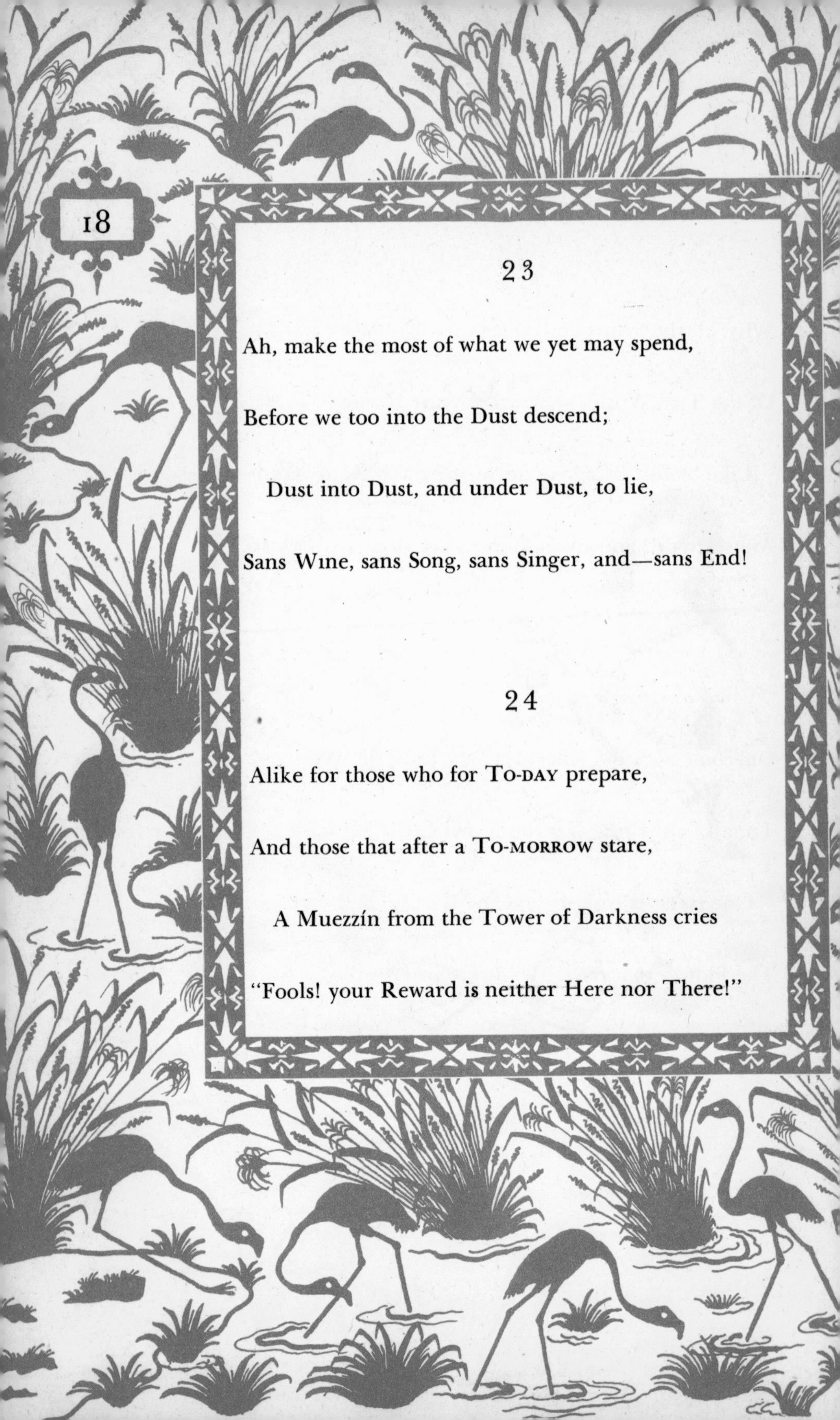

23

Ah, make the most of what we yet may spend,
Before we too into the Dust descend;
  Dust into Dust, and under Dust, to lie,
Sans Wine, sans Song, sans Singer, and—sans End!

24

Alike for those who for To-day prepare,
And those that after a To-morrow stare,
  A Muezzín from the Tower of Darkness cries
"Fools! your Reward is neither Here nor There!"

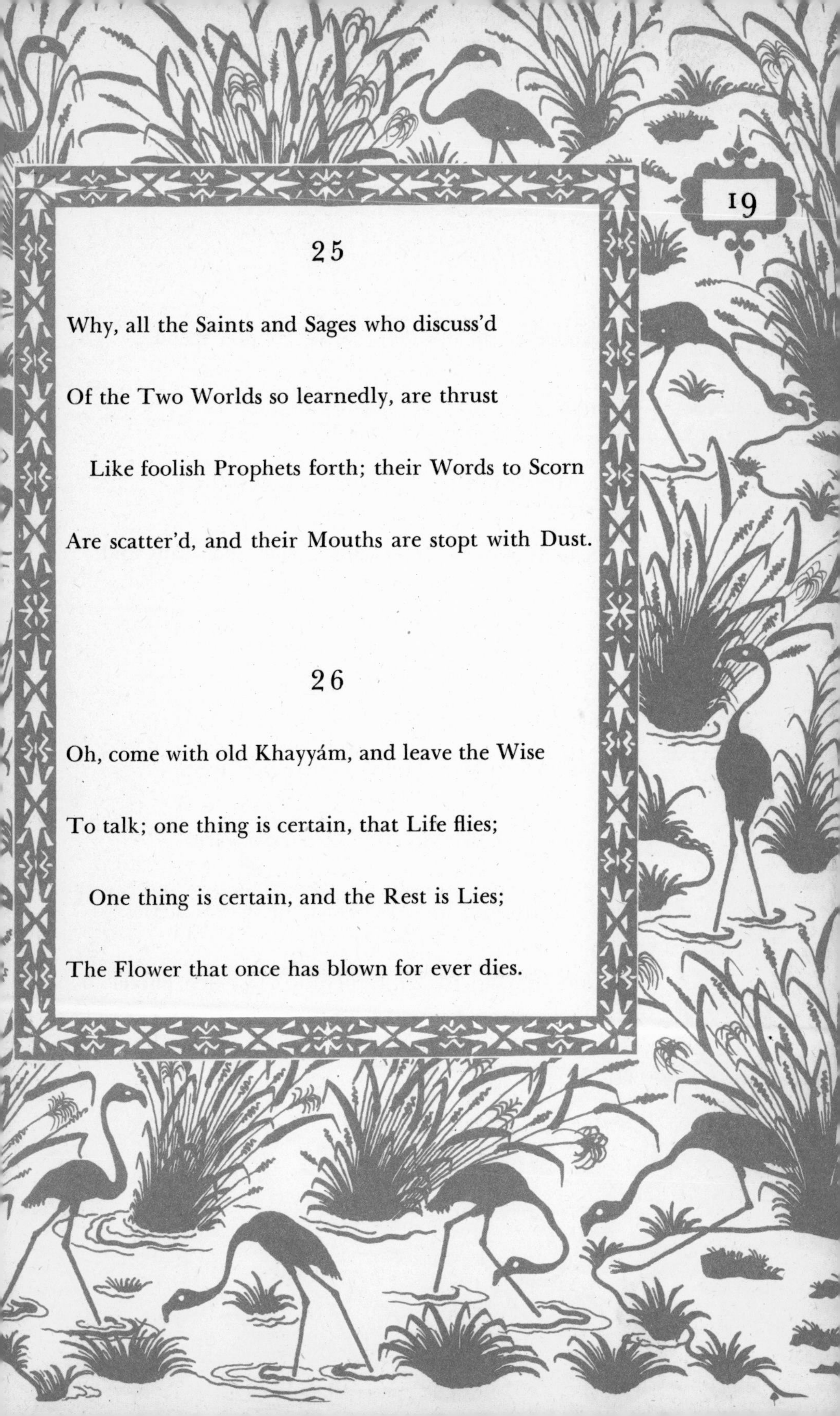

25

Why, all the Saints and Sages who discuss'd
Of the Two Worlds so learnedly, are thrust
  Like foolish Prophets forth; their Words to Scorn
Are scatter'd, and their Mouths are stopt with Dust.

26

Oh, come with old Khayyám, and leave the Wise
To talk; one thing is certain, that Life flies;
  One thing is certain, and the Rest is Lies;
The Flower that once has blown for ever dies.

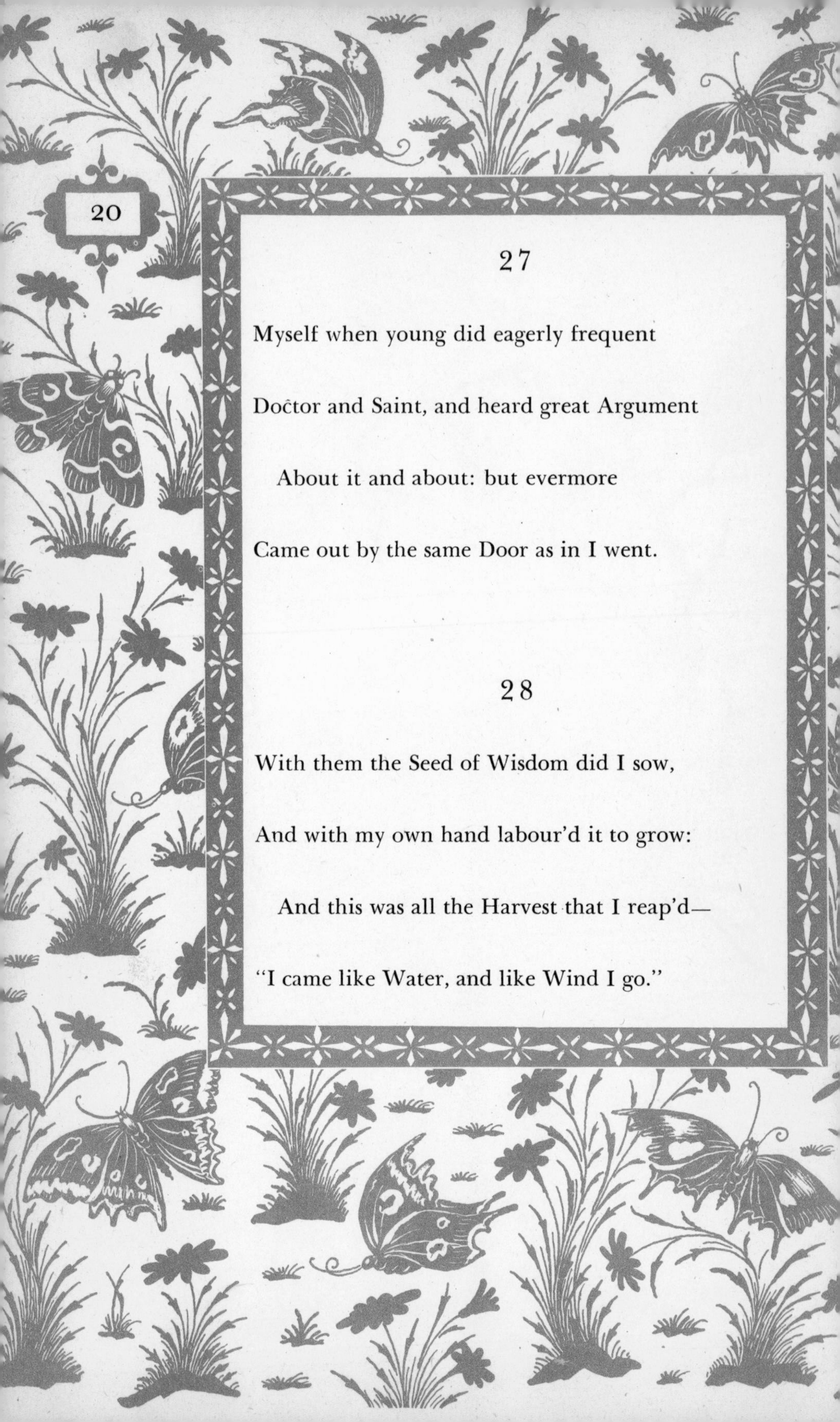

27

Myself when young did eagerly frequent
Doctor and Saint, and heard great Argument
About it and about: but evermore
Came out by the same Door as in I went.

28

With them the Seed of Wisdom did I sow,
And with my own hand labour'd it to grow:
And this was all the Harvest that I reap'd—
"I came like Water, and like Wind I go."

21
M. Sayah

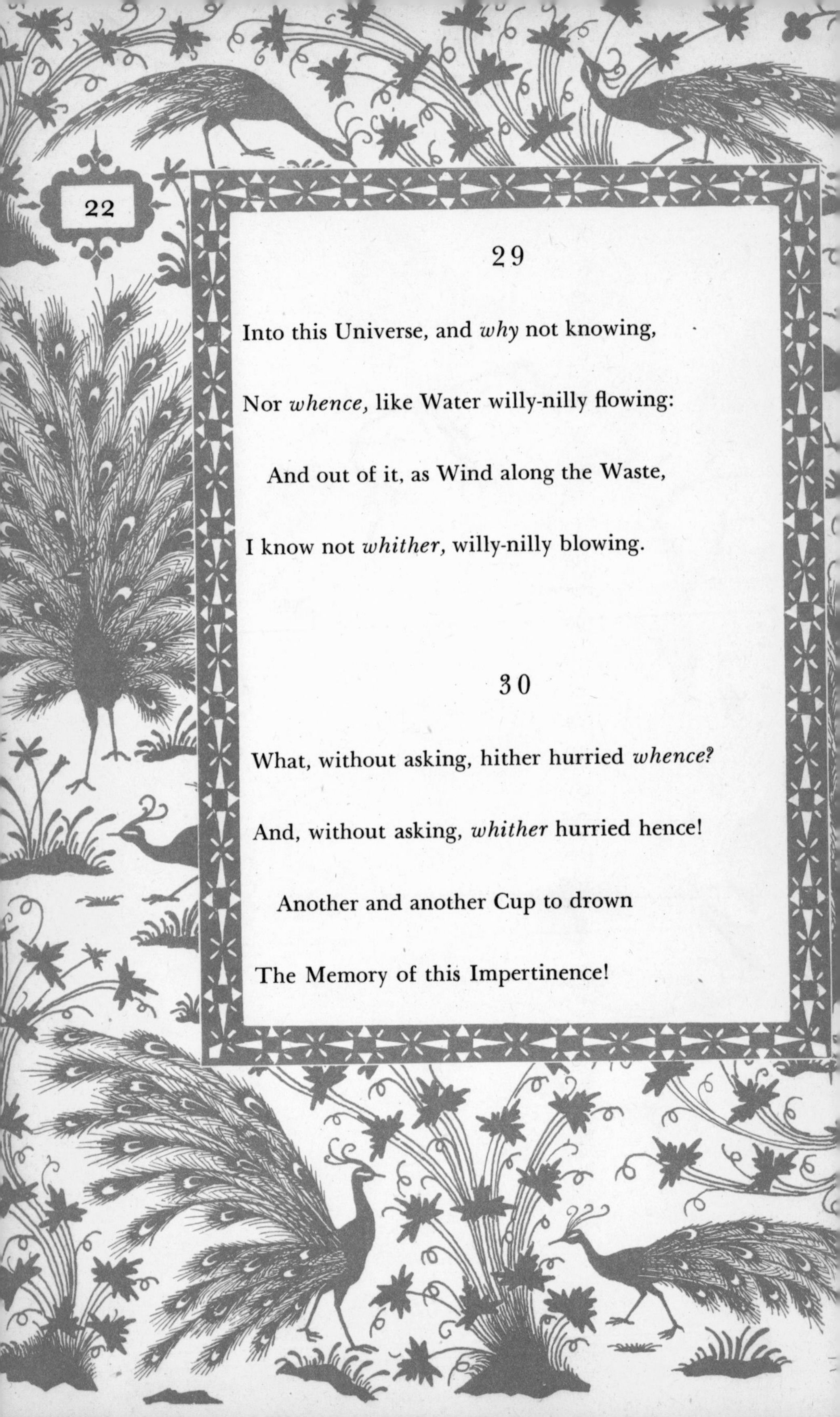

29

Into this Universe, and *why* not knowing,
Nor *whence,* like Water willy-nilly flowing:
  And out of it, as Wind along the Waste,
I know not *whither,* willy-nilly blowing.

30

What, without asking, hither hurried *whence?*
And, without asking, *whither* hurried hence!
  Another and another Cup to drown
The Memory of this Impertinence!

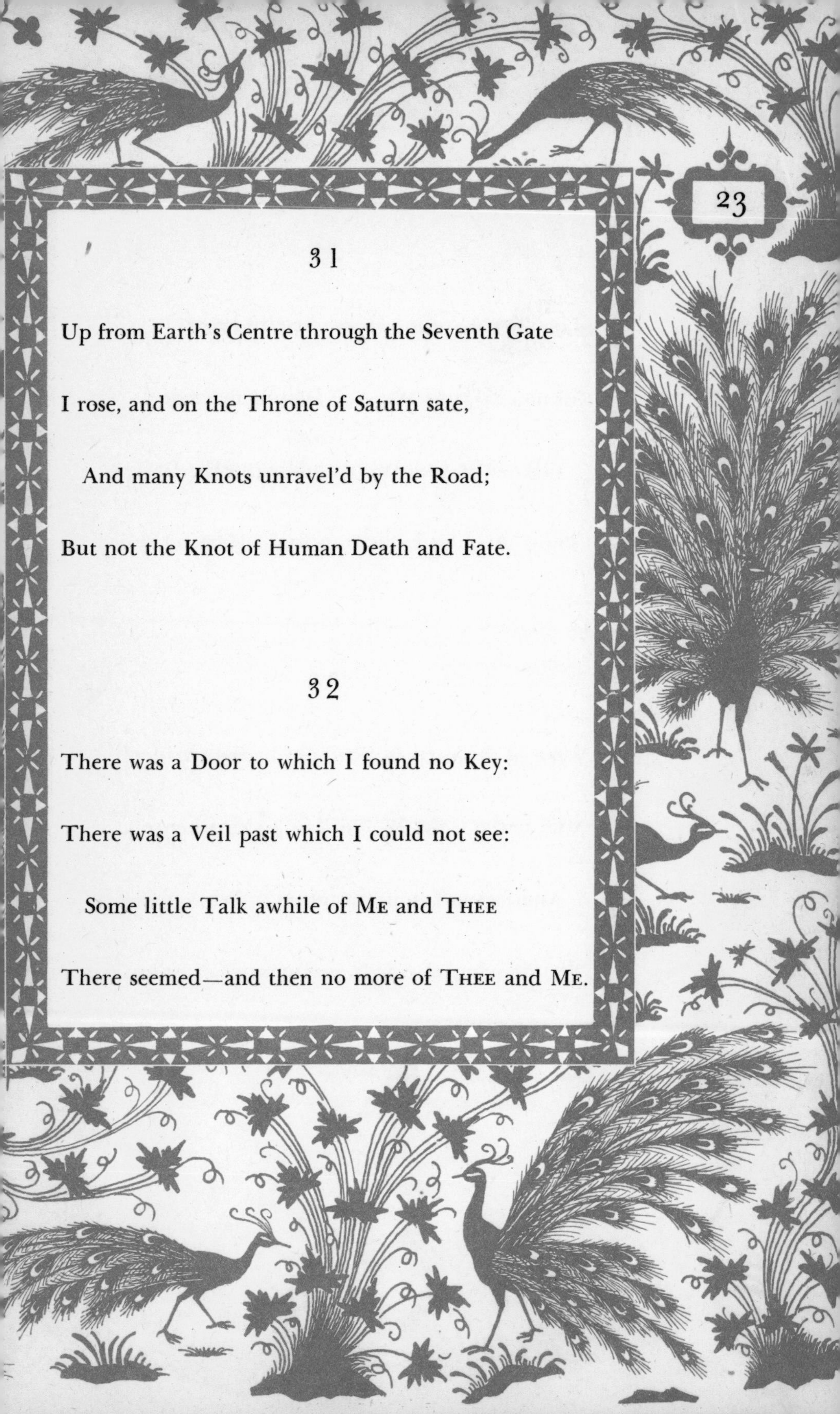

31

Up from Earth's Centre through the Seventh Gate
I rose, and on the Throne of Saturn sate,
And many Knots unravel'd by the Road;
But not the Knot of Human Death and Fate.

32

There was a Door to which I found no Key:
There was a Veil past which I could not see:
Some little Talk awhile of Me and Thee
There seemed—and then no more of Thee and Me.

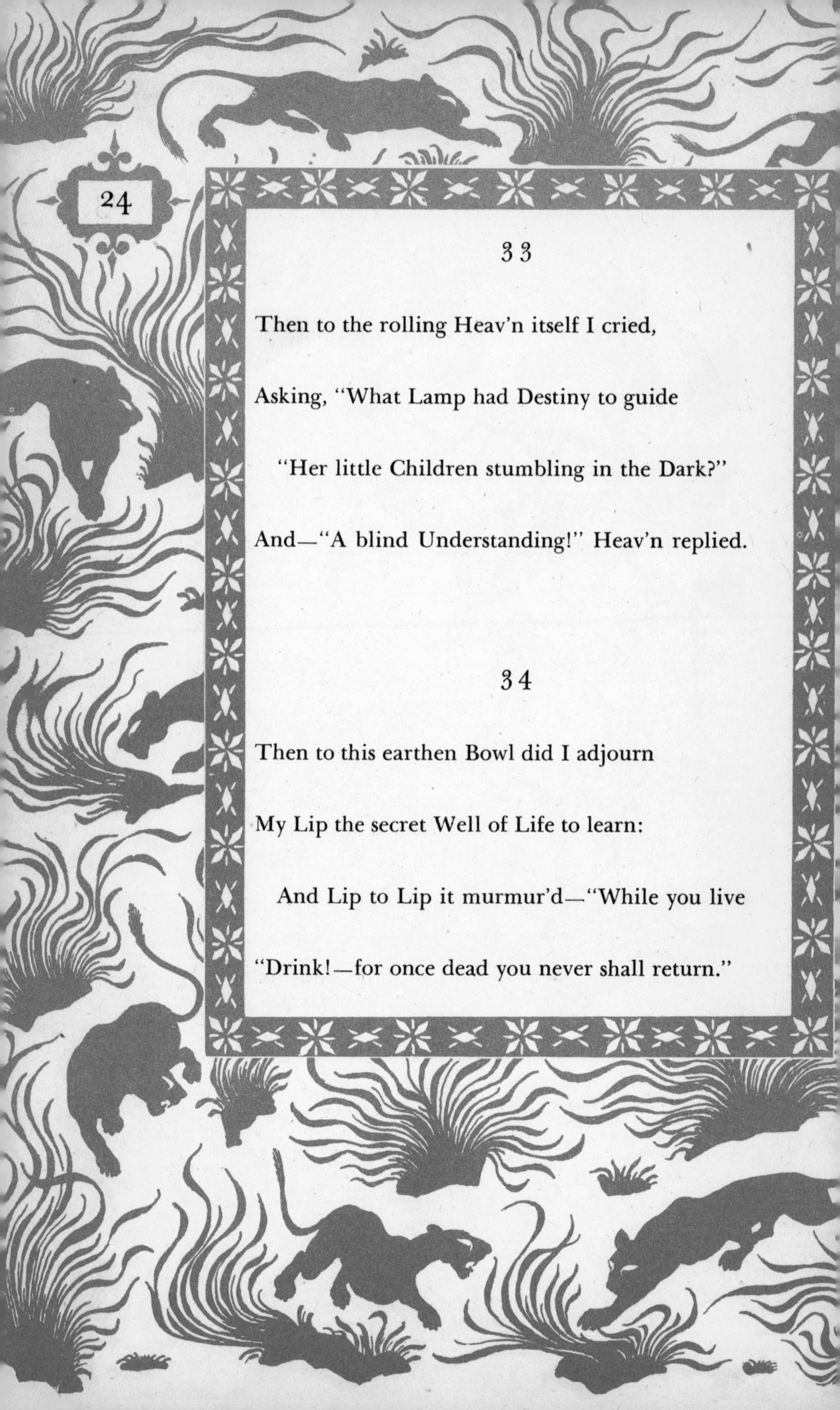

33

Then to the rolling Heav'n itself I cried,
Asking, "What Lamp had Destiny to guide
"Her little Children stumbling in the Dark?"
And—"A blind Understanding!" Heav'n replied.

34

Then to this earthen Bowl did I adjourn
My Lip the secret Well of Life to learn:
And Lip to Lip it murmur'd—"While you live
"Drink!—for once dead you never shall return."

25
M. Sayah

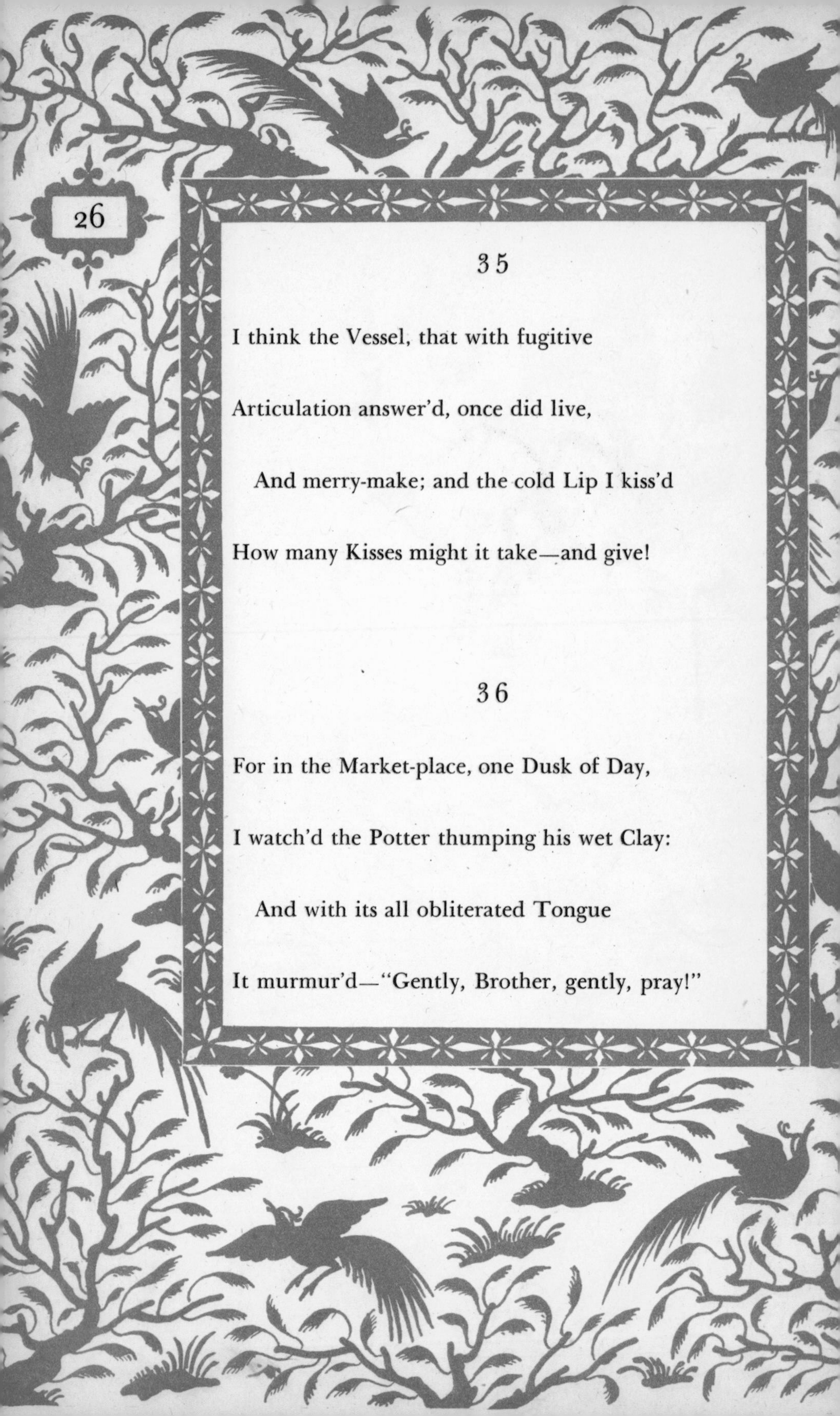

35

I think the Vessel, that with fugitive
Articulation answer'd, once did live,
And merry-make; and the cold Lip I kiss'd
How many Kisses might it take—and give!

36

For in the Market-place, one Dusk of Day,
I watch'd the Potter thumping his wet Clay:
And with its all obliterated Tongue
It murmur'd—"Gently, Brother, gently, pray!"

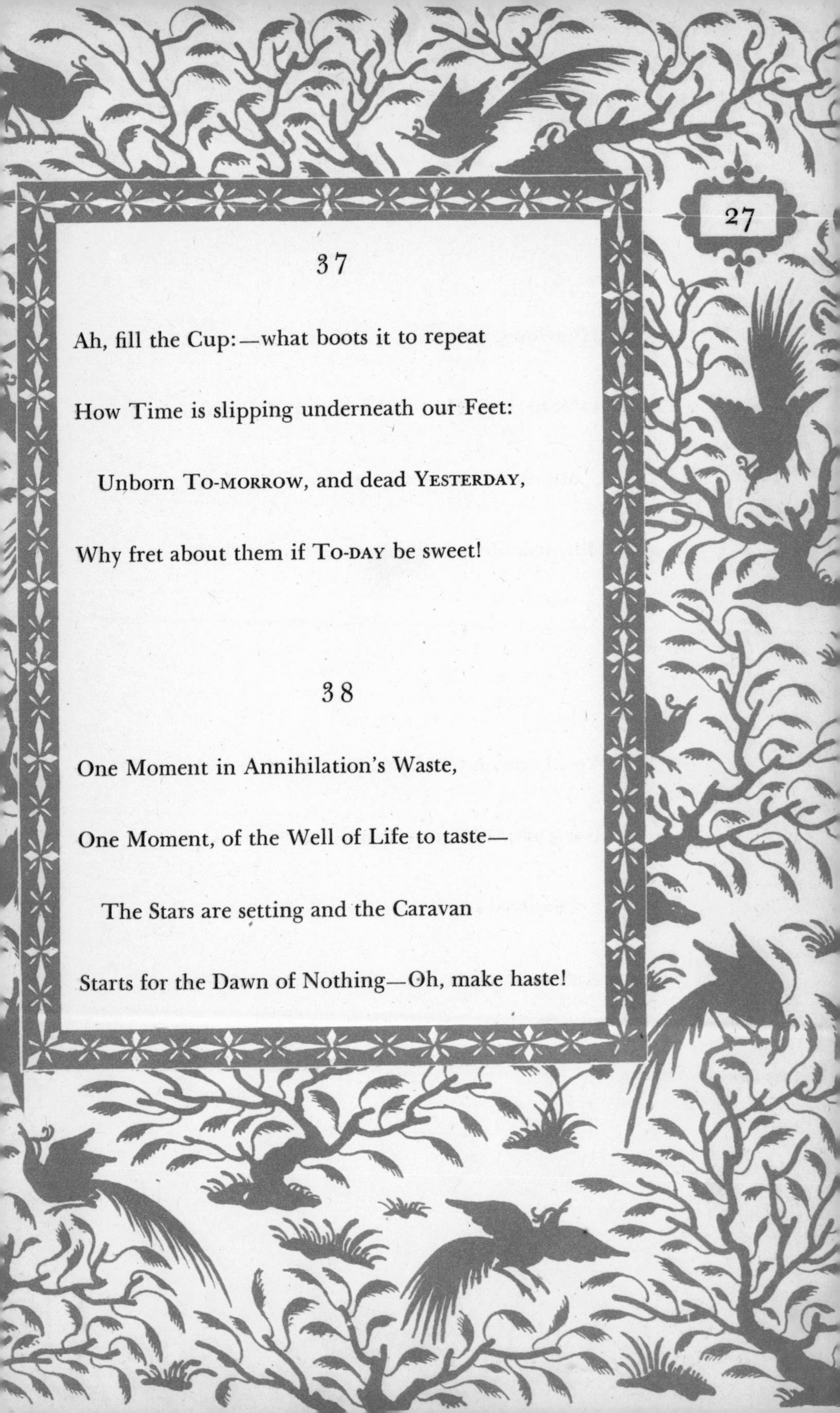

37

Ah, fill the Cup:—what boots it to repeat
How Time is slipping underneath our Feet:
  Unborn To-morrow, and dead Yesterday,
Why fret about them if To-day be sweet!

38

One Moment in Annihilation's Waste,
One Moment, of the Well of Life to taste—
  The Stars are setting and the Caravan
Starts for the Dawn of Nothing—Oh, make haste!

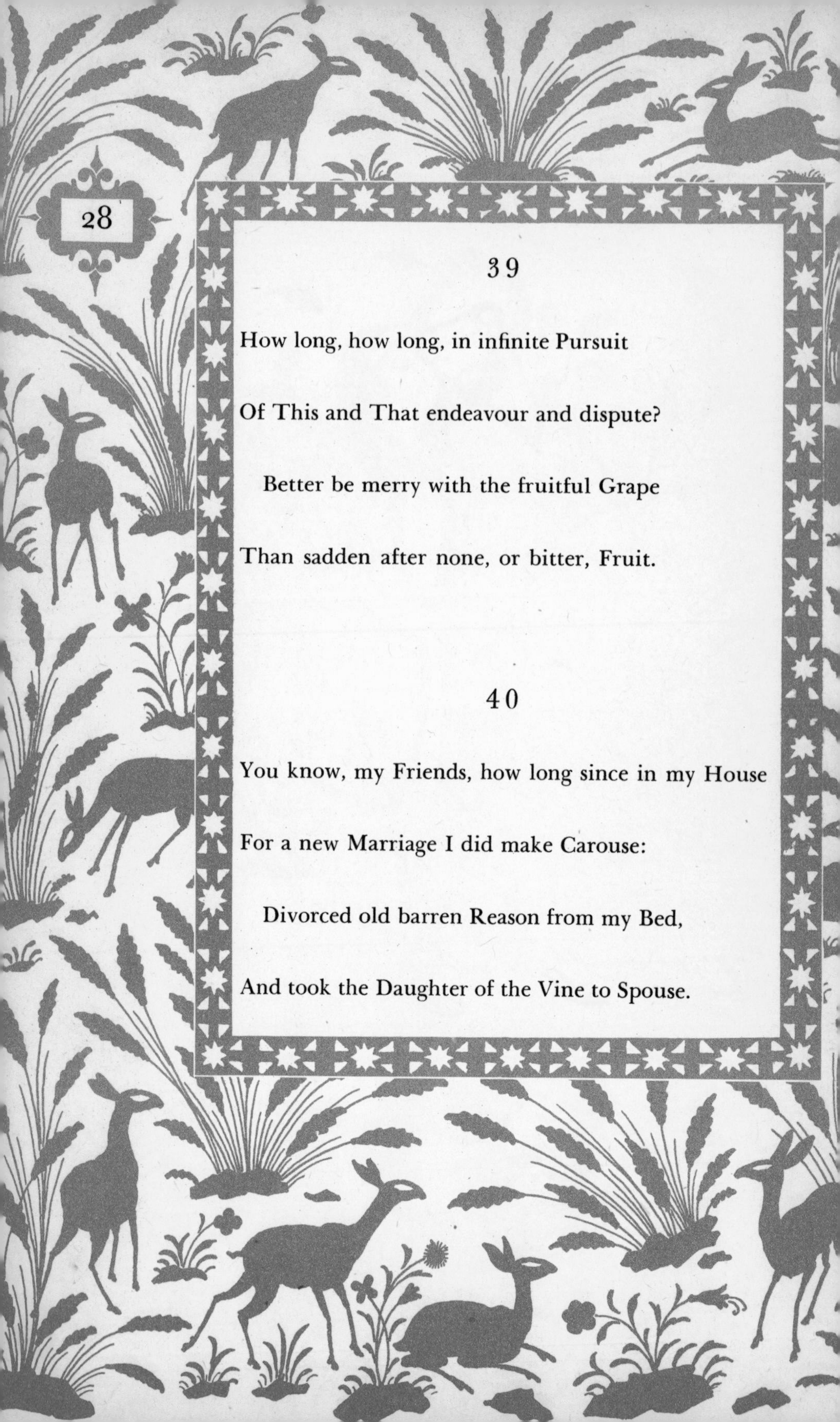

39

How long, how long, in infinite Pursuit
Of This and That endeavour and dispute?
  Better be merry with the fruitful Grape
Than sadden after none, or bitter, Fruit.

40

You know, my Friends, how long since in my House
For a new Marriage I did make Carouse:
  Divorced old barren Reason from my Bed,
And took the Daughter of the Vine to Spouse.

M. Sayah

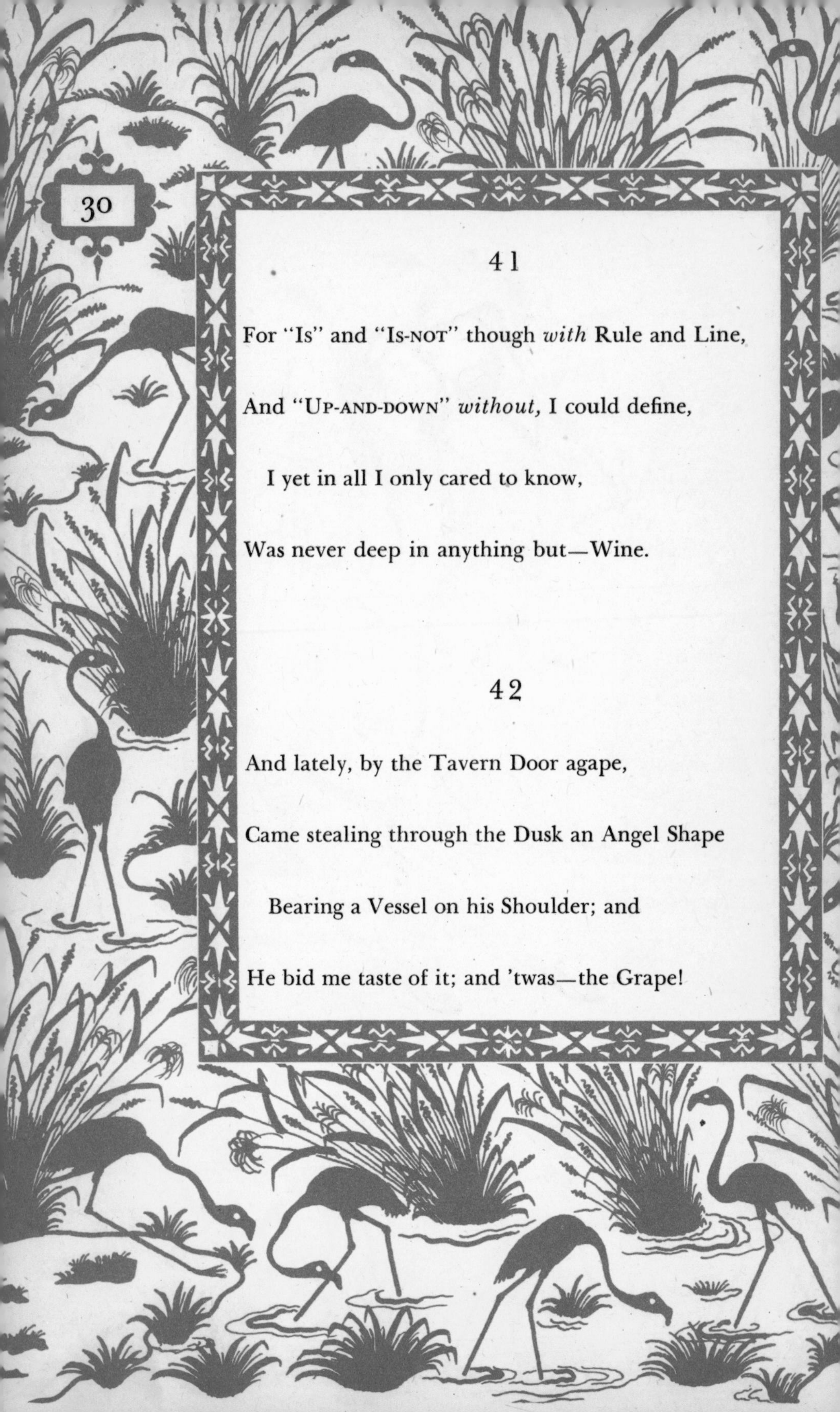

41

For "Is" and "Is-not" though *with* Rule and Line,
And "Up-and-down" *without,* I could define,
I yet in all I only cared to know,
Was never deep in anything but—Wine.

42

And lately, by the Tavern Door agape,
Came stealing through the Dusk an Angel Shape
Bearing a Vessel on his Shoulder; and
He bid me taste of it; and 'twas—the Grape!

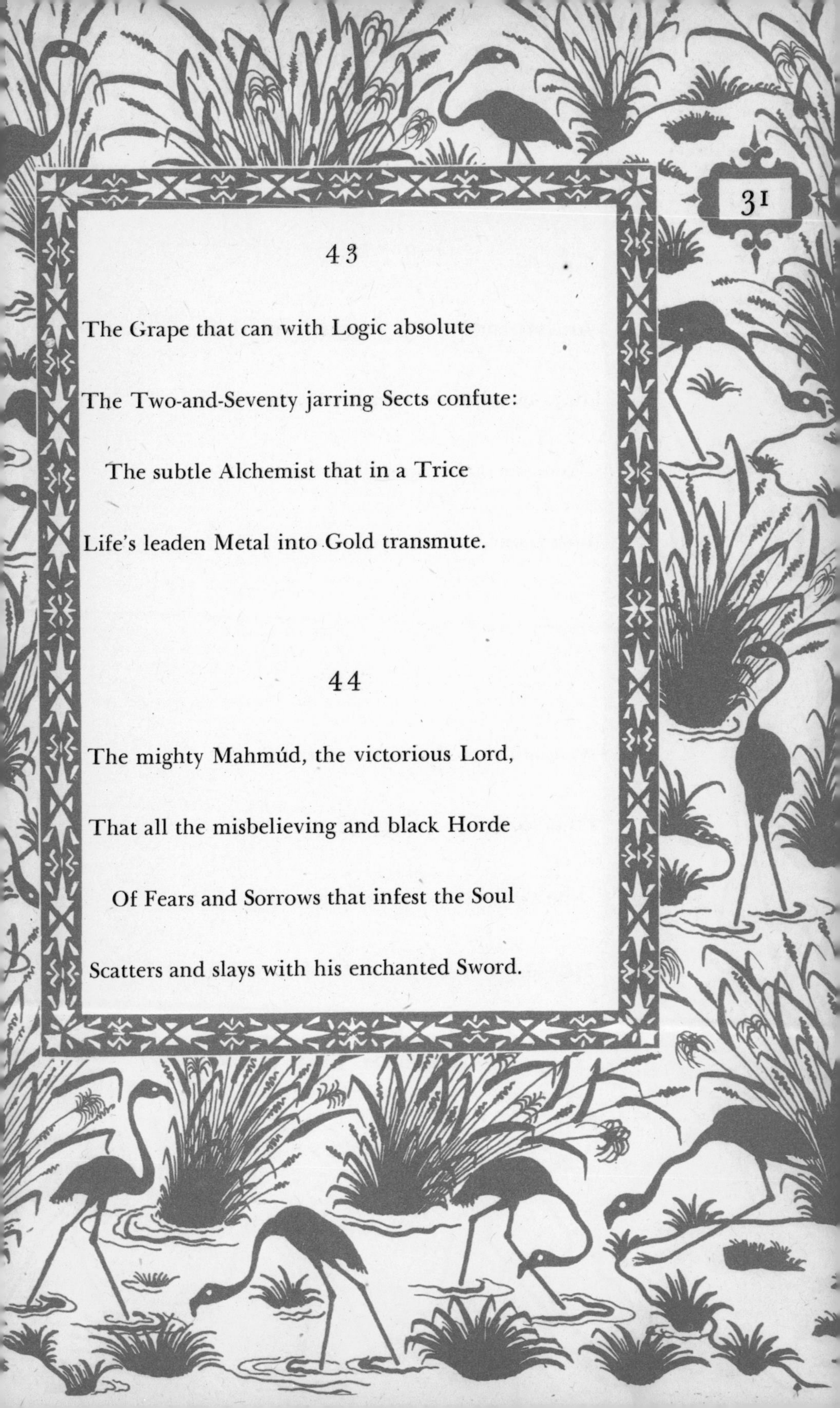

43

The Grape that can with Logic absolute
The Two-and-Seventy jarring Sects confute:
The subtle Alchemist that in a Trice
Life's leaden Metal into Gold transmute.

44

The mighty Mahmúd, the victorious Lord,
That all the misbelieving and black Horde
Of Fears and Sorrows that infest the Soul
Scatters and slays with his enchanted Sword.

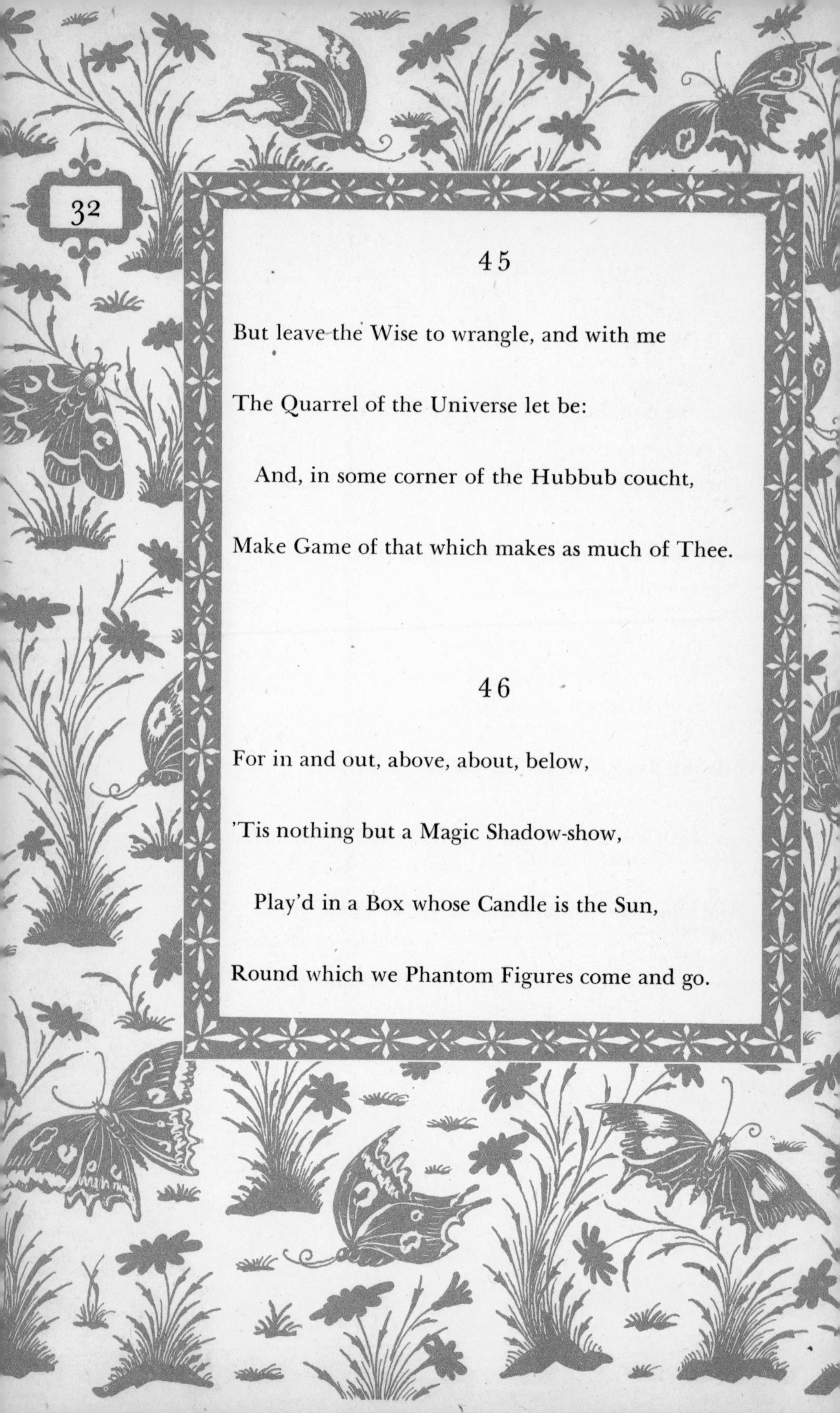

45

But leave the Wise to wrangle, and with me
The Quarrel of the Universe let be:
  And, in some corner of the Hubbub coucht,
Make Game of that which makes as much of Thee.

46

For in and out, above, about, below,
'Tis nothing but a Magic Shadow-show,
  Play'd in a Box whose Candle is the Sun,
Round which we Phantom Figures come and go.

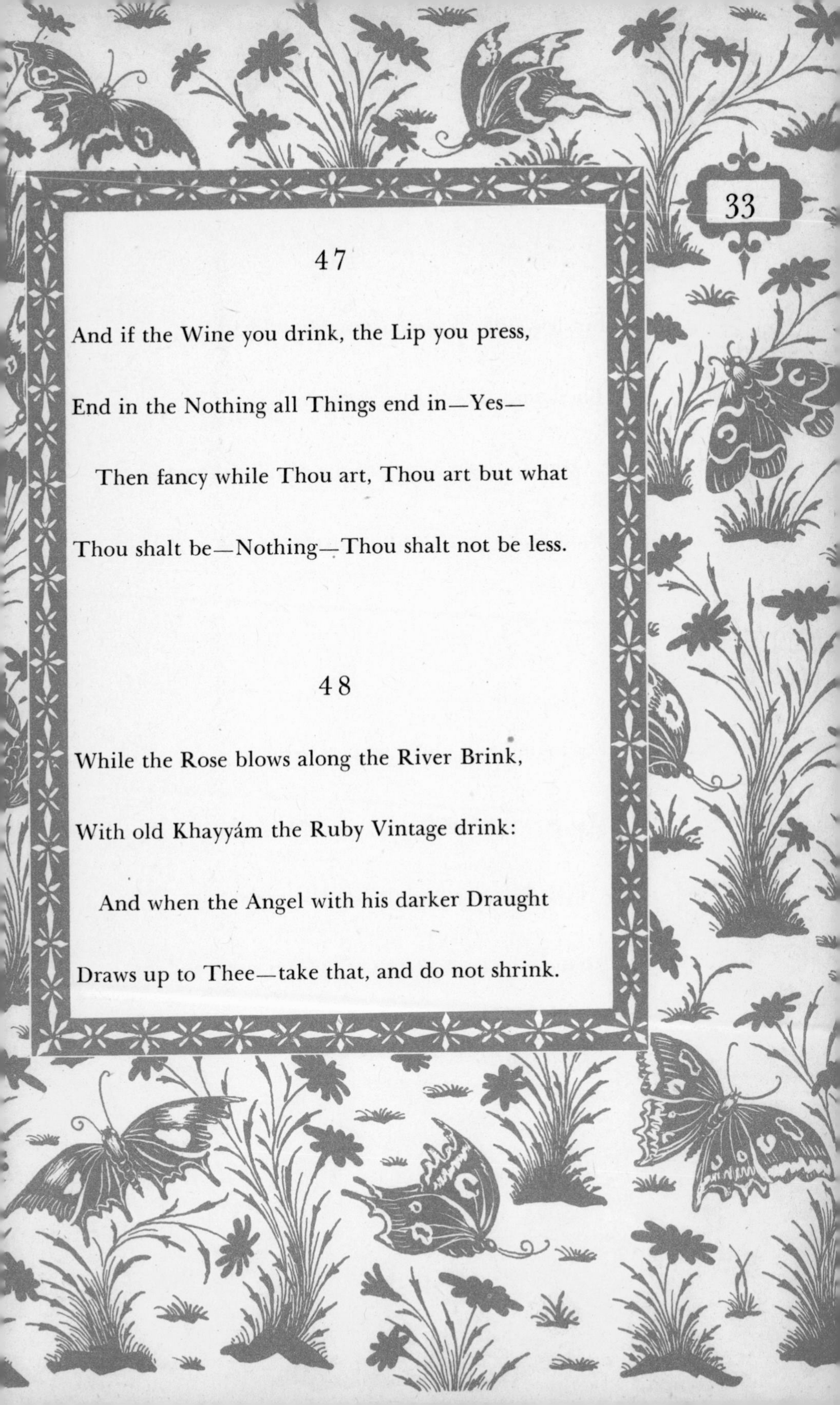

47

And if the Wine you drink, the Lip you press,
End in the Nothing all Things end in—Yes—
Then fancy while Thou art, Thou art but what
Thou shalt be—Nothing—Thou shalt not be less.

48

While the Rose blows along the River Brink,
With old Khayyám the Ruby Vintage drink:
And when the Angel with his darker Draught
Draws up to Thee—take that, and do not shrink.

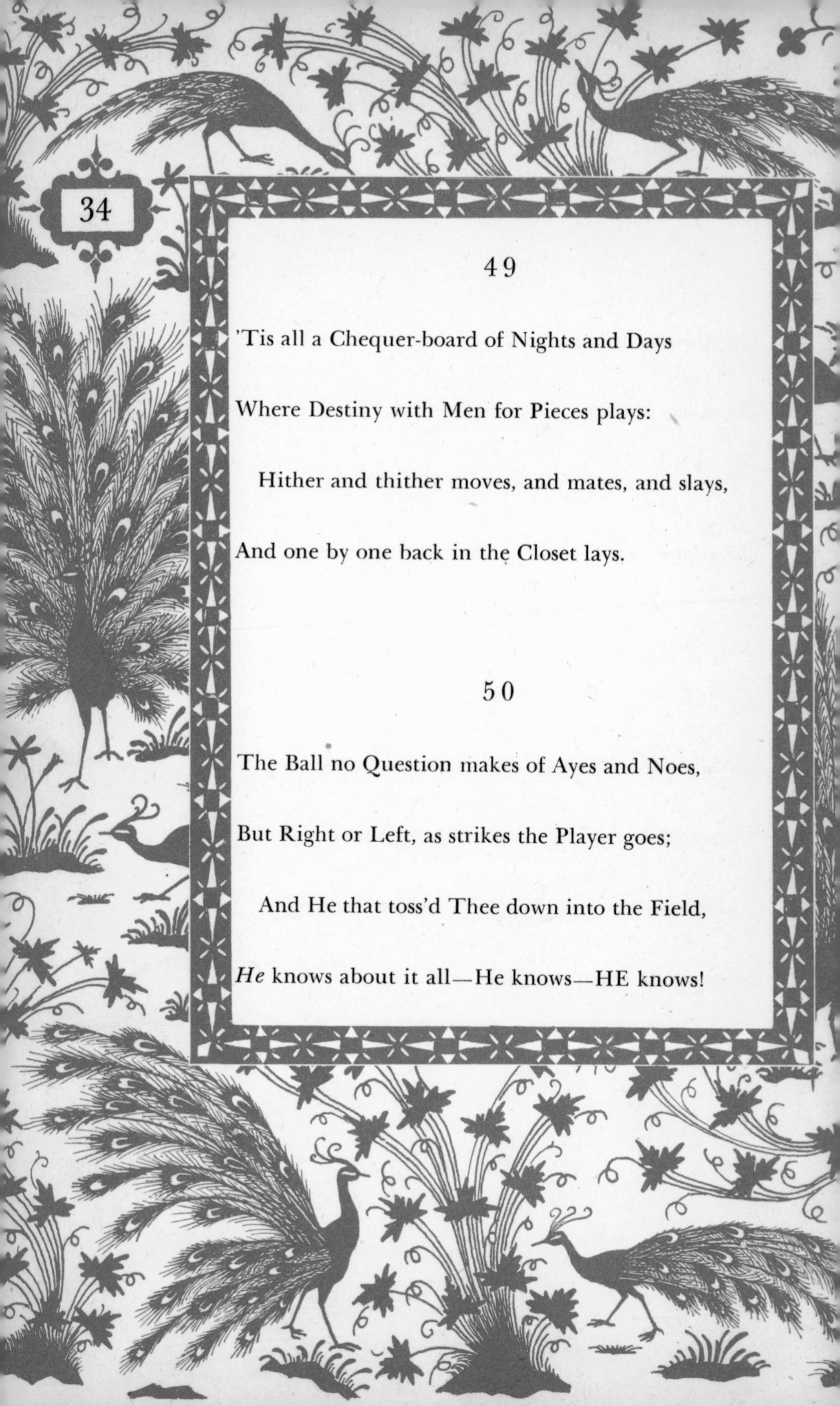

49

'Tis all a Chequer-board of Nights and Days
Where Destiny with Men for Pieces plays:
  Hither and thither moves, and mates, and slays,
And one by one back in the Closet lays.

50

The Ball no Question makes of Ayes and Noes,
But Right or Left, as strikes the Player goes;
  And He that toss'd Thee down into the Field,
He knows about it all—He knows—HE knows!

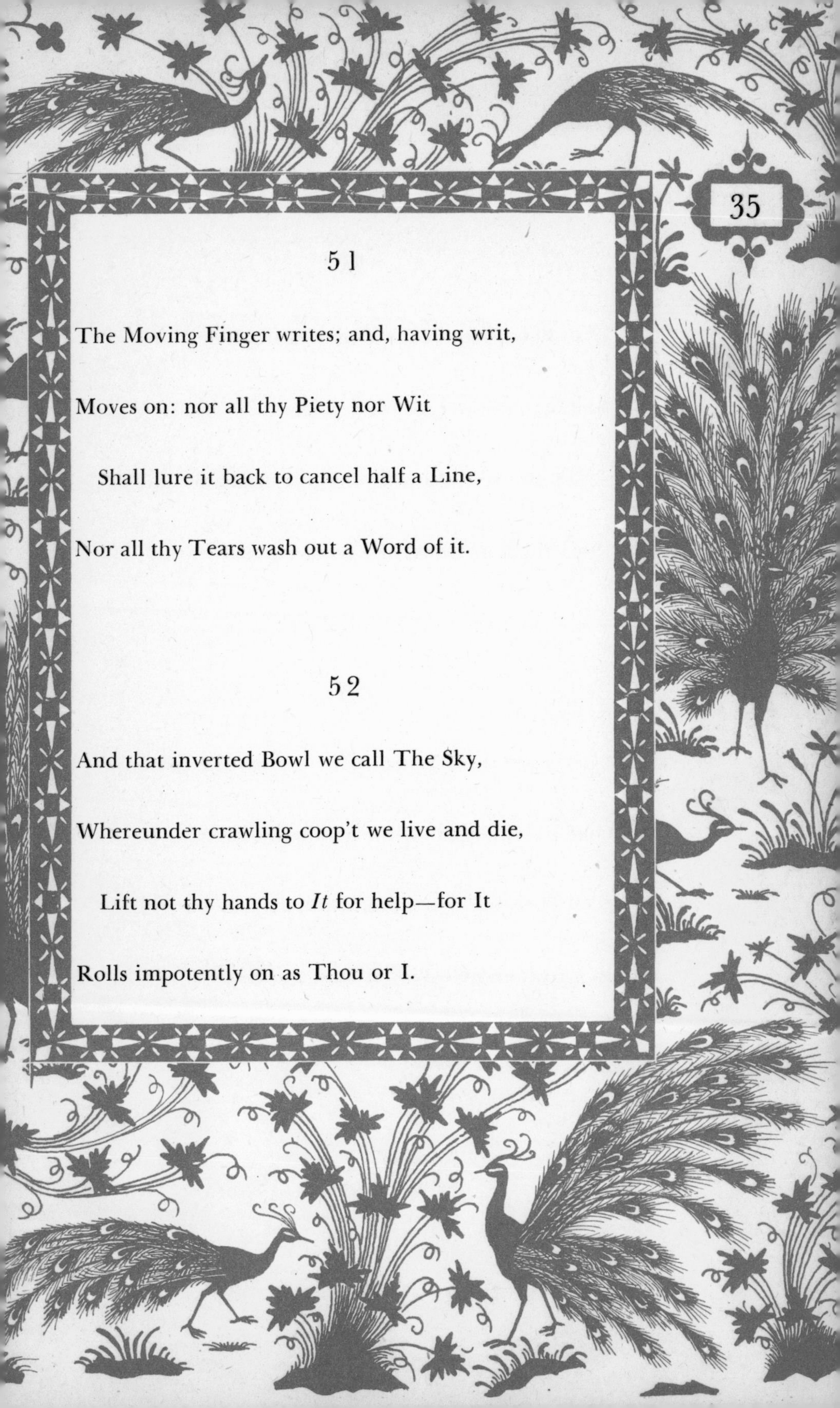

51

The Moving Finger writes; and, having writ,
Moves on: nor all thy Piety nor Wit
  Shall lure it back to cancel half a Line,
Nor all thy Tears wash out a Word of it.

52

And that inverted Bowl we call The Sky,
Whereunder crawling coop't we live and die,
  Lift not thy hands to *It* for help—for It
Rolls impotently on as Thou or I.

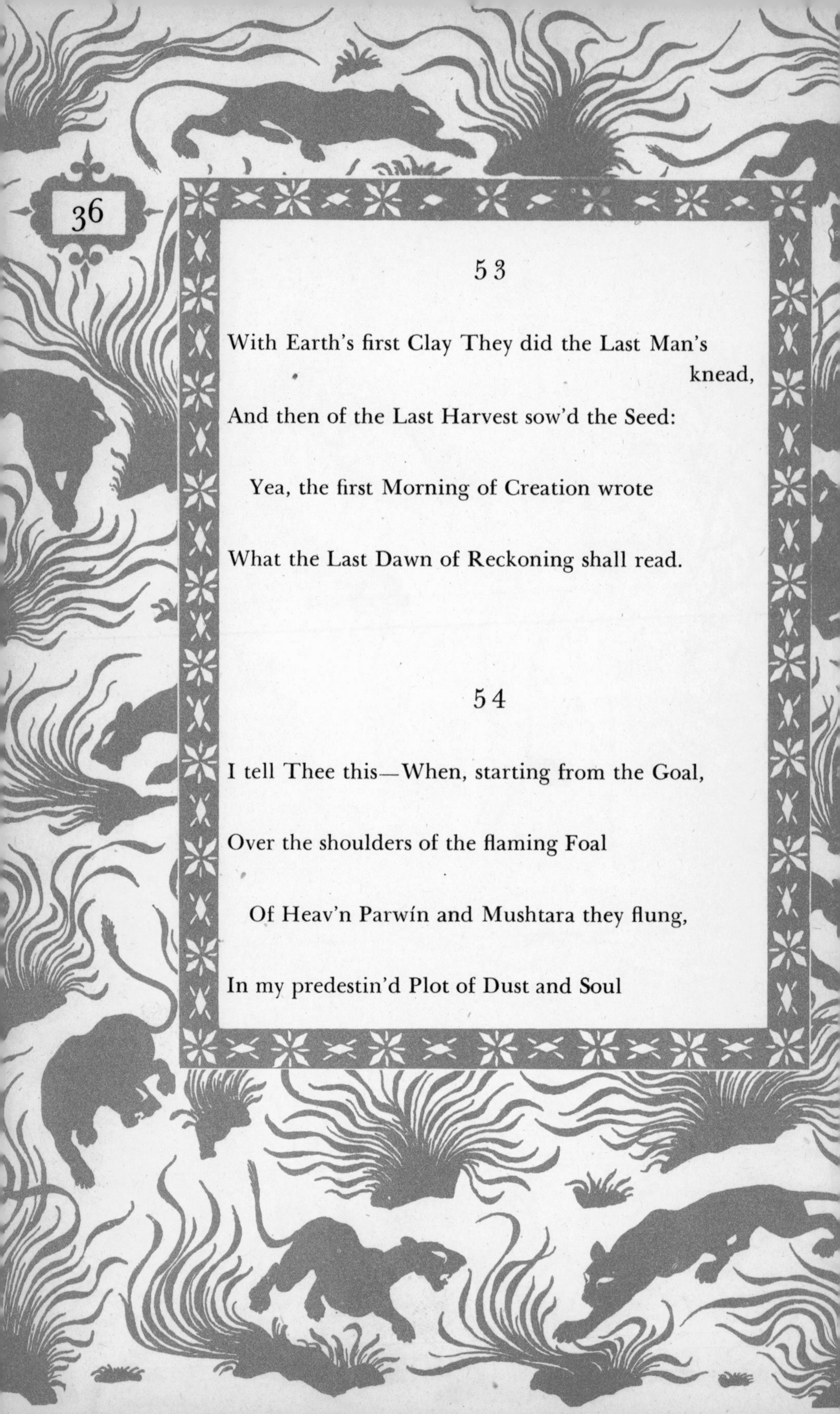

53

With Earth's first Clay They did the Last Man's knead,
And then of the Last Harvest sow'd the Seed:
Yea, the first Morning of Creation wrote
What the Last Dawn of Reckoning shall read.

54

I tell Thee this—When, starting from the Goal,
Over the shoulders of the flaming Foal
Of Heav'n Parwín and Mushtara they flung,
In my predestin'd Plot of Dust and Soul

37

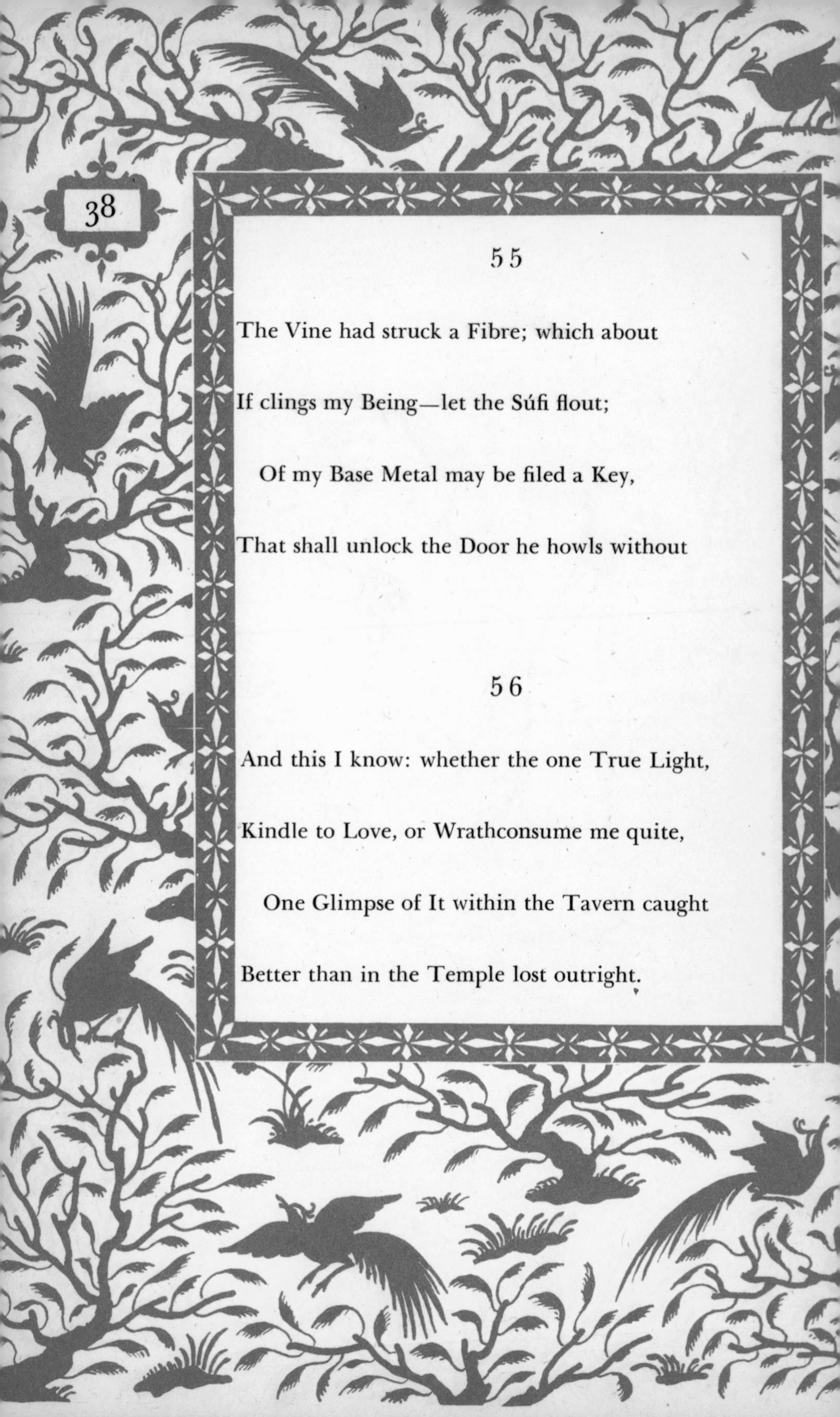

55

The Vine had struck a Fibre; which about
If clings my Being—let the Súfi flout;
   Of my Base Metal may be filed a Key,
That shall unlock the Door he howls without

56

And this I know: whether the one True Light,
Kindle to Love, or Wrathconsume me quite,
   One Glimpse of It within the Tavern caught
Better than in the Temple lost outright.

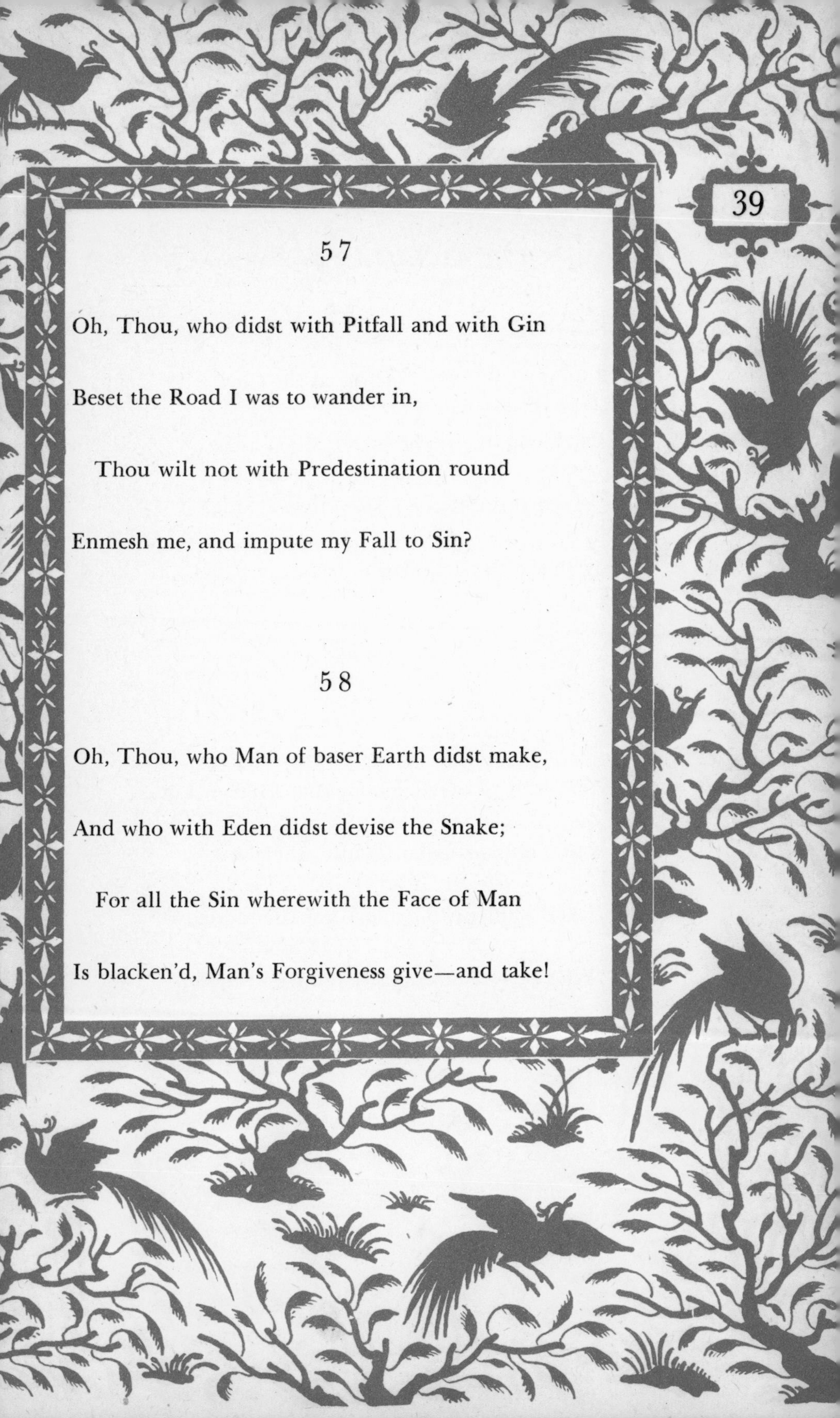

57

Oh, Thou, who didst with Pitfall and with Gin
Beset the Road I was to wander in,
Thou wilt not with Predestination round
Enmesh me, and impute my Fall to Sin?

58

Oh, Thou, who Man of baser Earth didst make,
And who with Eden didst devise the Snake;
For all the Sin wherewith the Face of Man
Is blacken'd, Man's Forgiveness give—and take!

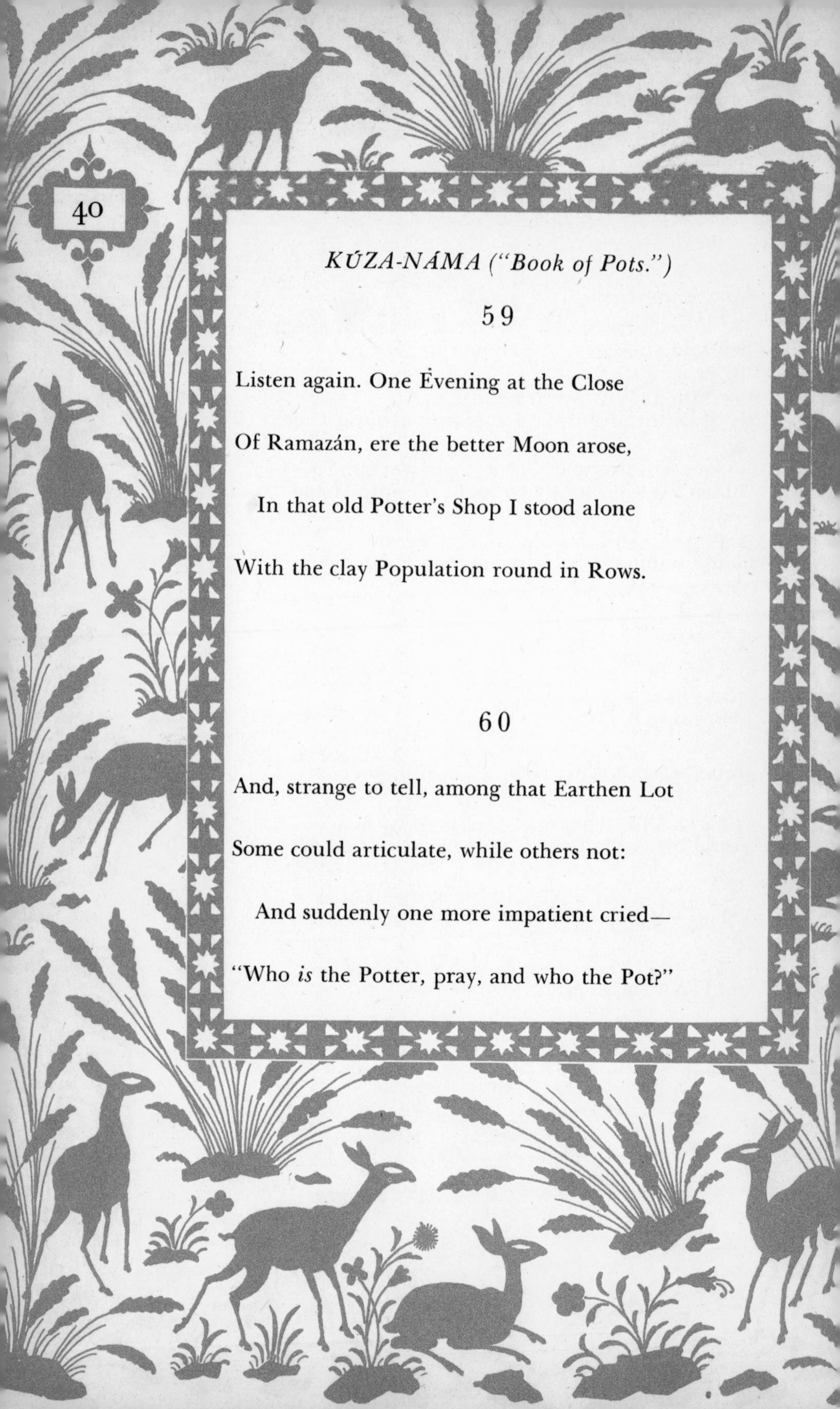

KÚZA-NÁMA ("*Book of Pots.*")

59

Listen again. One Evening at the Close
Of Ramazán, ere the better Moon arose,
In that old Potter's Shop I stood alone
With the clay Population round in Rows.

60

And, strange to tell, among that Earthen Lot
Some could articulate, while others not:
And suddenly one more impatient cried—
"Who *is* the Potter, pray, and who the Pot?"

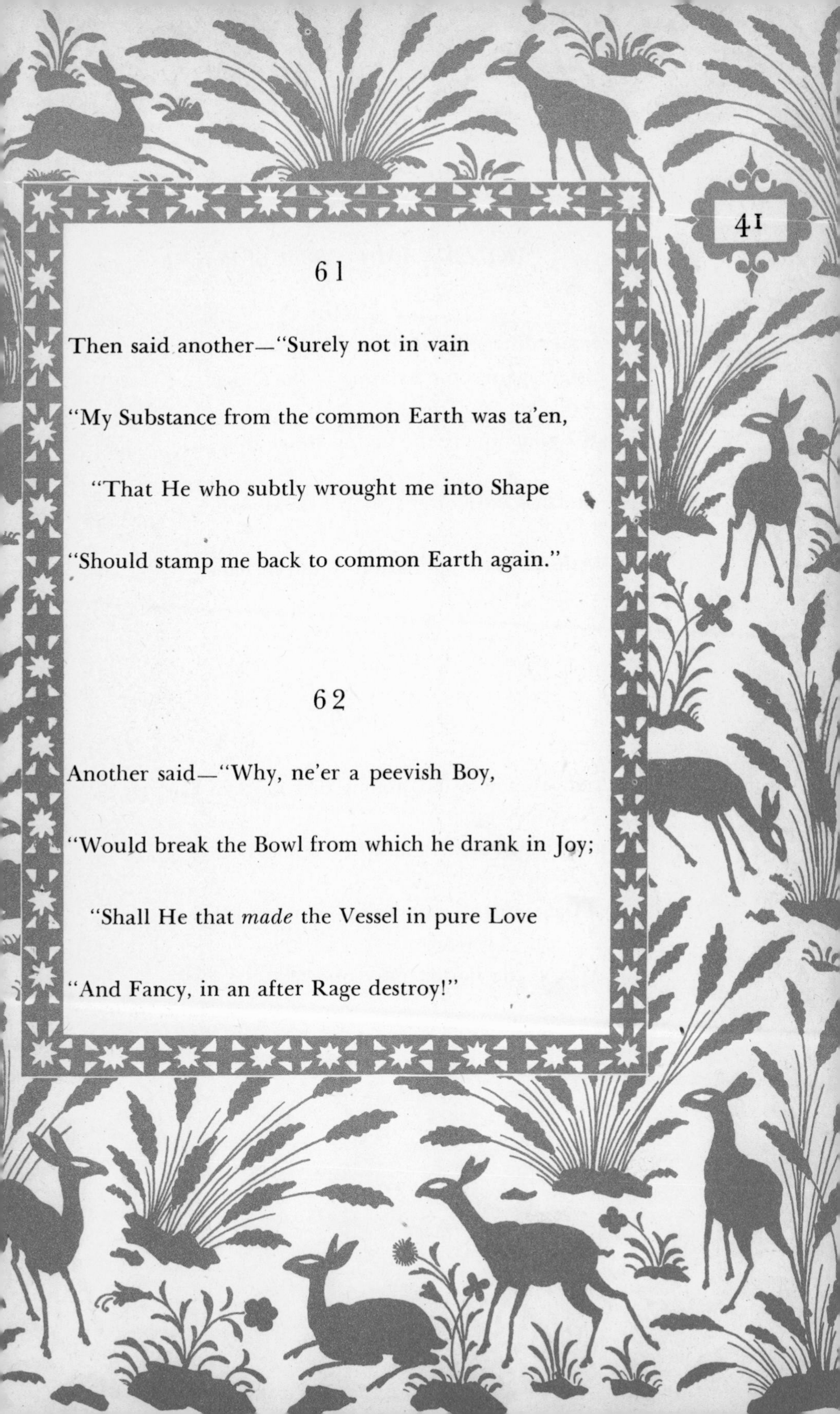

61

Then said another—"Surely not in vain

"My Substance from the common Earth was ta'en,

"That He who subtly wrought me into Shape

"Should stamp me back to common Earth again."

62

Another said—"Why, ne'er a peevish Boy,

"Would break the Bowl from which he drank in Joy;

"Shall He that *made* the Vessel in pure Love

"And Fancy, in an after Rage destroy!"

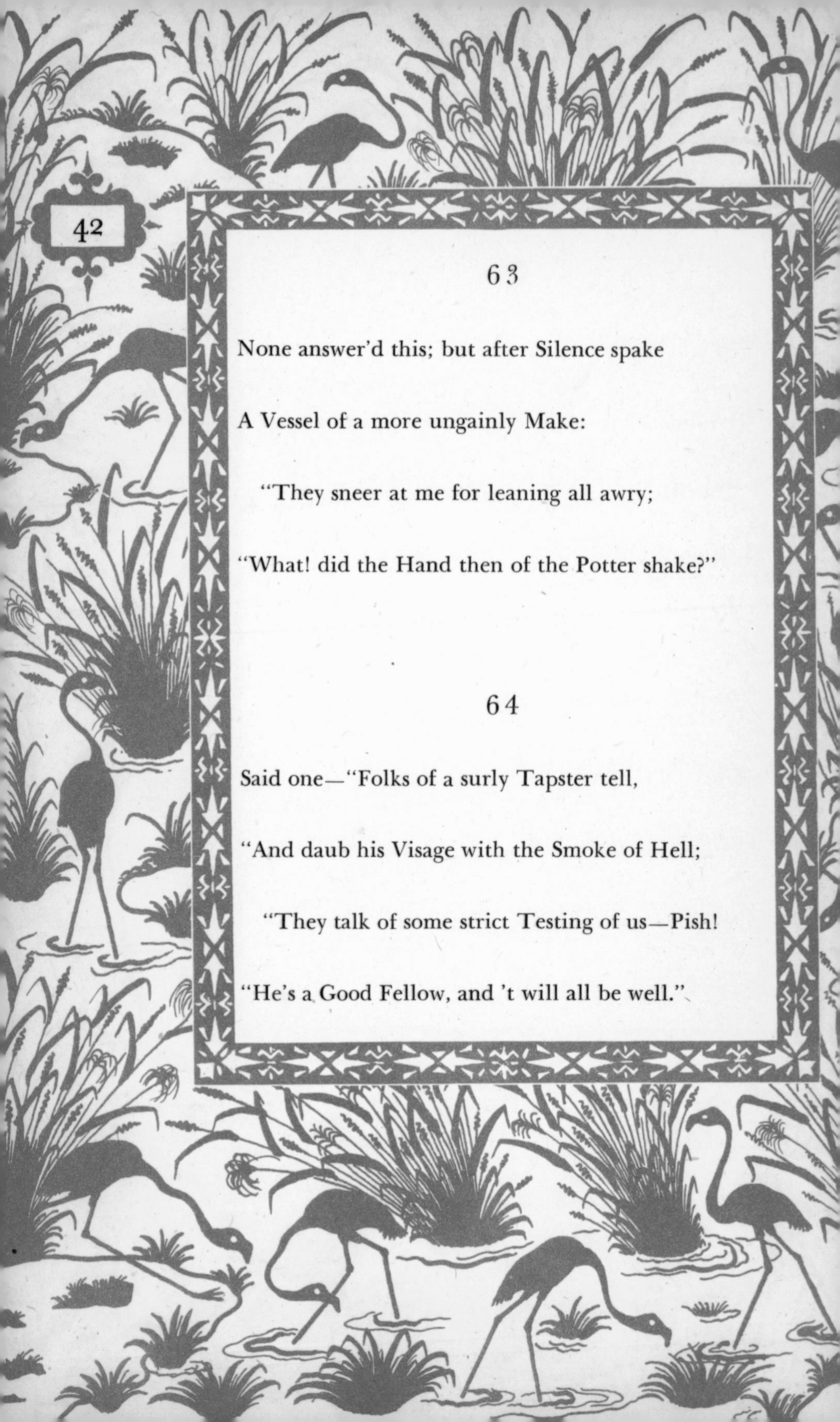

63

None answer'd this; but after Silence spake
A Vessel of a more ungainly Make:
"They sneer at me for leaning all awry;
"What! did the Hand then of the Potter shake?"

64

Said one—"Folks of a surly Tapster tell,
"And daub his Visage with the Smoke of Hell;
"They talk of some strict Testing of us—Pish!
"He's a Good Fellow, and 't will all be well."

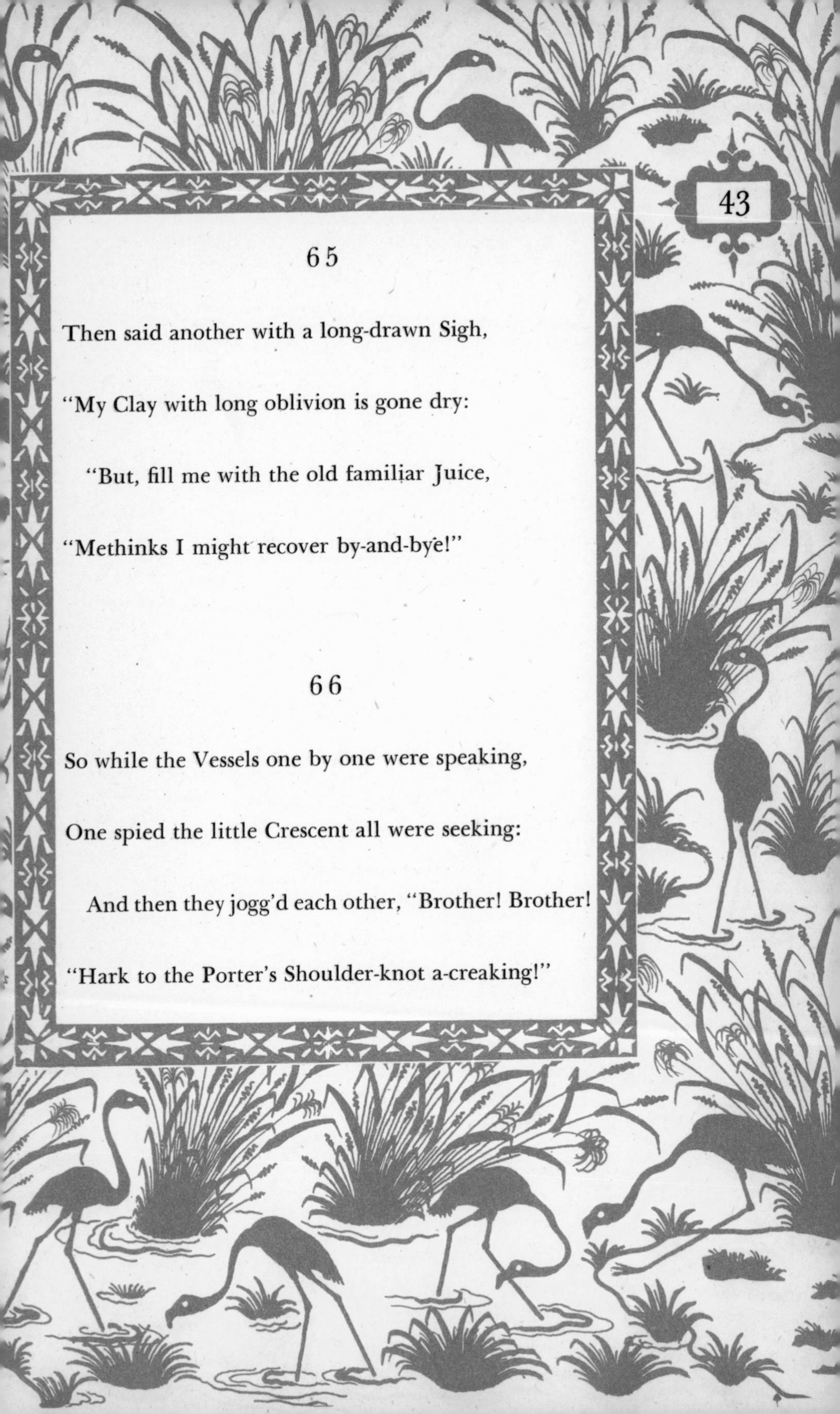

65

Then said another with a long-drawn Sigh,

"My Clay with long oblivion is gone dry:

"But, fill me with the old familiar Juice,

"Methinks I might recover by-and-bye!"

66

So while the Vessels one by one were speaking,

One spied the little Crescent all were seeking:

And then they jogg'd each other, "Brother! Brother!

"Hark to the Porter's Shoulder-knot a-creaking!"

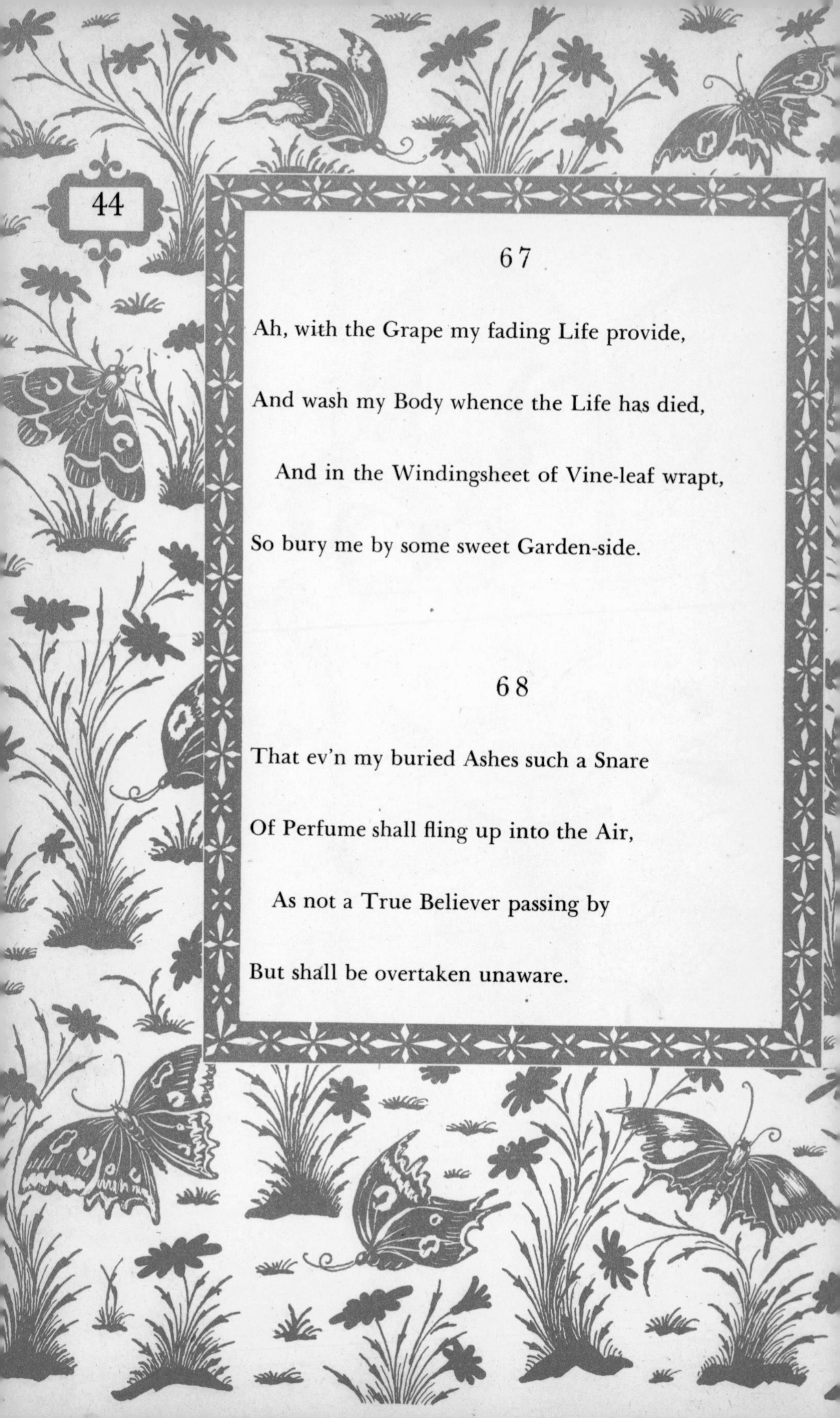

67

Ah, with the Grape my fading Life provide,
And wash my Body whence the Life has died,
  And in the Windingsheet of Vine-leaf wrapt,
So bury me by some sweet Garden-side.

68

That ev'n my buried Ashes such a Snare
Of Perfume shall fling up into the Air,
  As not a True Believer passing by
But shall be overtaken unaware.

45
M.S.

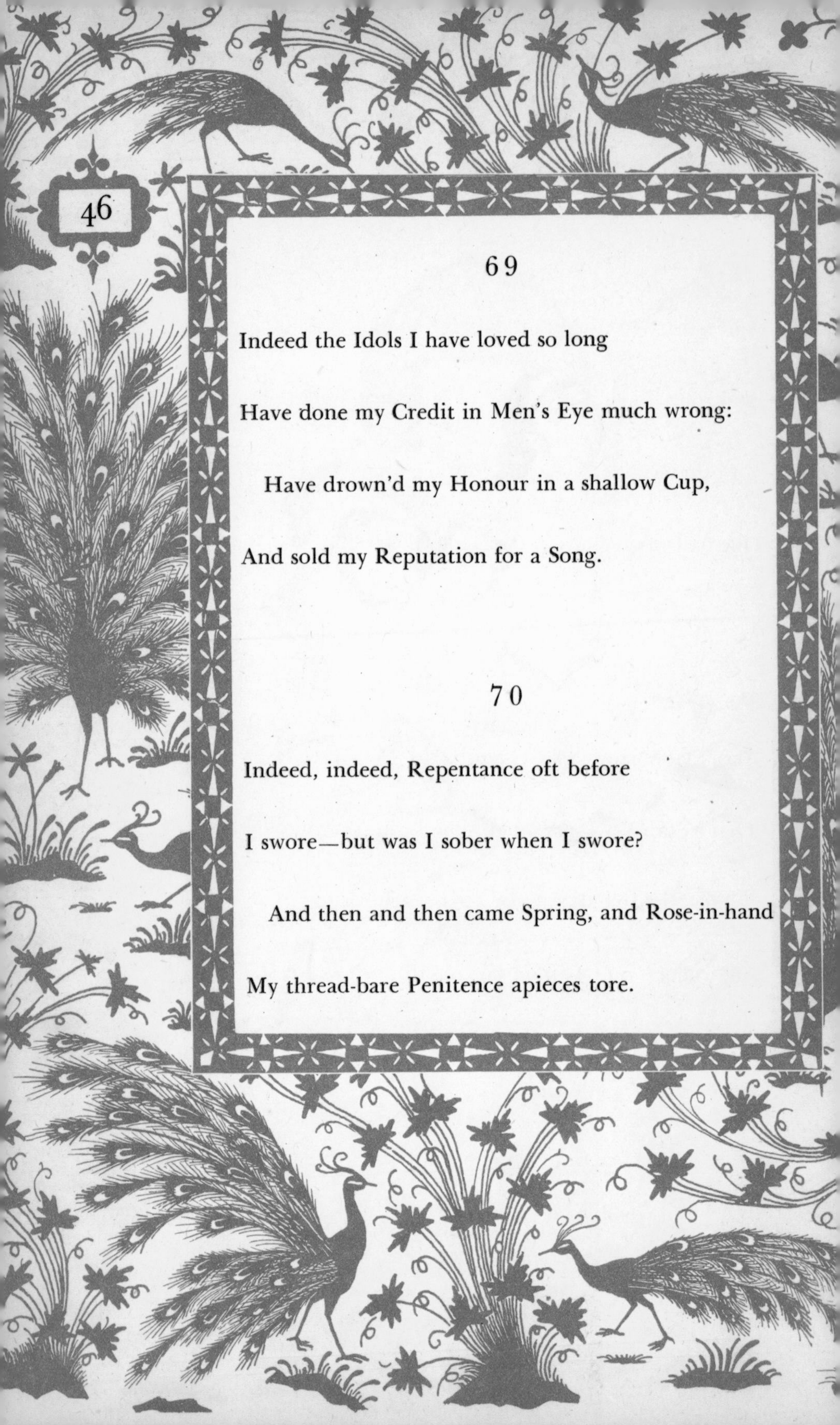

69

Indeed the Idols I have loved so long
Have done my Credit in Men's Eye much wrong:
Have drown'd my Honour in a shallow Cup,
And sold my Reputation for a Song.

70

Indeed, indeed, Repentance oft before
I swore—but was I sober when I swore?
And then and then came Spring, and Rose-in-hand
My thread-bare Penitence apieces tore.

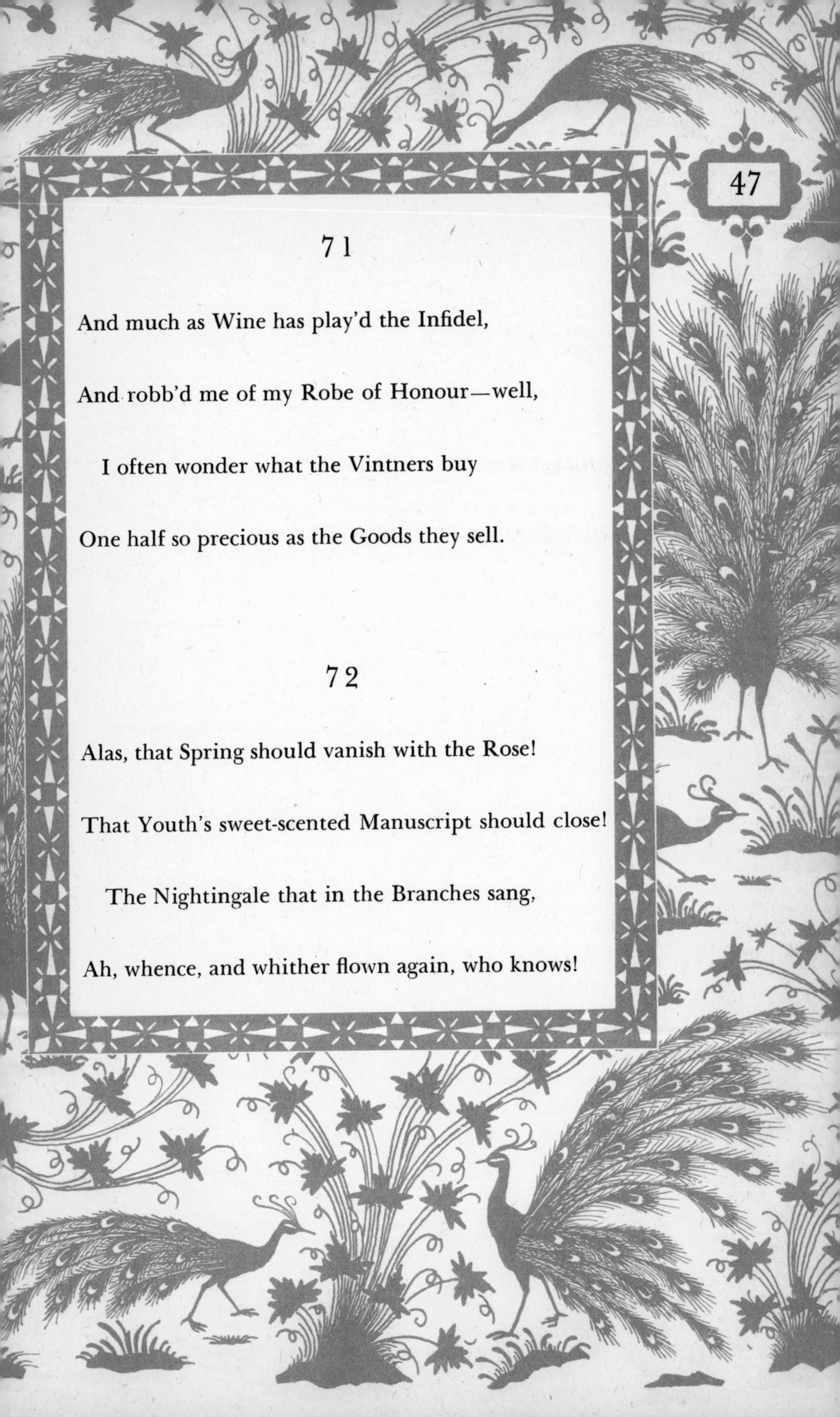

71

And much as Wine has play'd the Infidel,
And robb'd me of my Robe of Honour—well,
I often wonder what the Vintners buy
One half so precious as the Goods they sell.

72

Alas, that Spring should vanish with the Rose!
That Youth's sweet-scented Manuscript should close!
The Nightingale that in the Branches sang,
Ah, whence, and whither flown again, who knows!

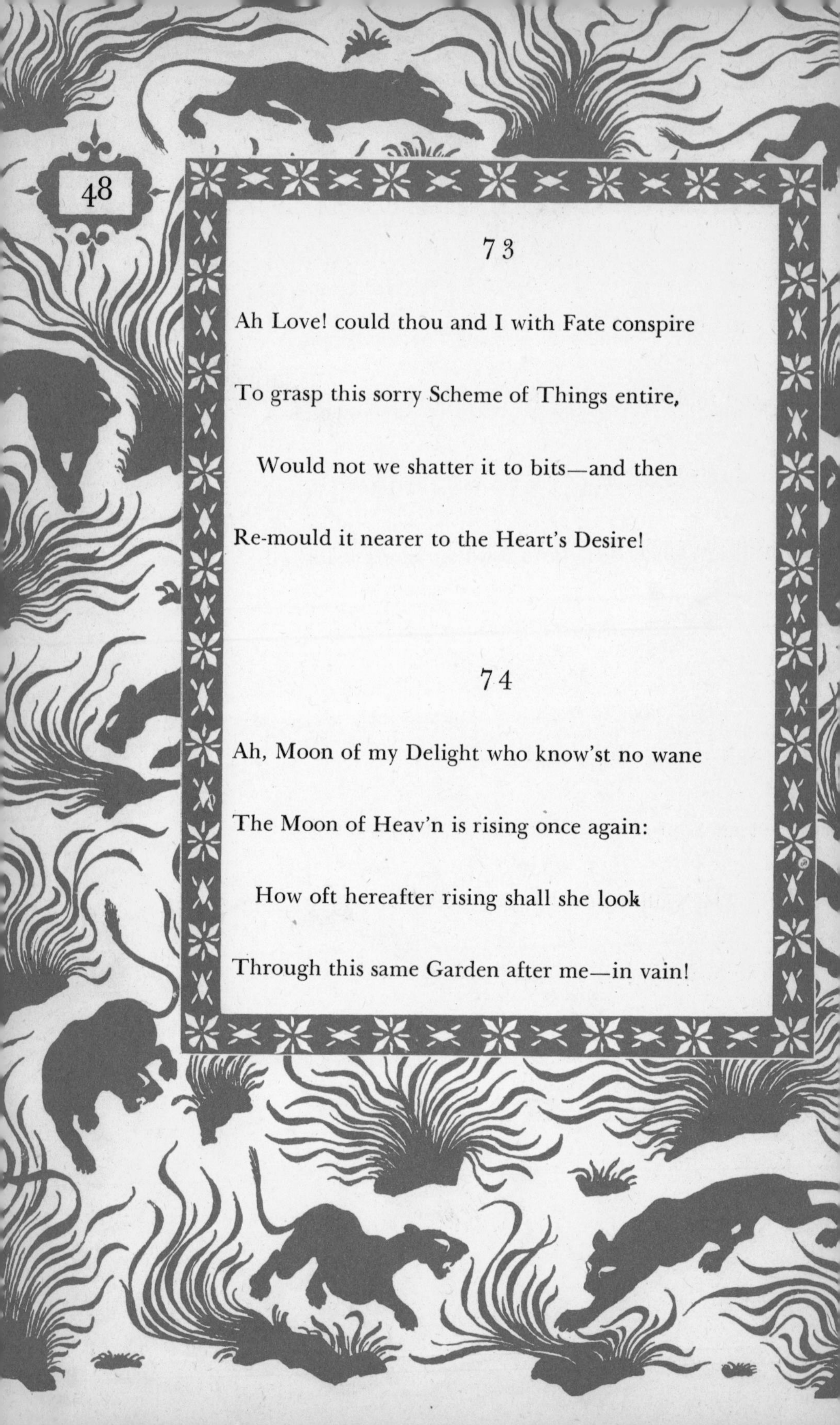

73

Ah Love! could thou and I with Fate conspire
To grasp this sorry Scheme of Things entire,
Would not we shatter it to bits—and then
Re-mould it nearer to the Heart's Desire!

74

Ah, Moon of my Delight who know'st no wane
The Moon of Heav'n is rising once again:
How oft hereafter rising shall she look
Through this same Garden after me—in vain!

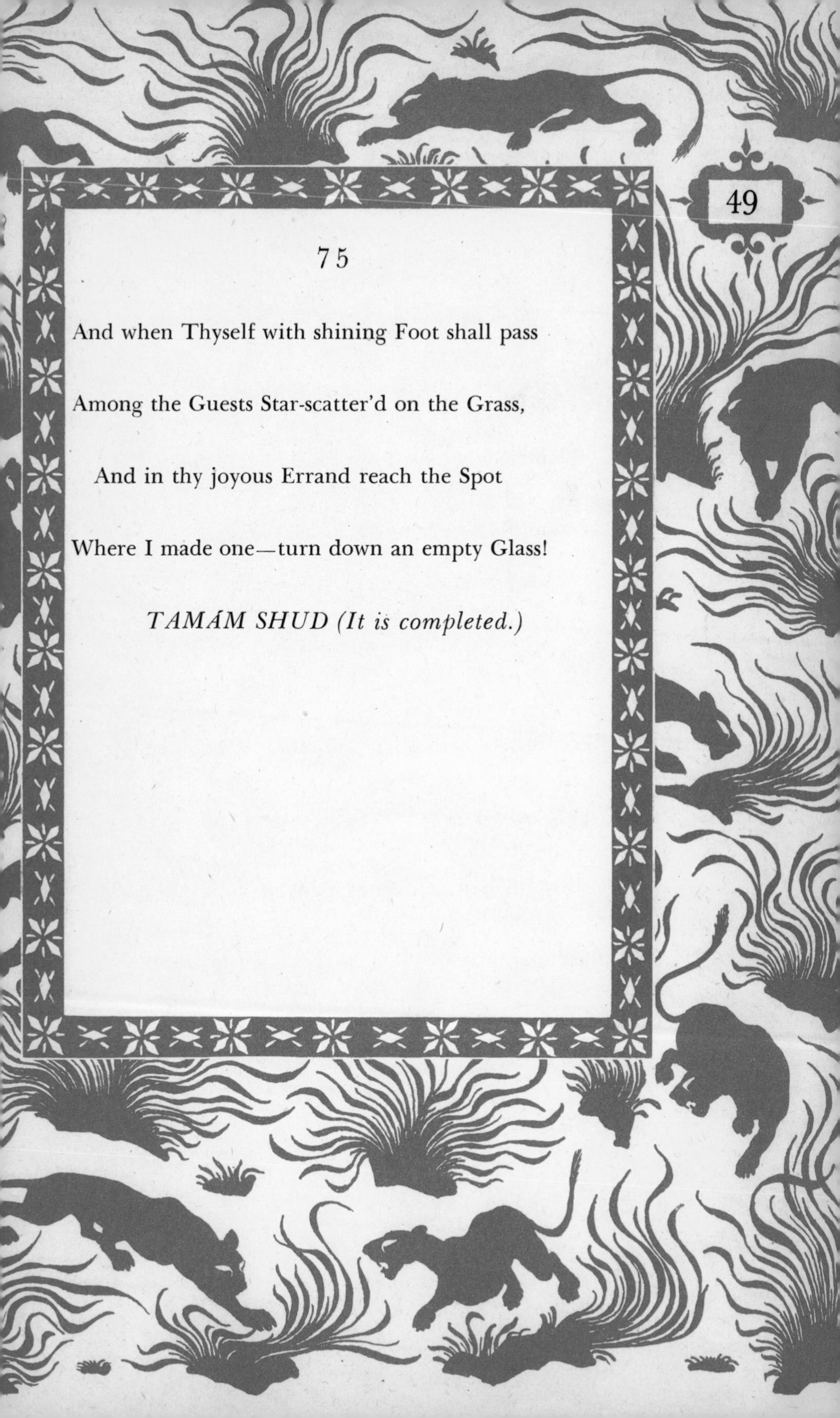

75

And when Thyself with shining Foot shall pass
Among the Guests Star-scatter'd on the Grass,
  And in thy joyous Errand reach the Spot
Where I made one—turn down an empty Glass!

TAMÁM SHUD (It is completed.)

RUBÁIYÁT OF
Omar Khayyám

Third Edition, 1872 · *Fourth Edition,* 1879
Fifth Edition, 1889

52
M. Sayah

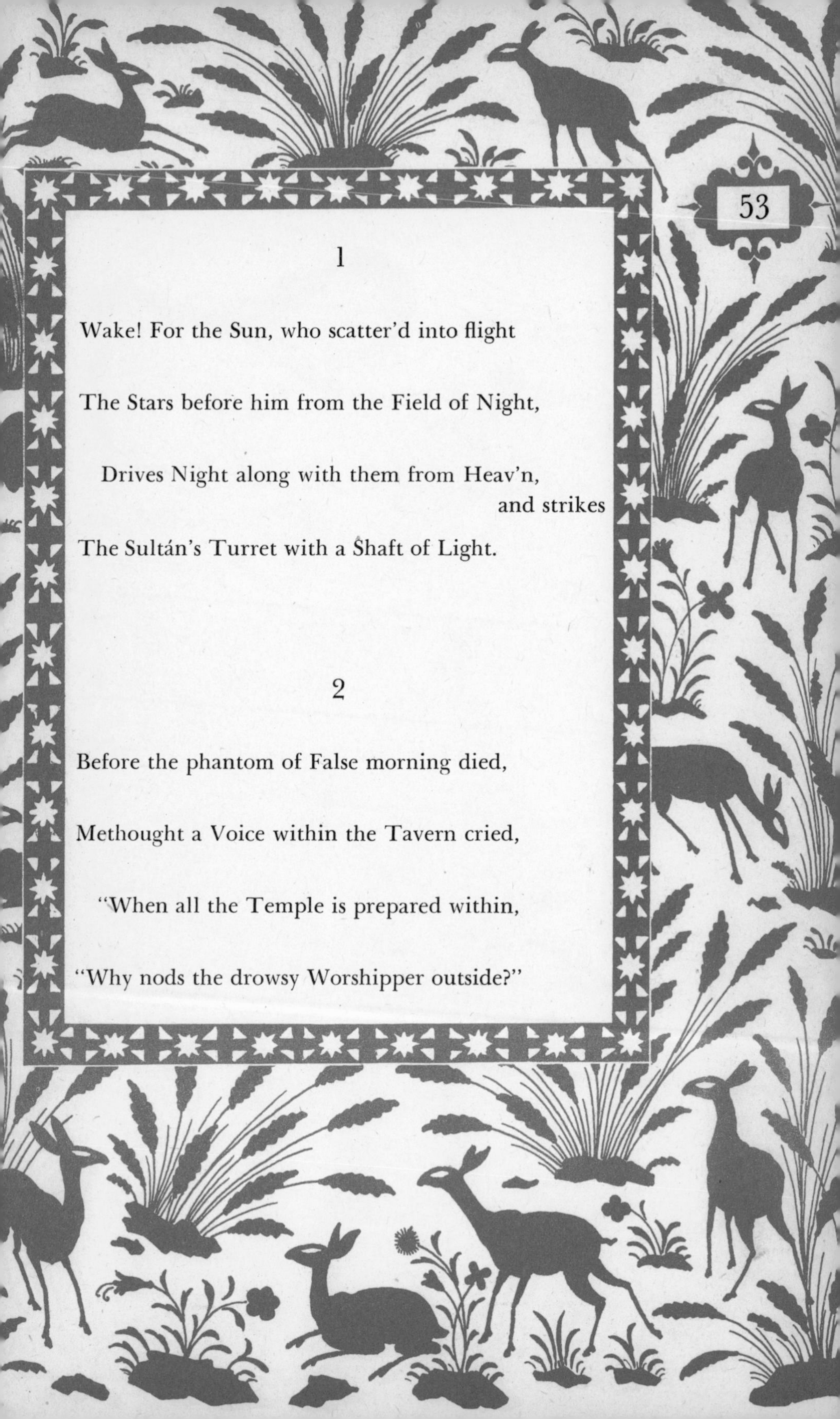

1

Wake! For the Sun, who scatter'd into flight
The Stars before him from the Field of Night,
Drives Night along with them from Heav'n, and strikes
The Sultán's Turret with a Shaft of Light.

2

Before the phantom of False morning died,
Methought a Voice within the Tavern cried,
"When all the Temple is prepared within,
"Why nods the drowsy Worshipper outside?"

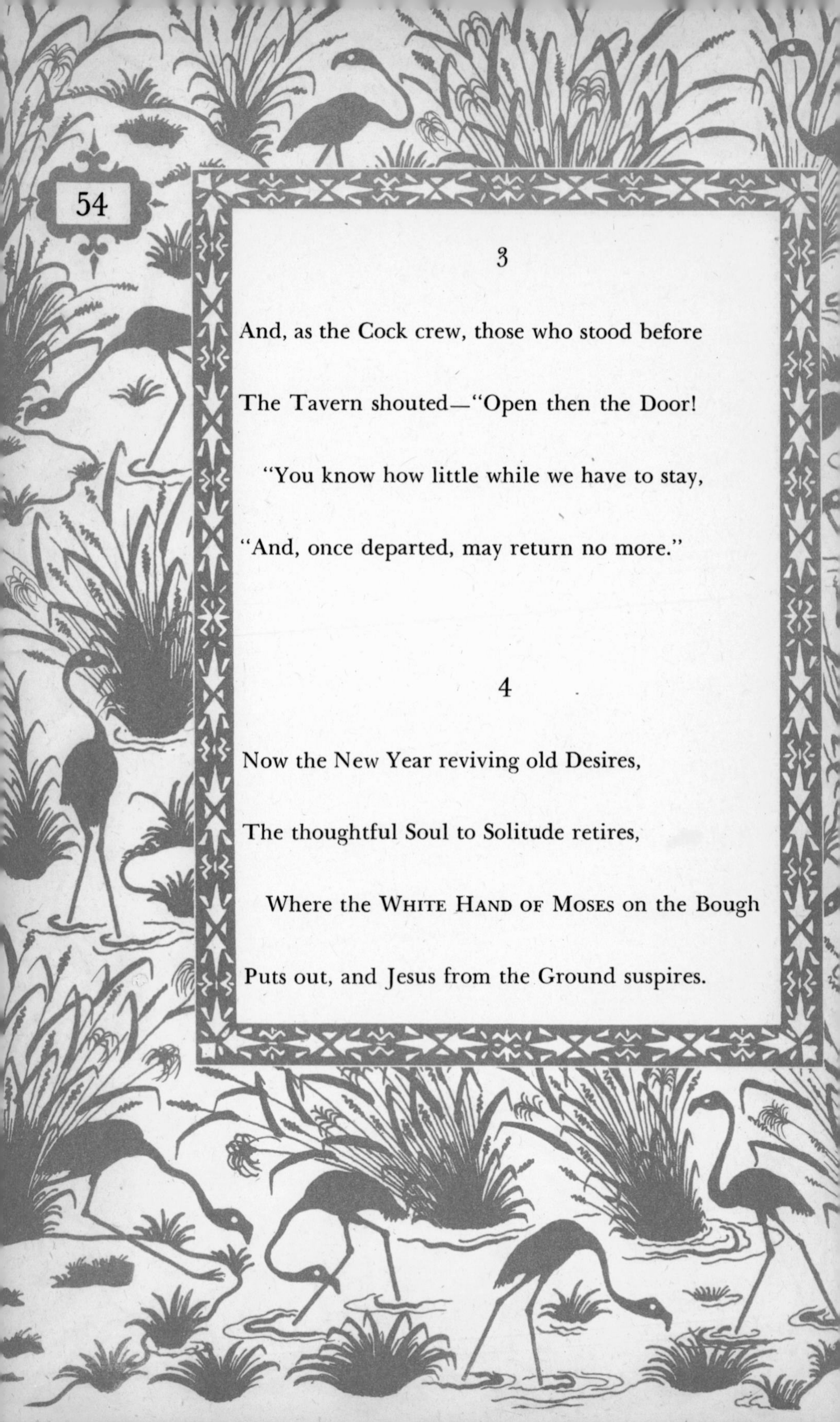

3

And, as the Cock crew, those who stood before
The Tavern shouted—"Open then the Door!
"You know how little while we have to stay,
"And, once departed, may return no more."

4

Now the New Year reviving old Desires,
The thoughtful Soul to Solitude retires,
Where the White Hand of Moses on the Bough
Puts out, and Jesus from the Ground suspires.

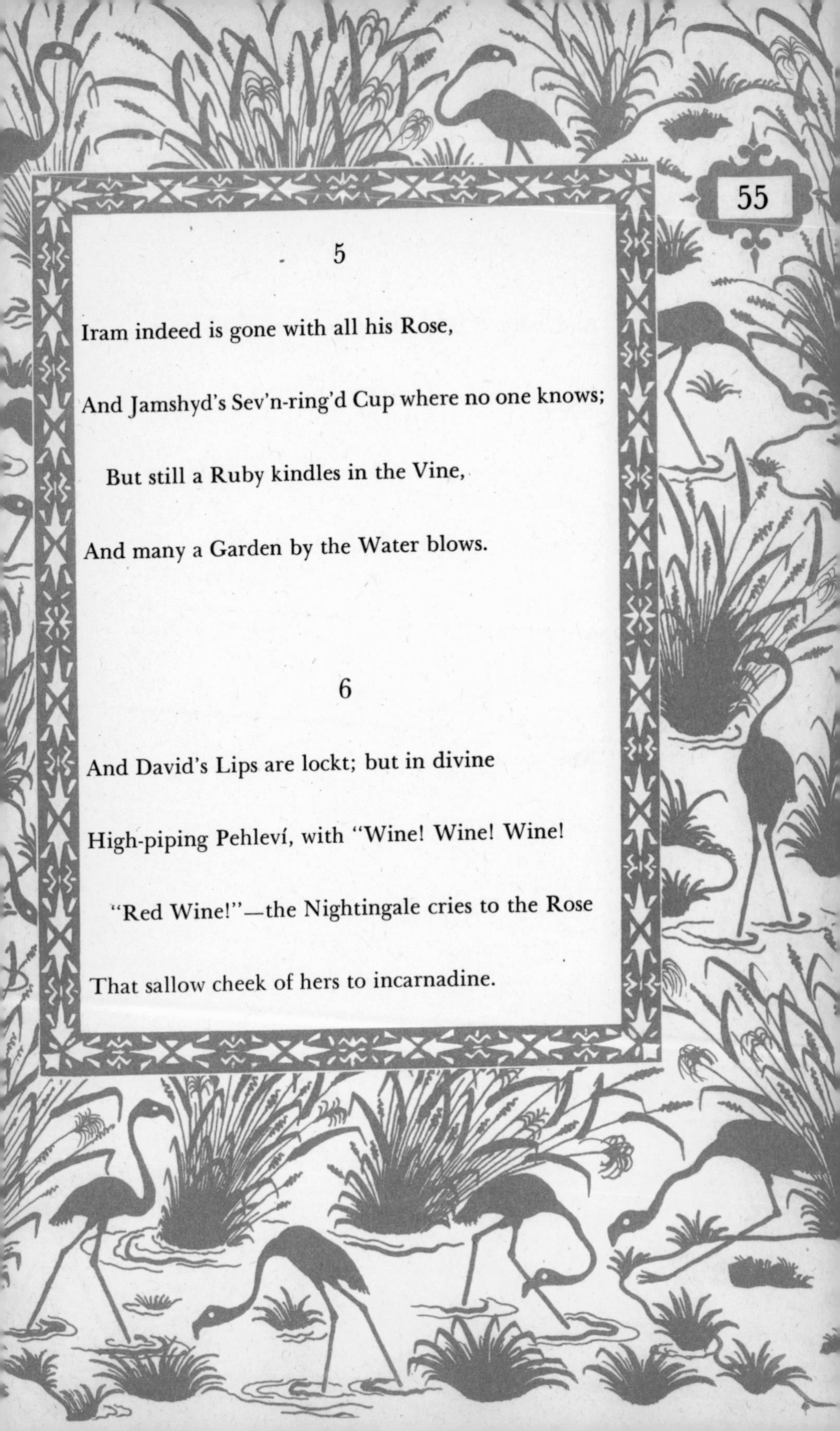

5

Iram indeed is gone with all his Rose,
And Jamshyd's Sev'n-ring'd Cup where no one knows;
 But still a Ruby kindles in the Vine,
And many a Garden by the Water blows.

6

And David's Lips are lockt; but in divine
High-piping Pehleví, with "Wine! Wine! Wine!
 "Red Wine!"—the Nightingale cries to the Rose
That sallow cheek of hers to incarnadine.

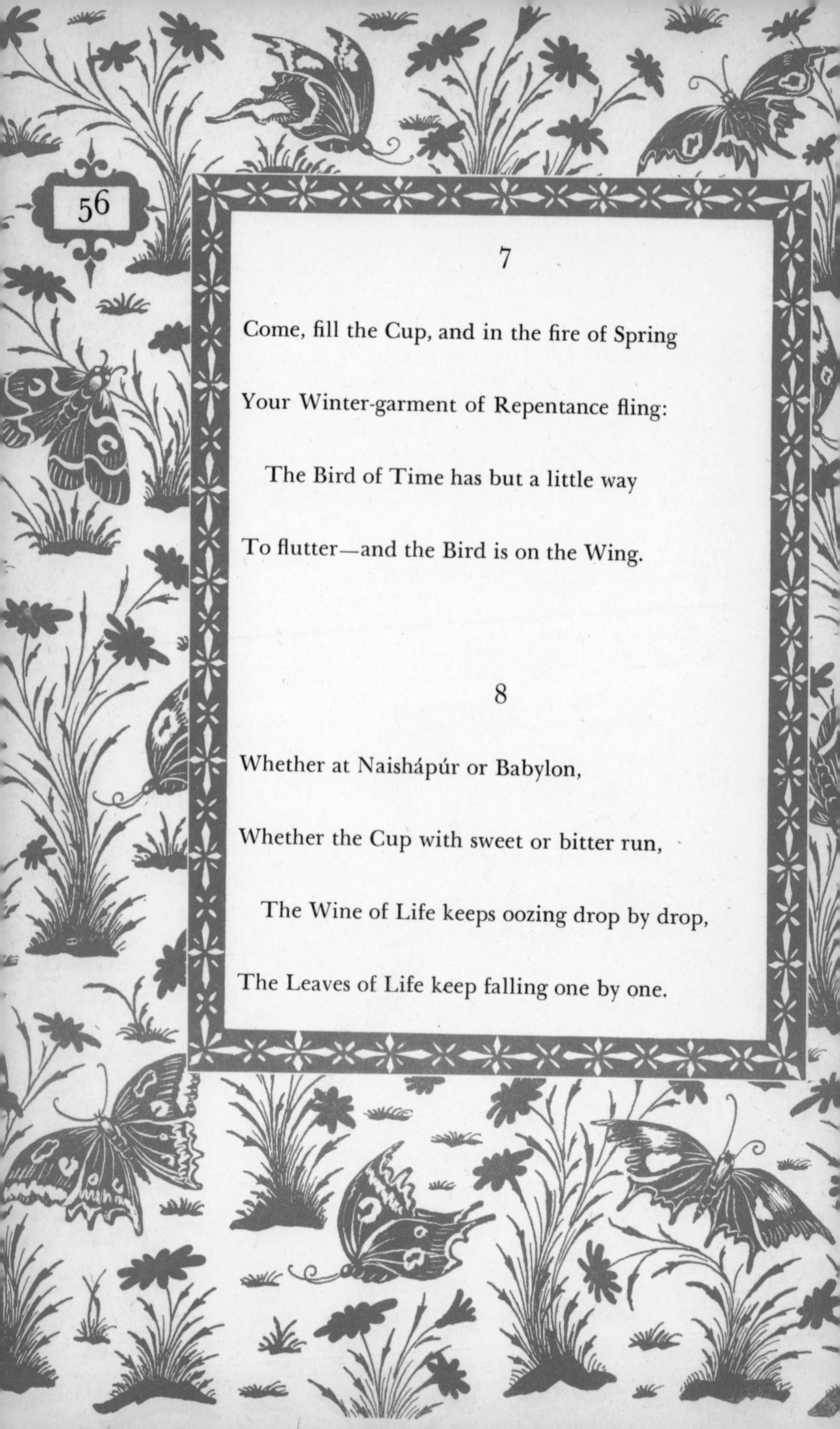

7

Come, fill the Cup, and in the fire of Spring
Your Winter-garment of Repentance fling:
    The Bird of Time has but a little way
To flutter—and the Bird is on the Wing.

8

Whether at Naishápúr or Babylon,
Whether the Cup with sweet or bitter run,
    The Wine of Life keeps oozing drop by drop,
The Leaves of Life keep falling one by one.

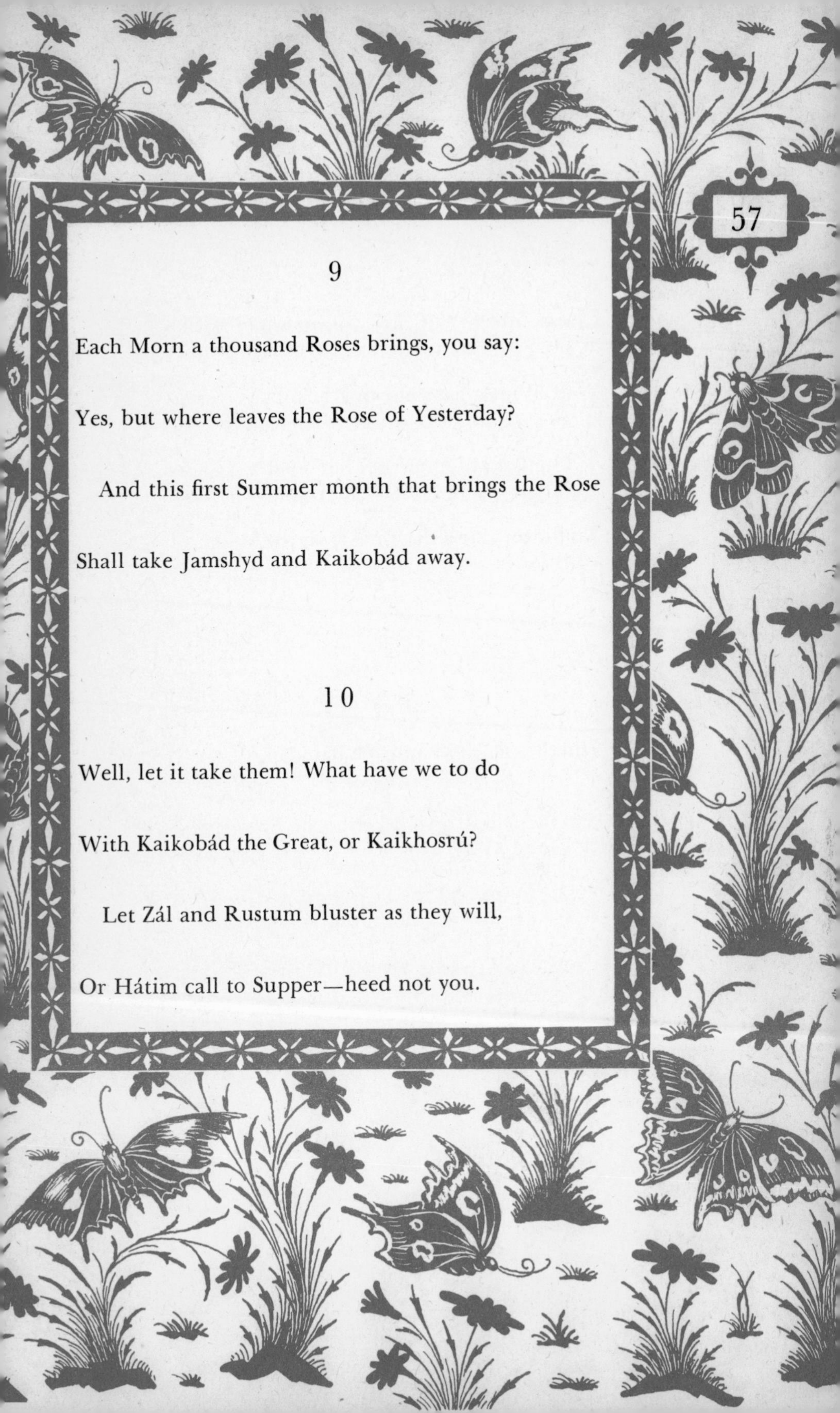

9

Each Morn a thousand Roses brings, you say:
Yes, but where leaves the Rose of Yesterday?
And this first Summer month that brings the Rose
Shall take Jamshyd and Kaikobád away.

10

Well, let it take them! What have we to do
With Kaikobád the Great, or Kaikhosrú?
Let Zál and Rustum bluster as they will,
Or Hátim call to Supper—heed not you.

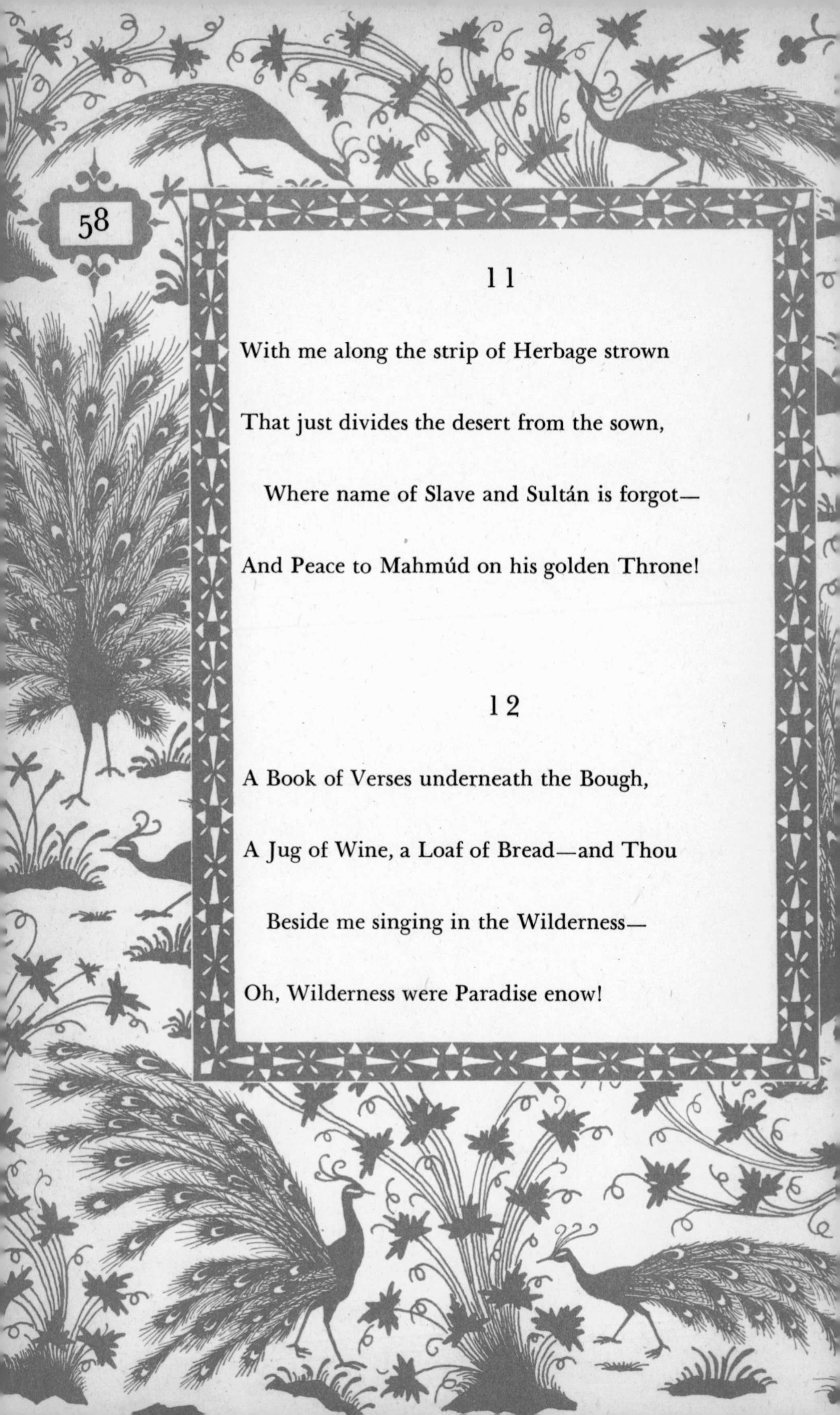

11

With me along the strip of Herbage strown
That just divides the desert from the sown,
   Where name of Slave and Sultán is forgot—
And Peace to Mahmúd on his golden Throne!

12

A Book of Verses underneath the Bough,
A Jug of Wine, a Loaf of Bread—and Thou
   Beside me singing in the Wilderness—
Oh, Wilderness were Paradise enow!

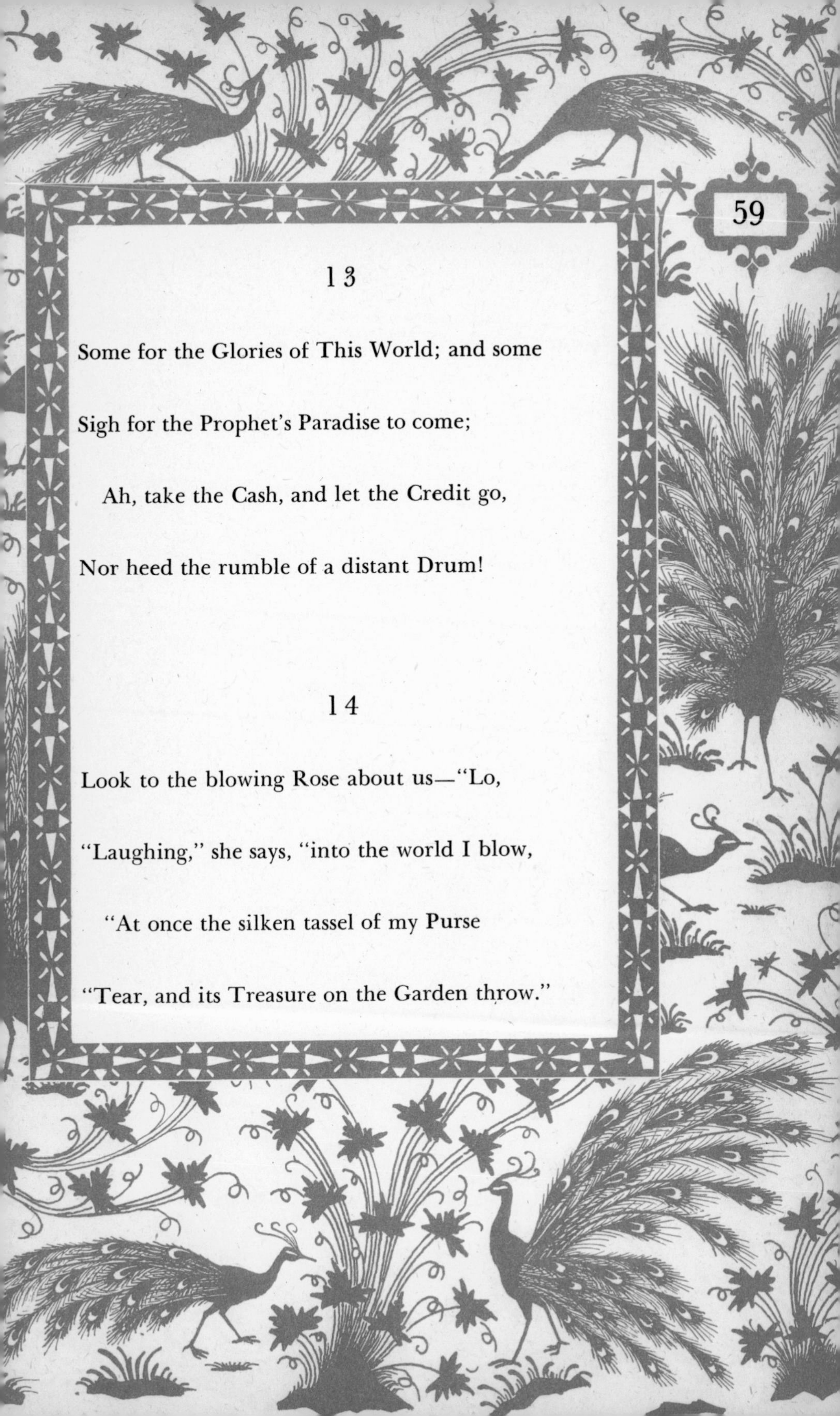

13

Some for the Glories of This World; and some
Sigh for the Prophet's Paradise to come;
Ah, take the Cash, and let the Credit go,
Nor heed the rumble of a distant Drum!

14

Look to the blowing Rose about us—"Lo,
"Laughing," she says, "into the world I blow,
"At once the silken tassel of my Purse
"Tear, and its Treasure on the Garden throw."

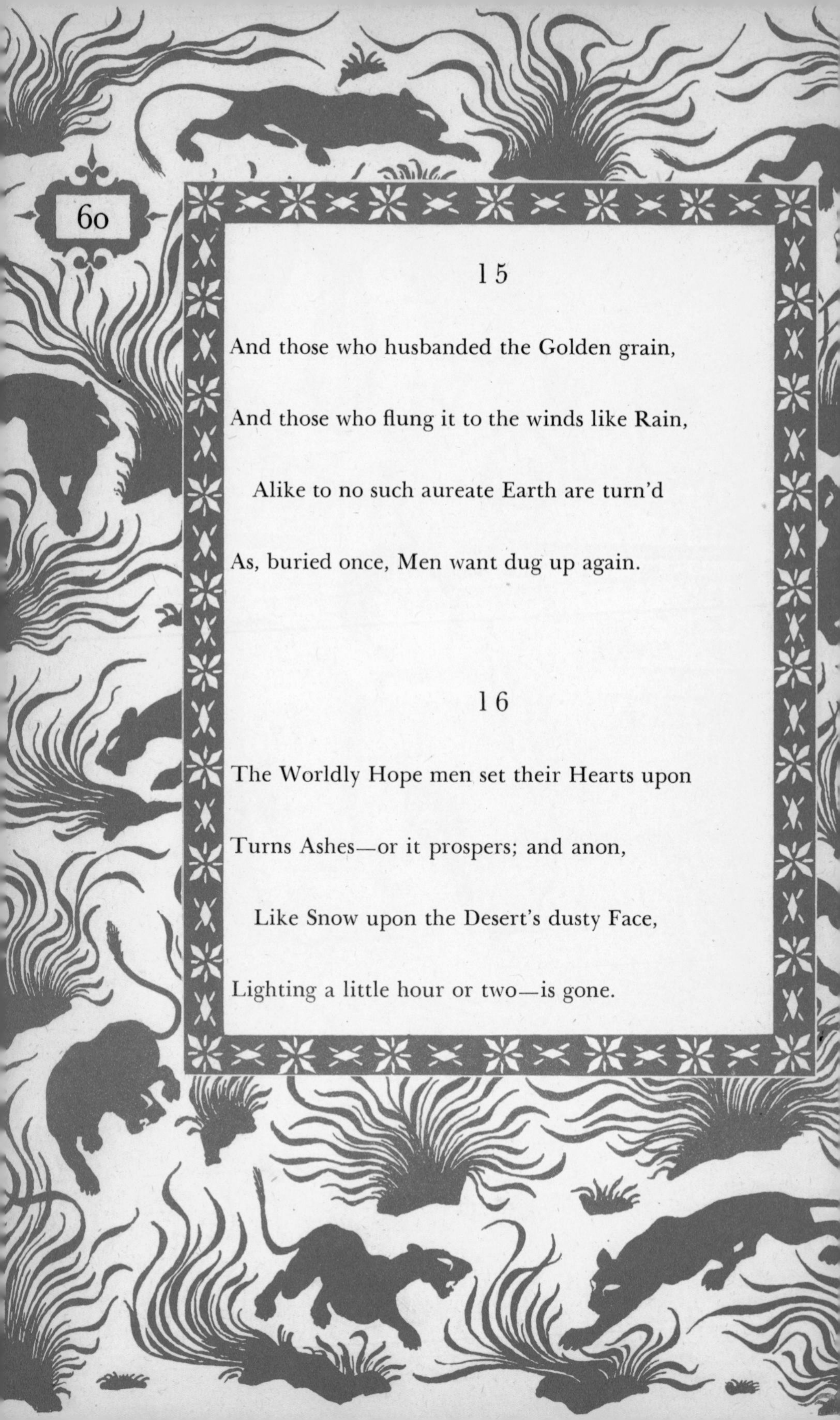

15

And those who husbanded the Golden grain,
And those who flung it to the winds like Rain,
  Alike to no such aureate Earth are turn'd
As, buried once, Men want dug up again.

16

The Worldly Hope men set their Hearts upon
Turns Ashes—or it prospers; and anon,
  Like Snow upon the Desert's dusty Face,
Lighting a little hour or two—is gone.

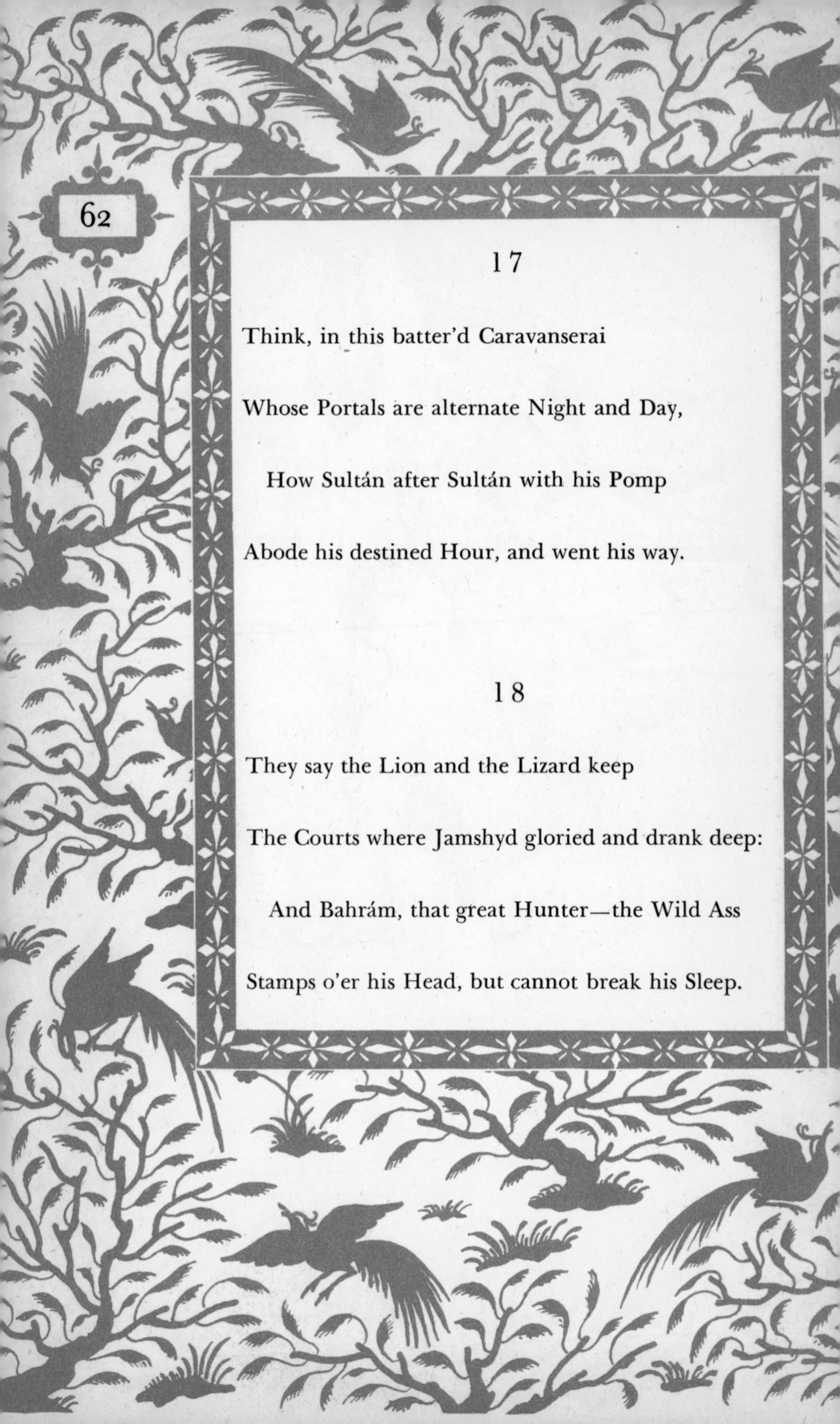

17

Think, in this batter'd Caravanserai
Whose Portals are alternate Night and Day,
How Sultán after Sultán with his Pomp
Abode his destined Hour, and went his way.

18

They say the Lion and the Lizard keep
The Courts where Jamshyd gloried and drank deep:
And Bahrám, that great Hunter—the Wild Ass
Stamps o'er his Head, but cannot break his Sleep.

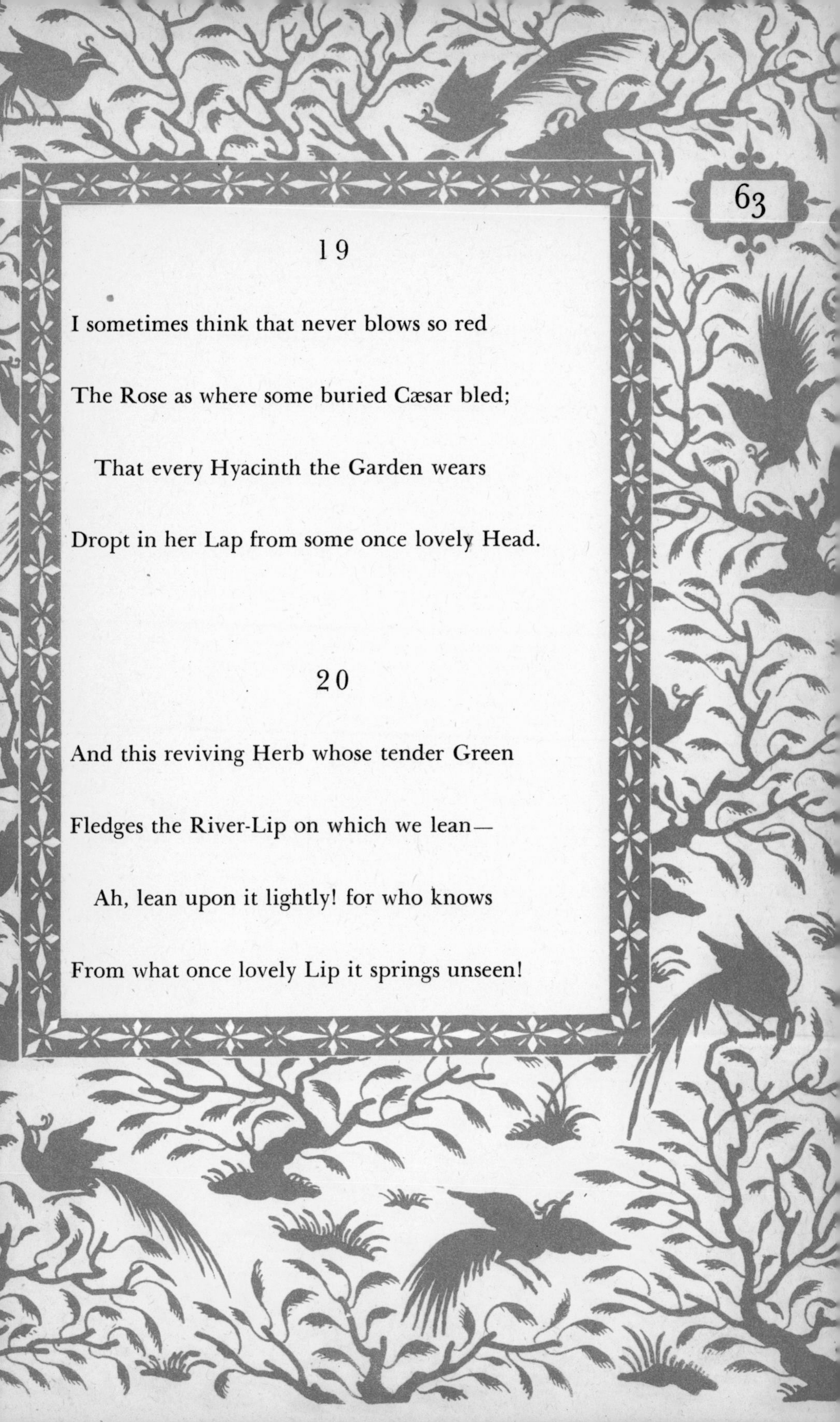

19

I sometimes think that never blows so red
The Rose as where some buried Cæsar bled;
   That every Hyacinth the Garden wears
Dropt in her Lap from some once lovely Head.

20

And this reviving Herb whose tender Green
Fledges the River-Lip on which we lean—
   Ah, lean upon it lightly! for who knows
From what once lovely Lip it springs unseen!

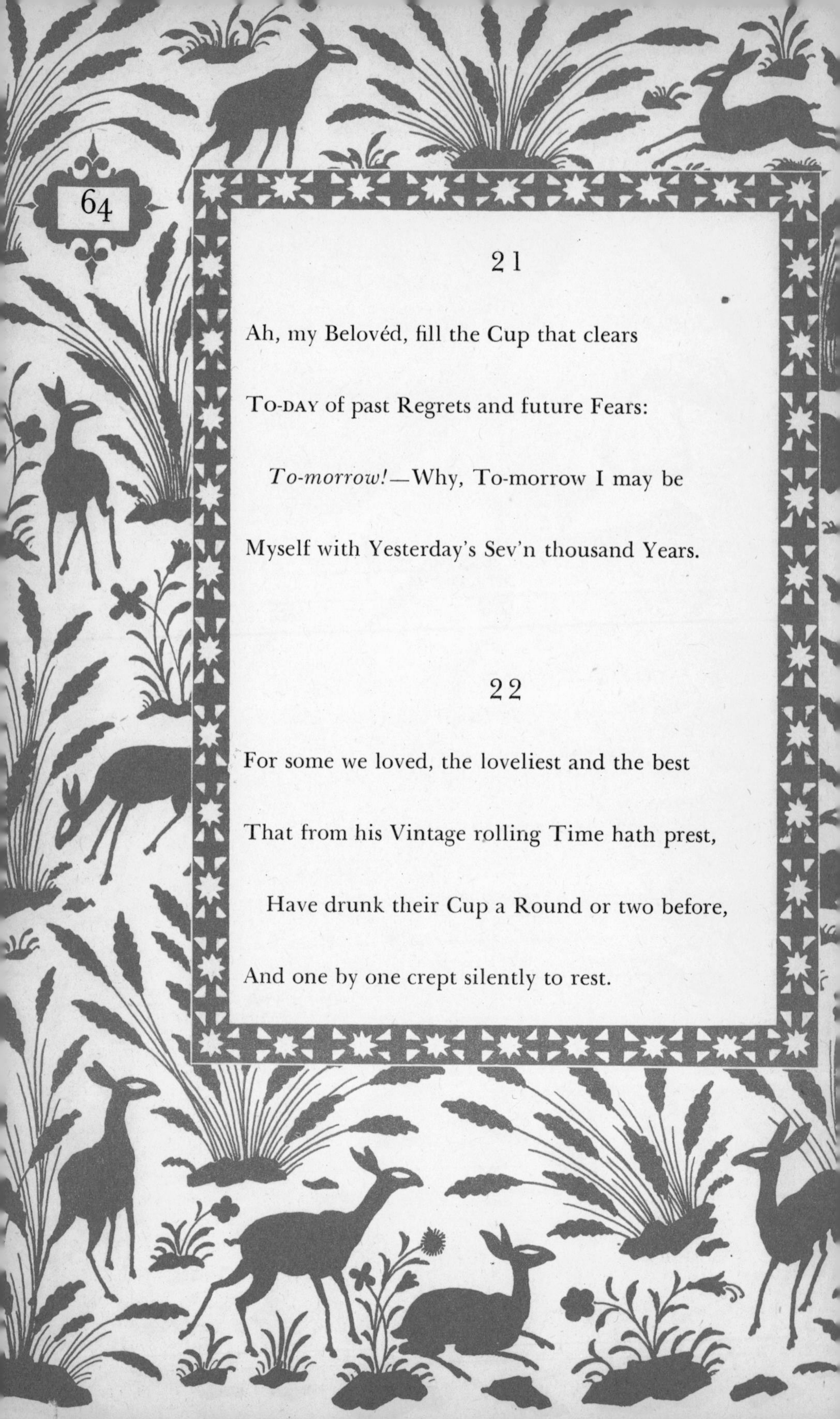

21

Ah, my Belovéd, fill the Cup that clears
To-day of past Regrets and future Fears:
To-morrow!—Why, To-morrow I may be
Myself with Yesterday's Sev'n thousand Years.

22

For some we loved, the loveliest and the best
That from his Vintage rolling Time hath prest,
Have drunk their Cup a Round or two before,
And one by one crept silently to rest.

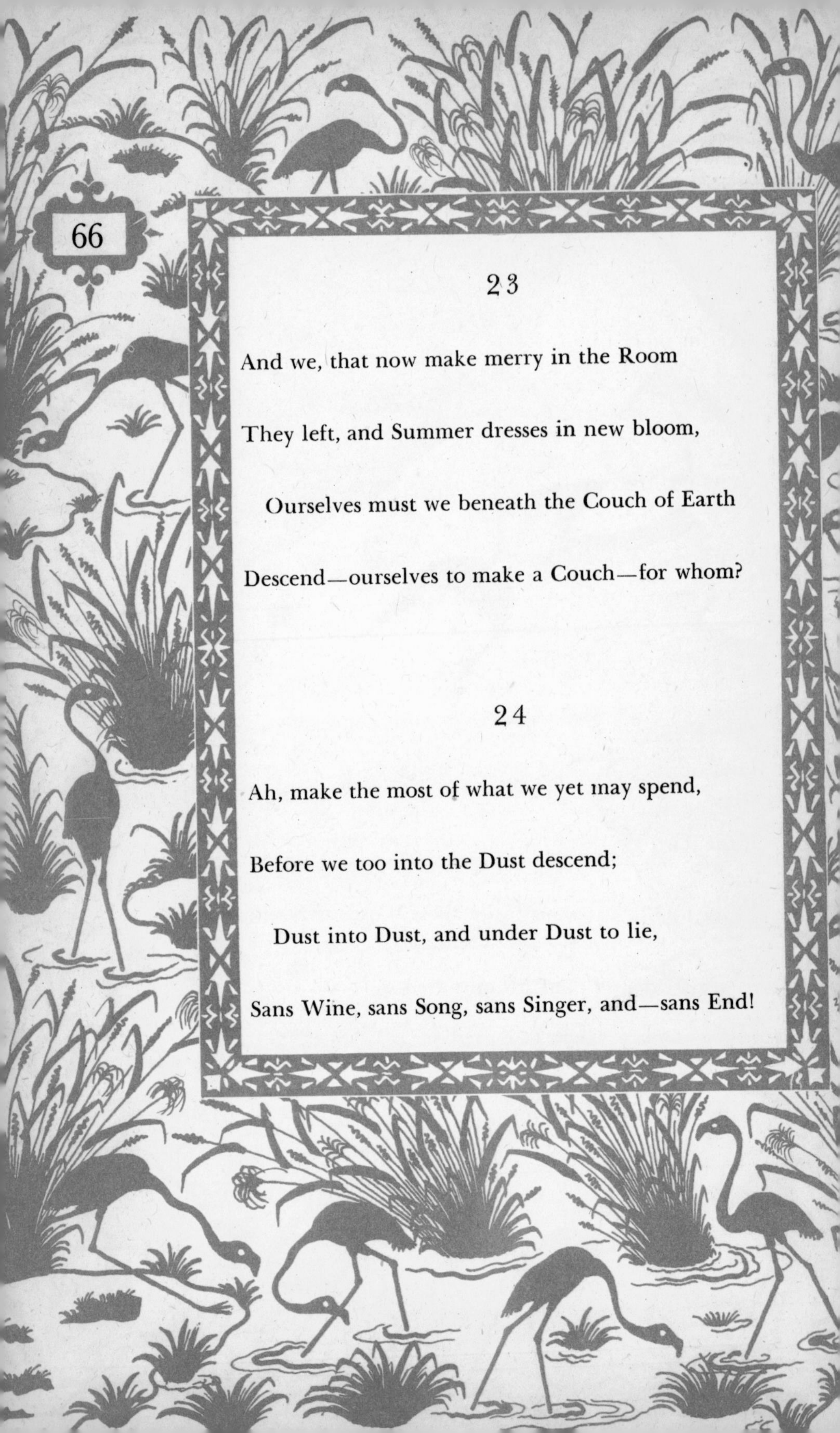

23

And we, that now make merry in the Room
They left, and Summer dresses in new bloom,
Ourselves must we beneath the Couch of Earth
Descend—ourselves to make a Couch—for whom?

24

Ah, make the most of what we yet may spend,
Before we too into the Dust descend;
Dust into Dust, and under Dust to lie,
Sans Wine, sans Song, sans Singer, and—sans End!

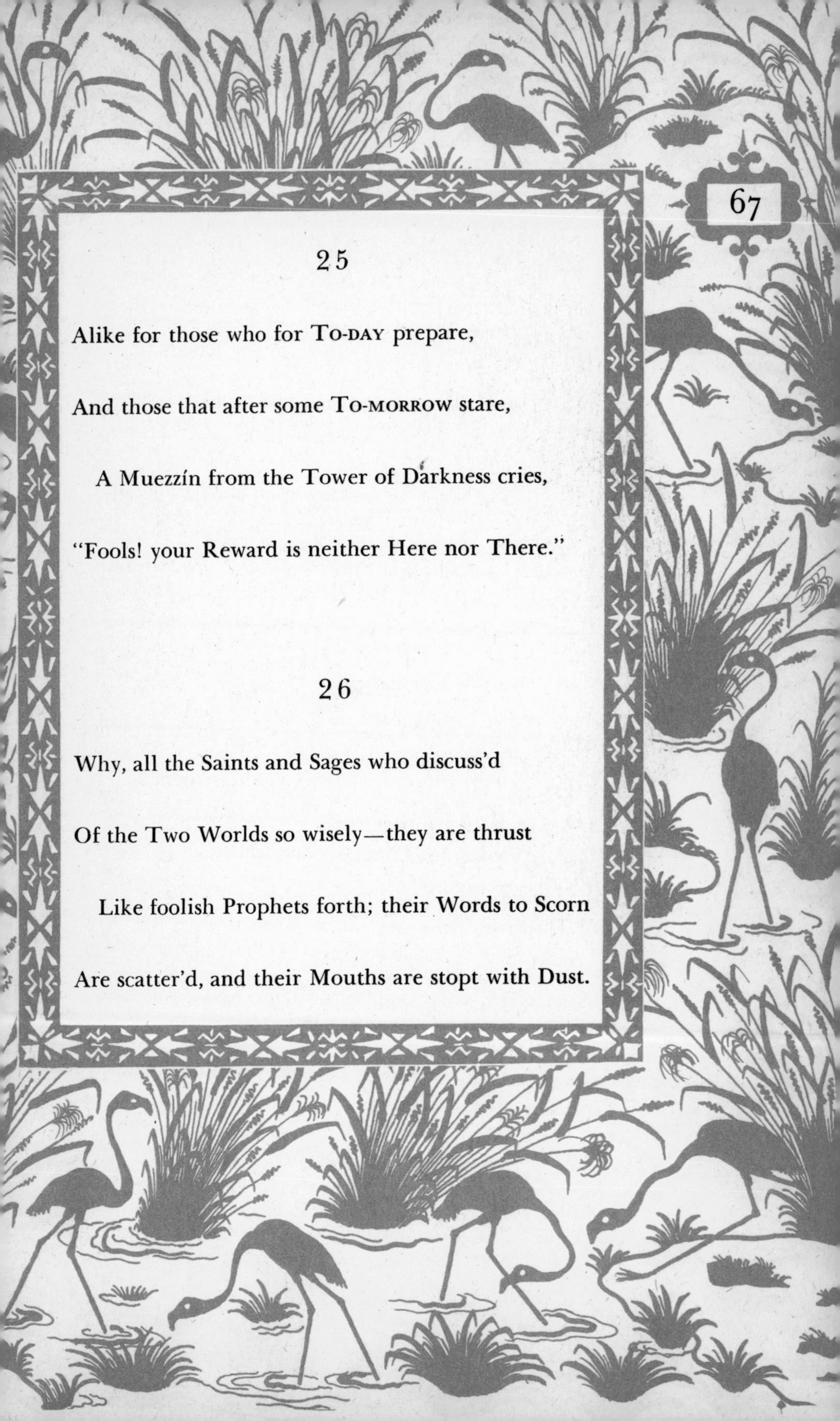

25

Alike for those who for To-day prepare,
And those that after some To-morrow stare,
  A Muezzín from the Tower of Darkness cries,
"Fools! your Reward is neither Here nor There."

26

Why, all the Saints and Sages who discuss'd
Of the Two Worlds so wisely—they are thrust
  Like foolish Prophets forth; their Words to Scorn
Are scatter'd, and their Mouths are stopt with Dust.

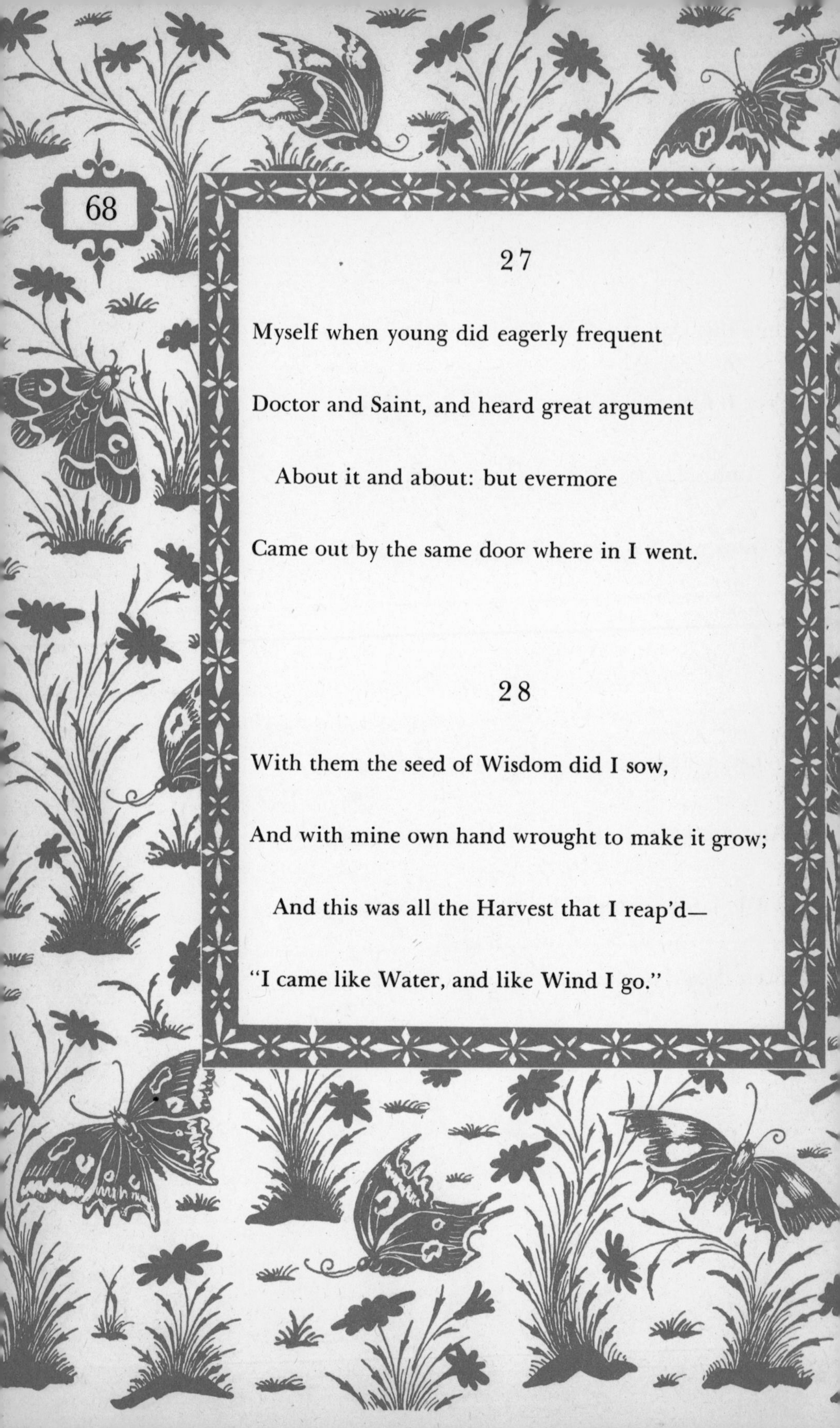

27

Myself when young did eagerly frequent
Doctor and Saint, and heard great argument
About it and about: but evermore
Came out by the same door where in I went.

28

With them the seed of Wisdom did I sow,
And with mine own hand wrought to make it grow;
And this was all the Harvest that I reap'd—
"I came like Water, and like Wind I go."

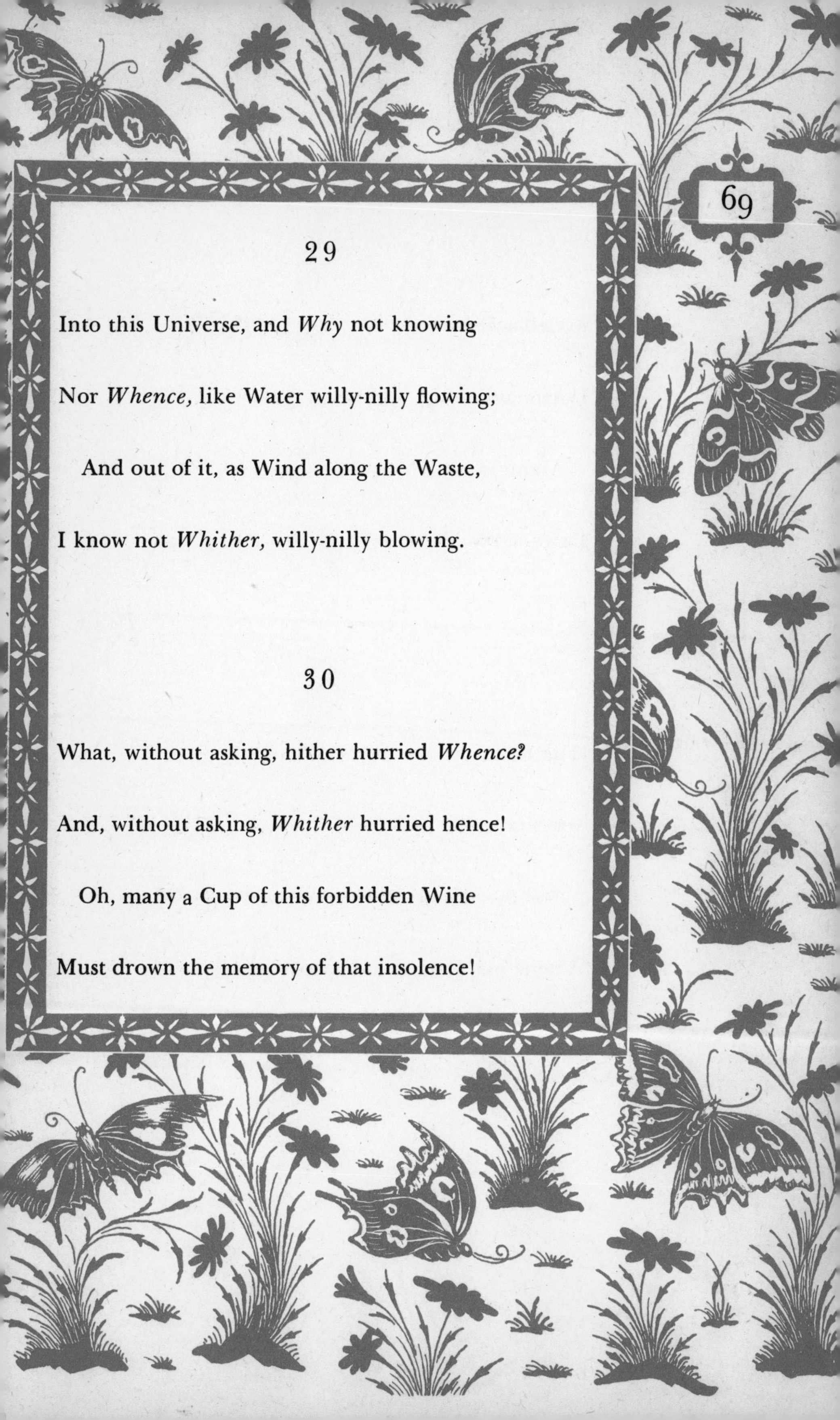

29

Into this Universe, and *Why* not knowing
Nor *Whence,* like Water willy-nilly flowing;
And out of it, as Wind along the Waste,
I know not *Whither,* willy-nilly blowing.

30

What, without asking, hither hurried *Whence?*
And, without asking, *Whither* hurried hence!
Oh, many a Cup of this forbidden Wine
Must drown the memory of that insolence!

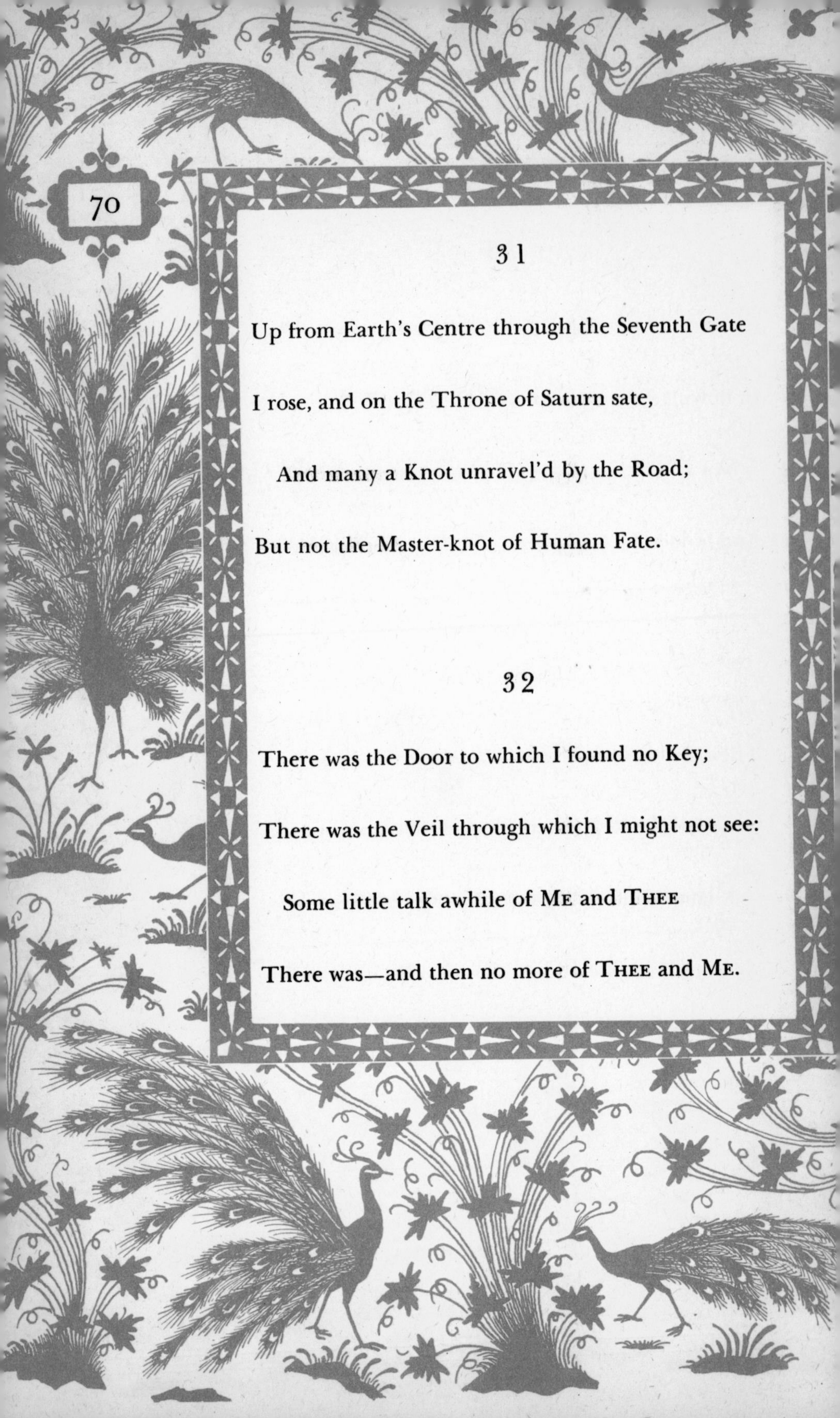

31

Up from Earth's Centre through the Seventh Gate
I rose, and on the Throne of Saturn sate,
  And many a Knot unravel'd by the Road;
But not the Master-knot of Human Fate.

32

There was the Door to which I found no Key;
There was the Veil through which I might not see:
  Some little talk awhile of Me and Thee
There was—and then no more of Thee and Me.

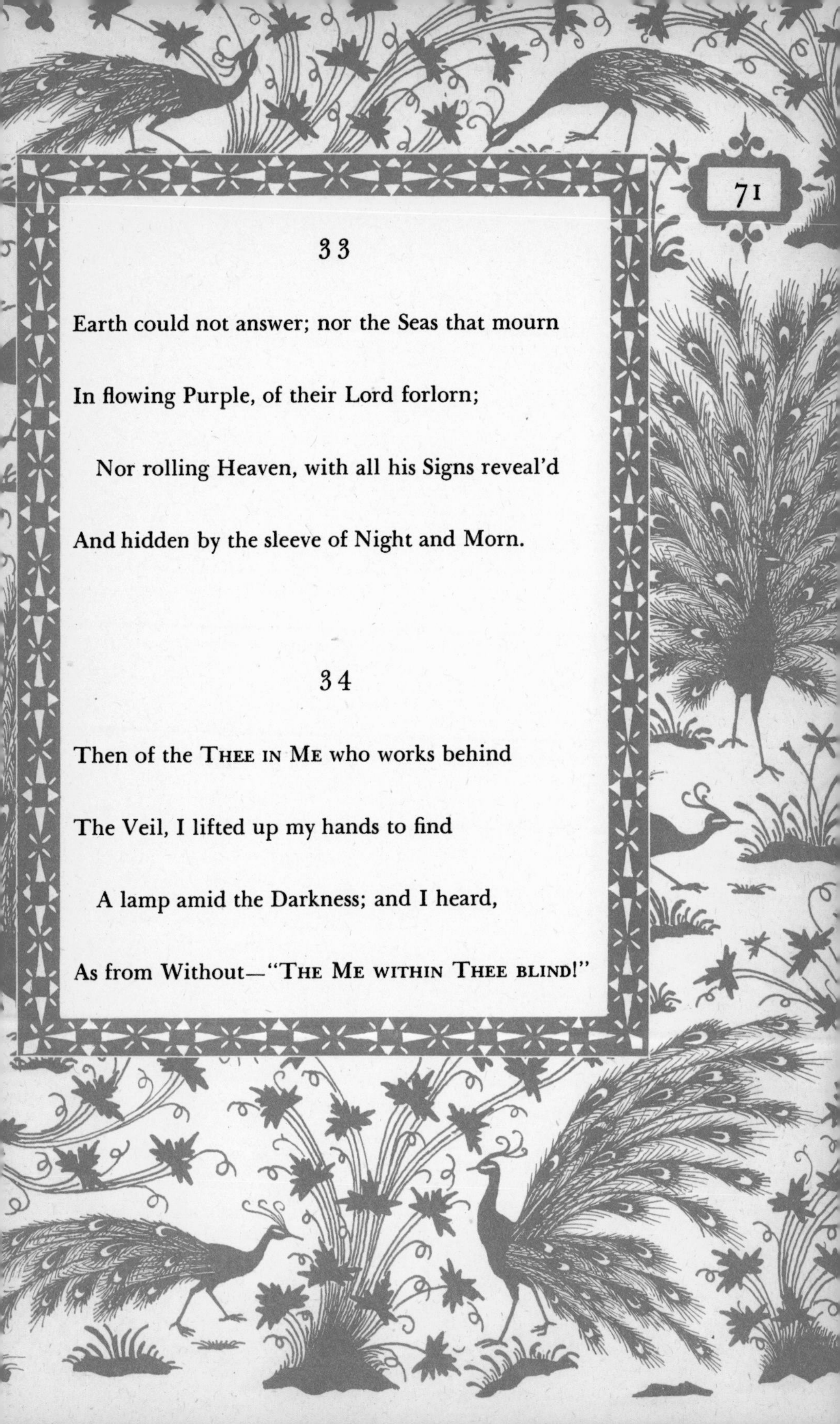

33

Earth could not answer; nor the Seas that mourn
In flowing Purple, of their Lord forlorn;
Nor rolling Heaven, with all his Signs reveal'd
And hidden by the sleeve of Night and Morn.

34

Then of the THEE IN ME who works behind
The Veil, I lifted up my hands to find
A lamp amid the Darkness; and I heard,
As from Without—"THE ME WITHIN THEE BLIND!"

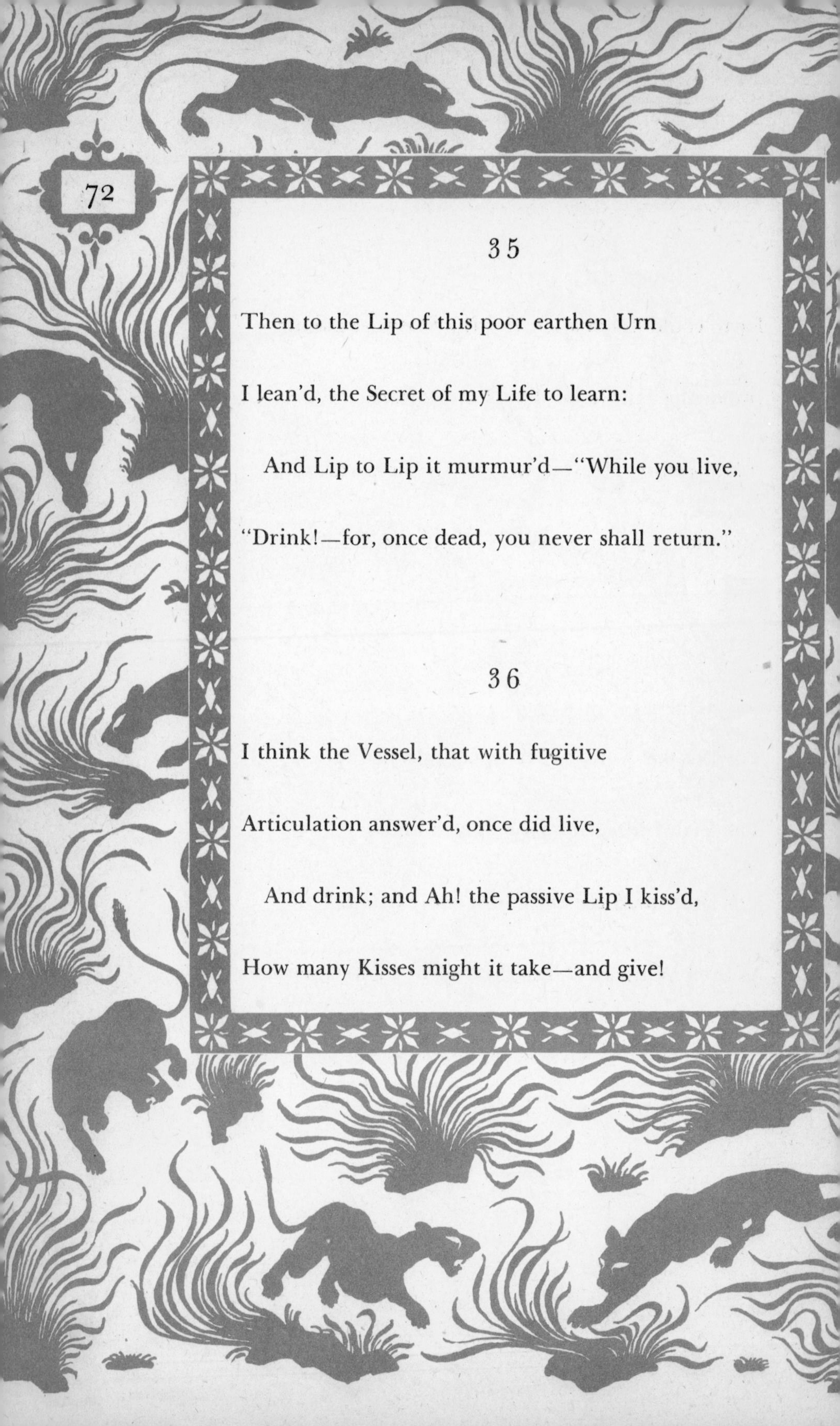

35

Then to the Lip of this poor earthen Urn
I lean'd, the Secret of my Life to learn:
   And Lip to Lip it murmur'd—"While you live,
"Drink!—for, once dead, you never shall return."

36

I think the Vessel, that with fugitive
Articulation answer'd, once did live,
   And drink; and Ah! the passive Lip I kiss'd,
How many Kisses might it take—and give!

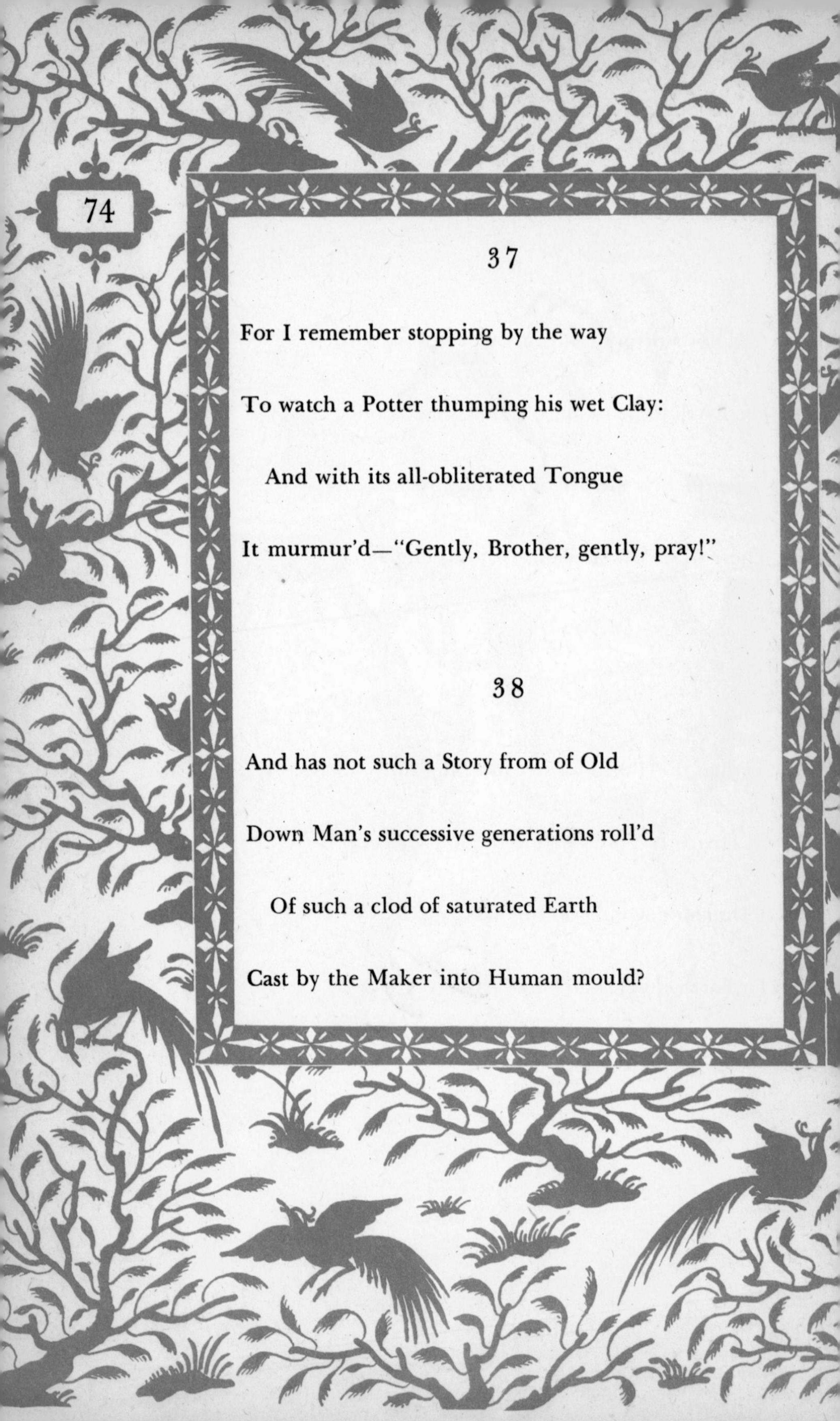

37

For I remember stopping by the way
To watch a Potter thumping his wet Clay:
And with its all-obliterated Tongue
It murmur'd—"Gently, Brother, gently, pray!"

38

And has not such a Story from of Old
Down Man's successive generations roll'd
Of such a clod of saturated Earth
Cast by the Maker into Human mould?

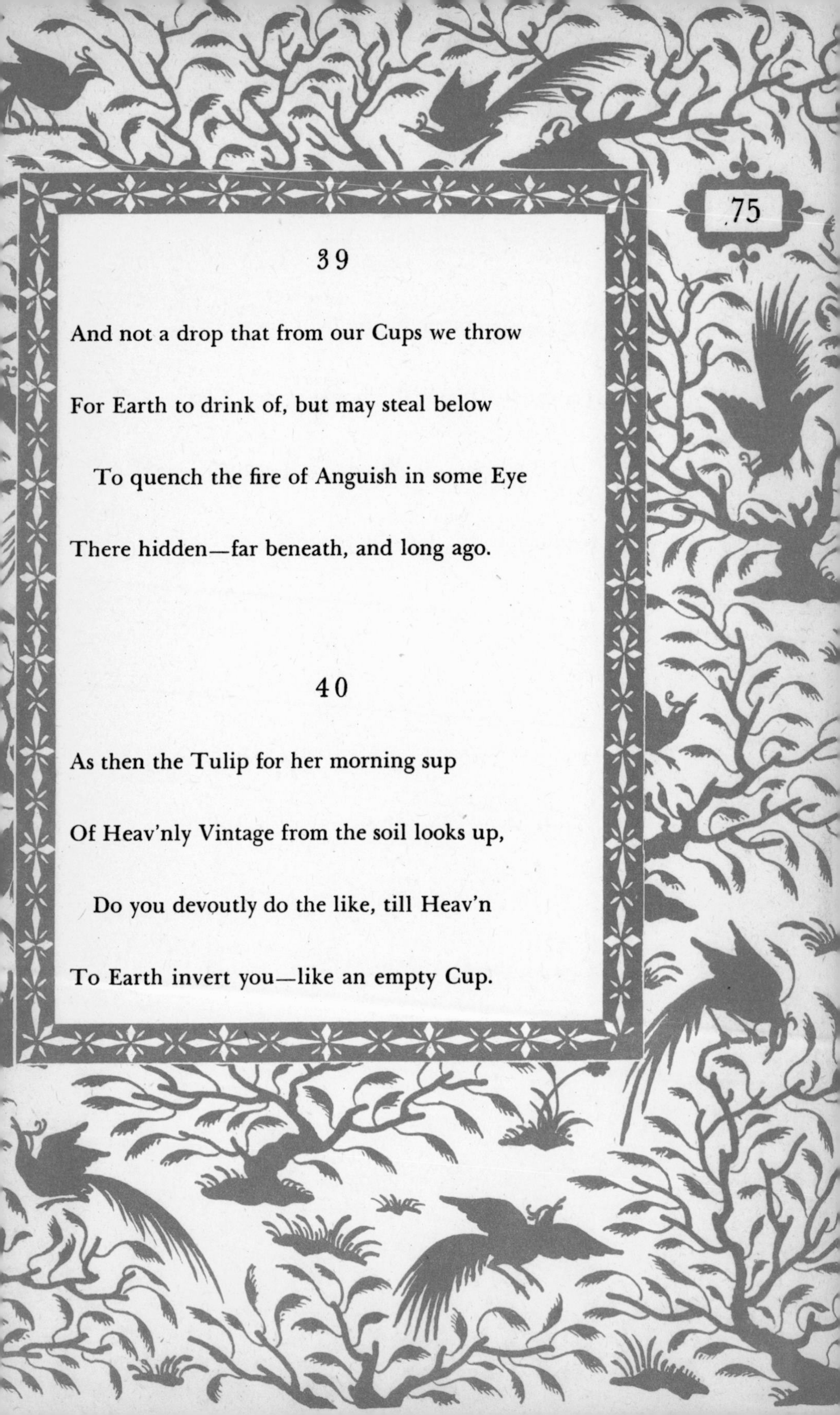

39

And not a drop that from our Cups we throw
For Earth to drink of, but may steal below
  To quench the fire of Anguish in some Eye
There hidden—far beneath, and long ago.

40

As then the Tulip for her morning sup
Of Heav'nly Vintage from the soil looks up,
  Do you devoutly do the like, till Heav'n
To Earth invert you—like an empty Cup.

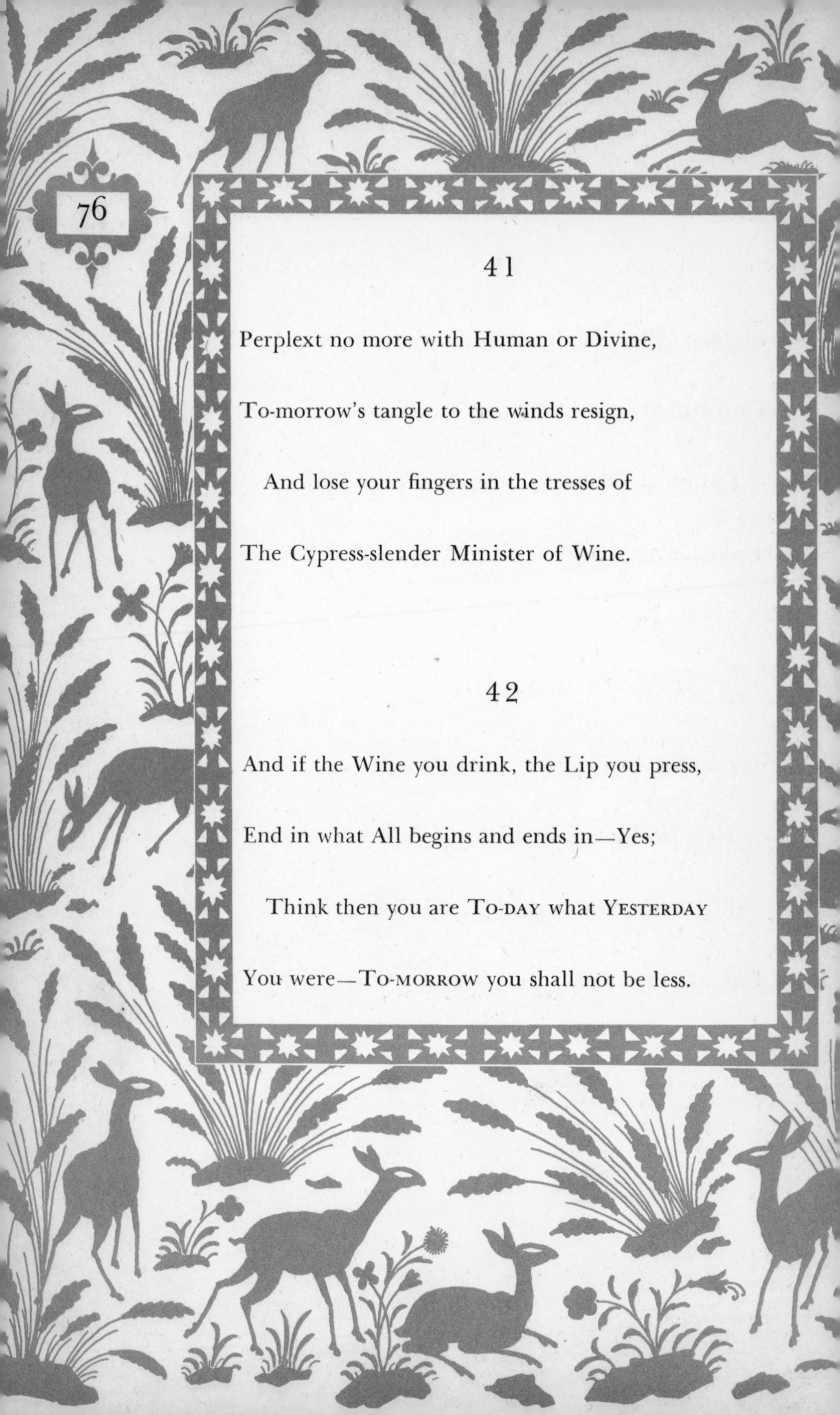

41

Perplext no more with Human or Divine,

To-morrow's tangle to the winds resign,

And lose your fingers in the tresses of

The Cypress-slender Minister of Wine.

42

And if the Wine you drink, the Lip you press,

End in what All begins and ends in—Yes;

Think then you are TO-DAY what YESTERDAY

You were—TO-MORROW you shall not be less.

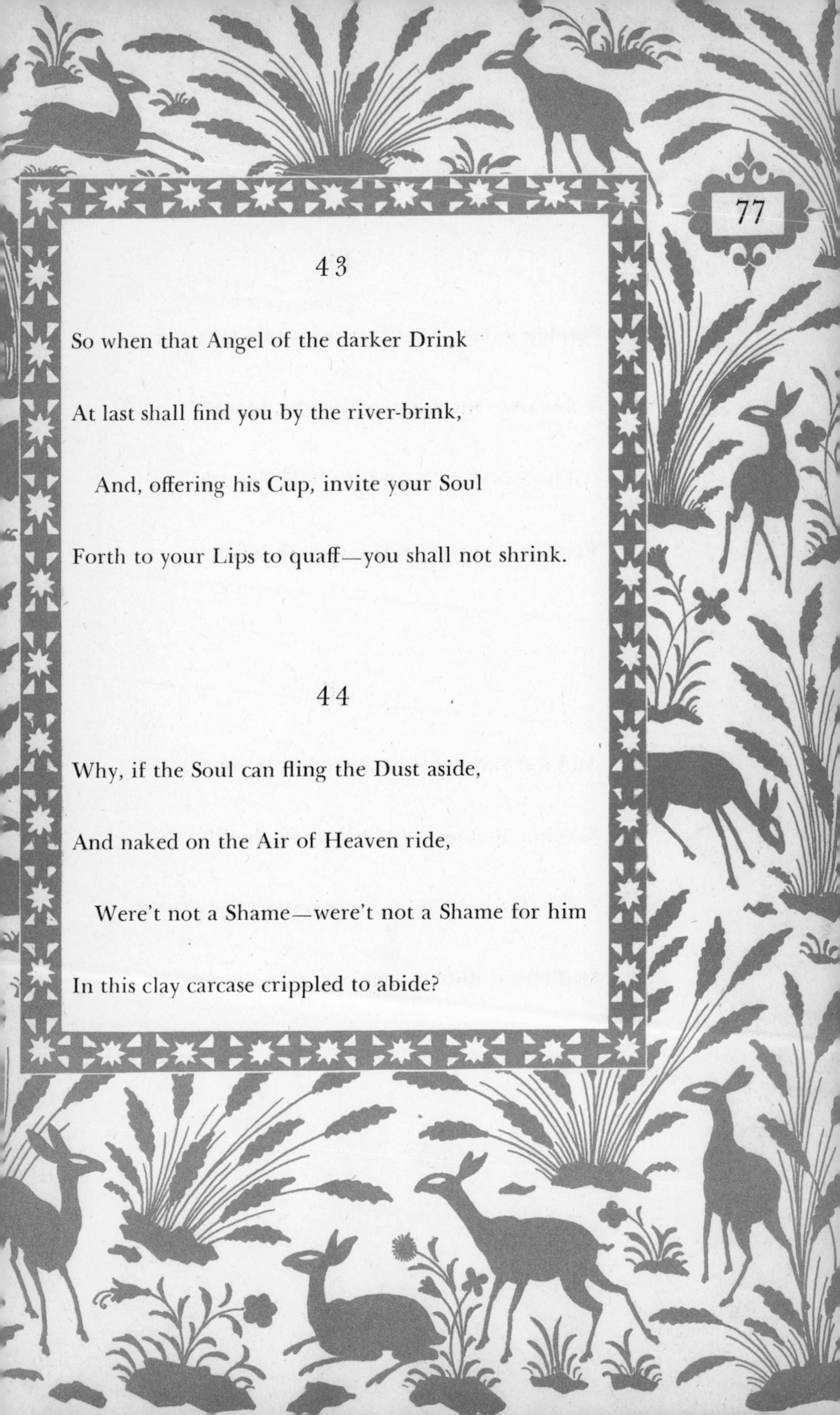

43

So when that Angel of the darker Drink
At last shall find you by the river-brink,
   And, offering his Cup, invite your Soul
Forth to your Lips to quaff—you shall not shrink.

44

Why, if the Soul can fling the Dust aside,
And naked on the Air of Heaven ride,
   Were't not a Shame—were't not a Shame for him
In this clay carcase crippled to abide?

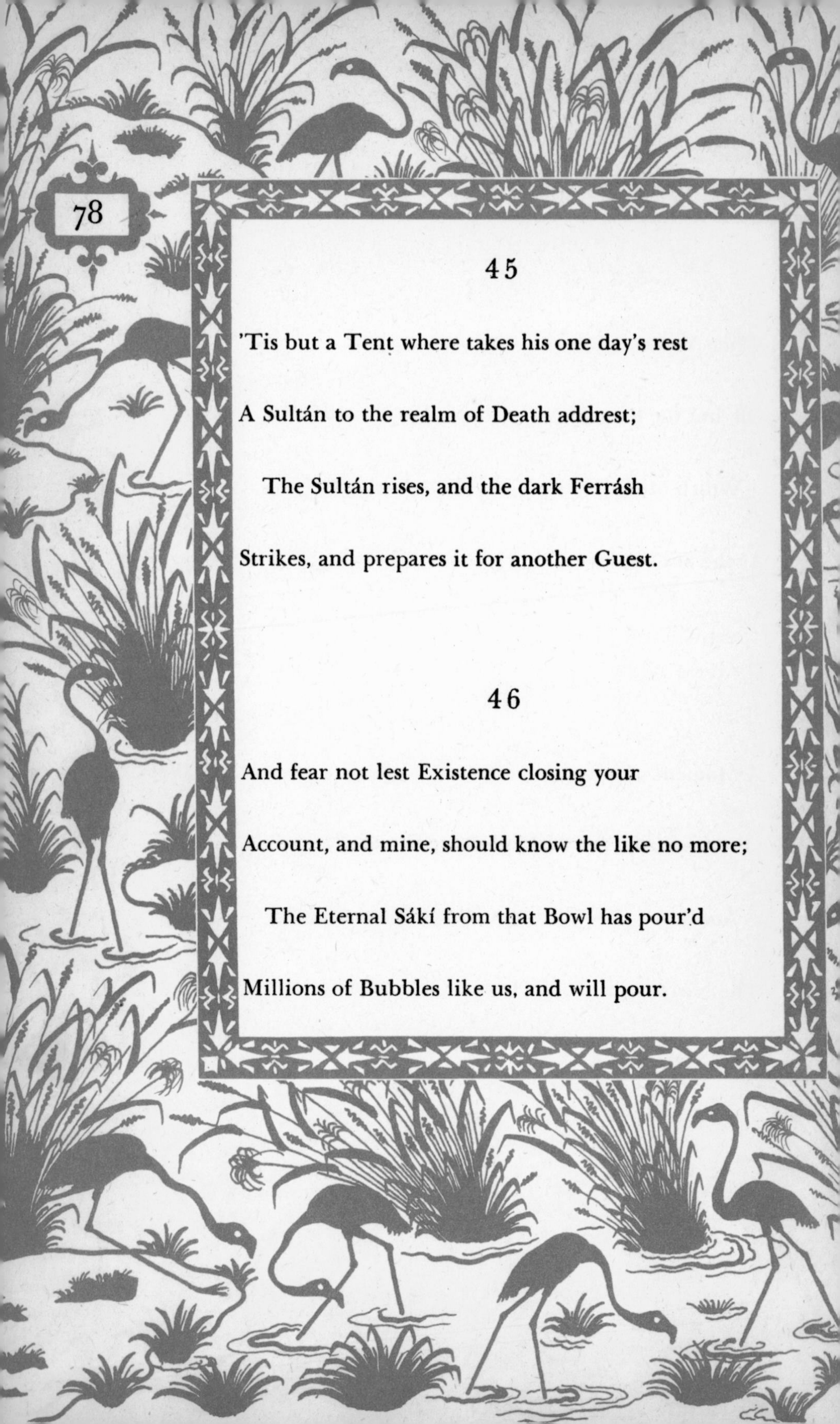

45

'Tis but a Tent where takes his one day's rest
A Sultán to the realm of Death addrest;
The Sultán rises, and the dark Ferrásh
Strikes, and prepares it for another Guest.

46

And fear not lest Existence closing your
Account, and mine, should know the like no more;
The Eternal Sákí from that Bowl has pour'd
Millions of Bubbles like us, and will pour.

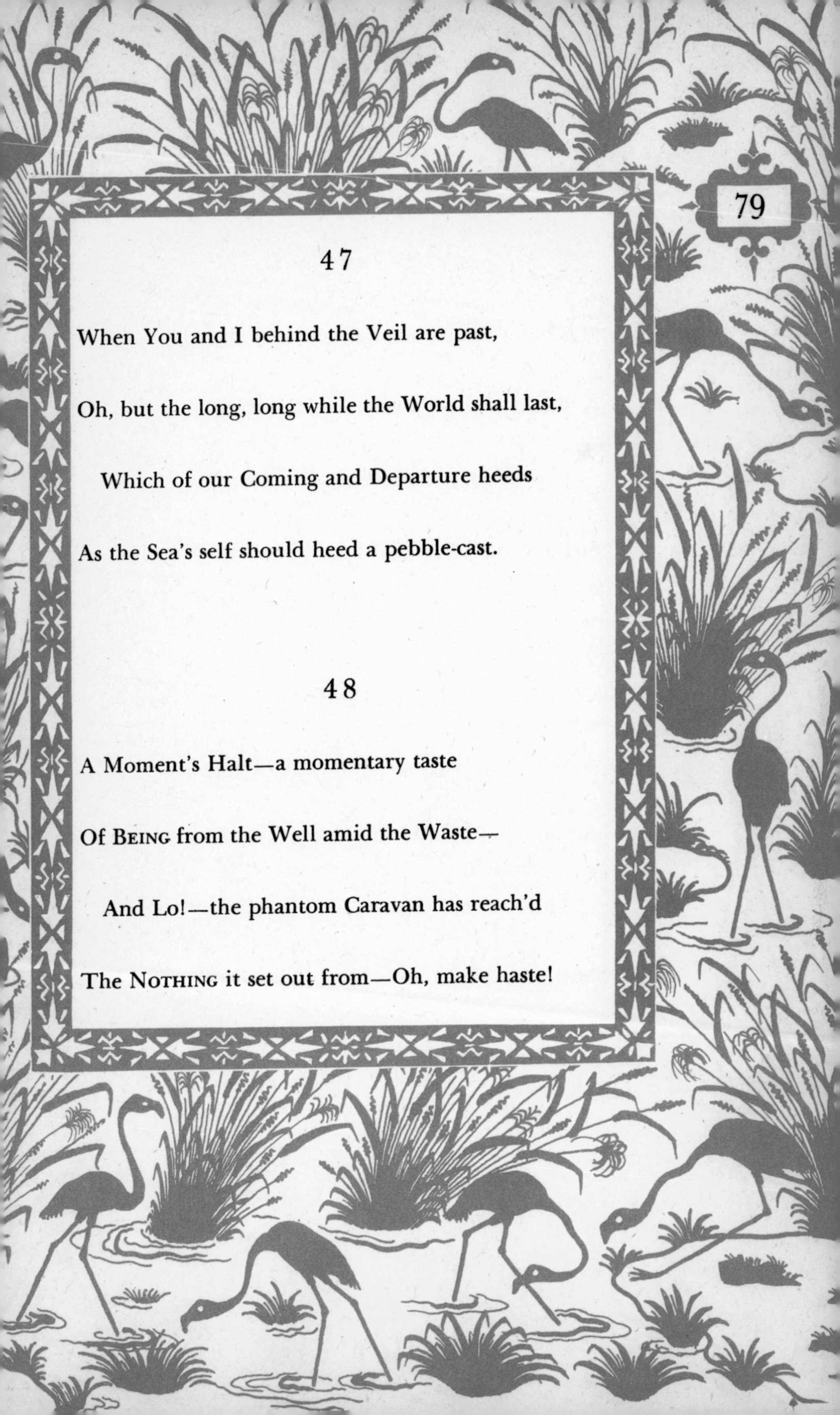

47

When You and I behind the Veil are past,
Oh, but the long, long while the World shall last,
Which of our Coming and Departure heeds
As the Sea's self should heed a pebble-cast.

48

A Moment's Halt—a momentary taste
Of Being from the Well amid the Waste—
And Lo!—the phantom Caravan has reach'd
The Nothing it set out from—Oh, make haste!

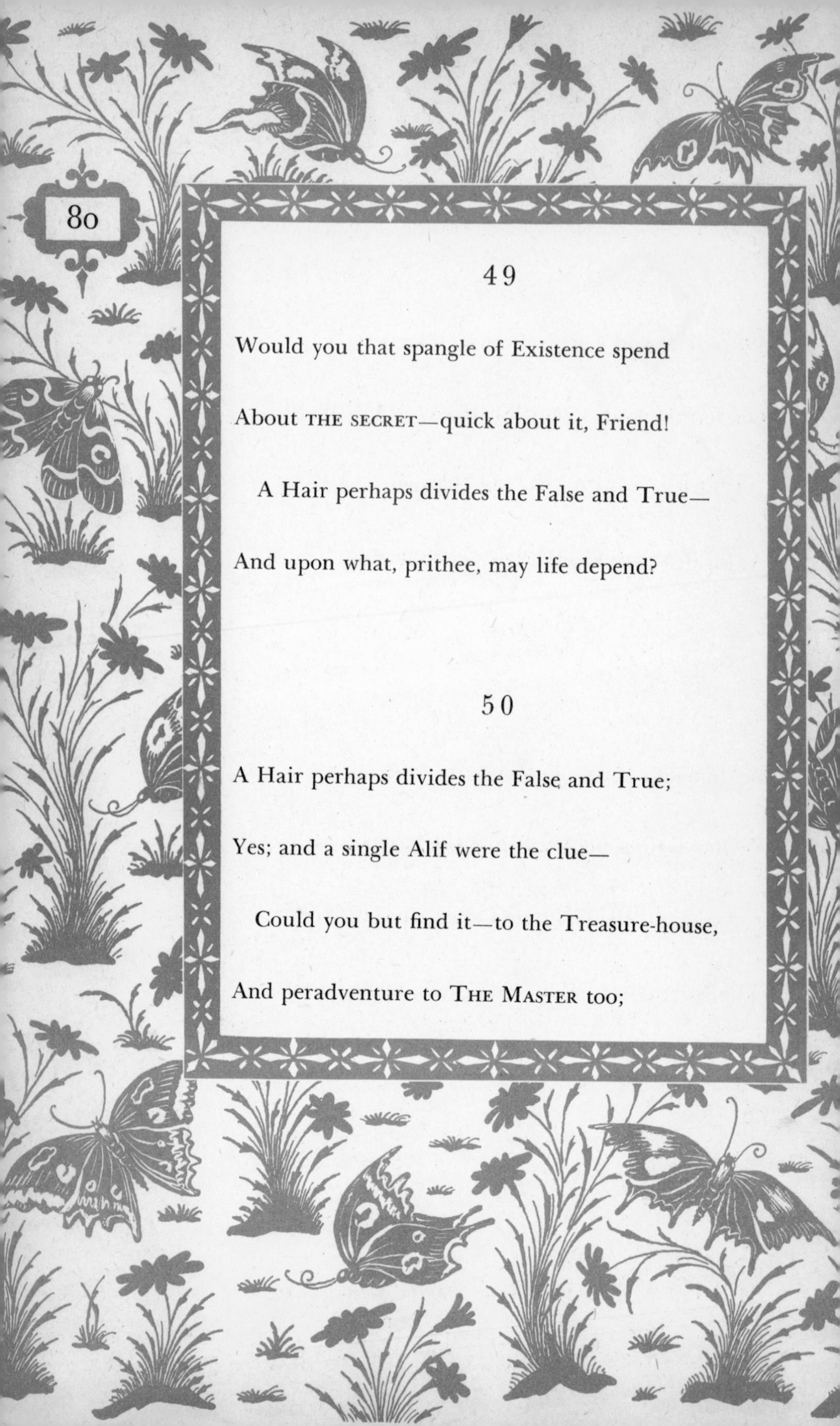

49

Would you that spangle of Existence spend
About THE SECRET—quick about it, Friend!
  A Hair perhaps divides the False and True—
And upon what, prithee, may life depend?

50

A Hair perhaps divides the False and True;
Yes; and a single Alif were the clue—
  Could you but find it—to the Treasure-house,
And peradventure to THE MASTER too;

81
M.S.

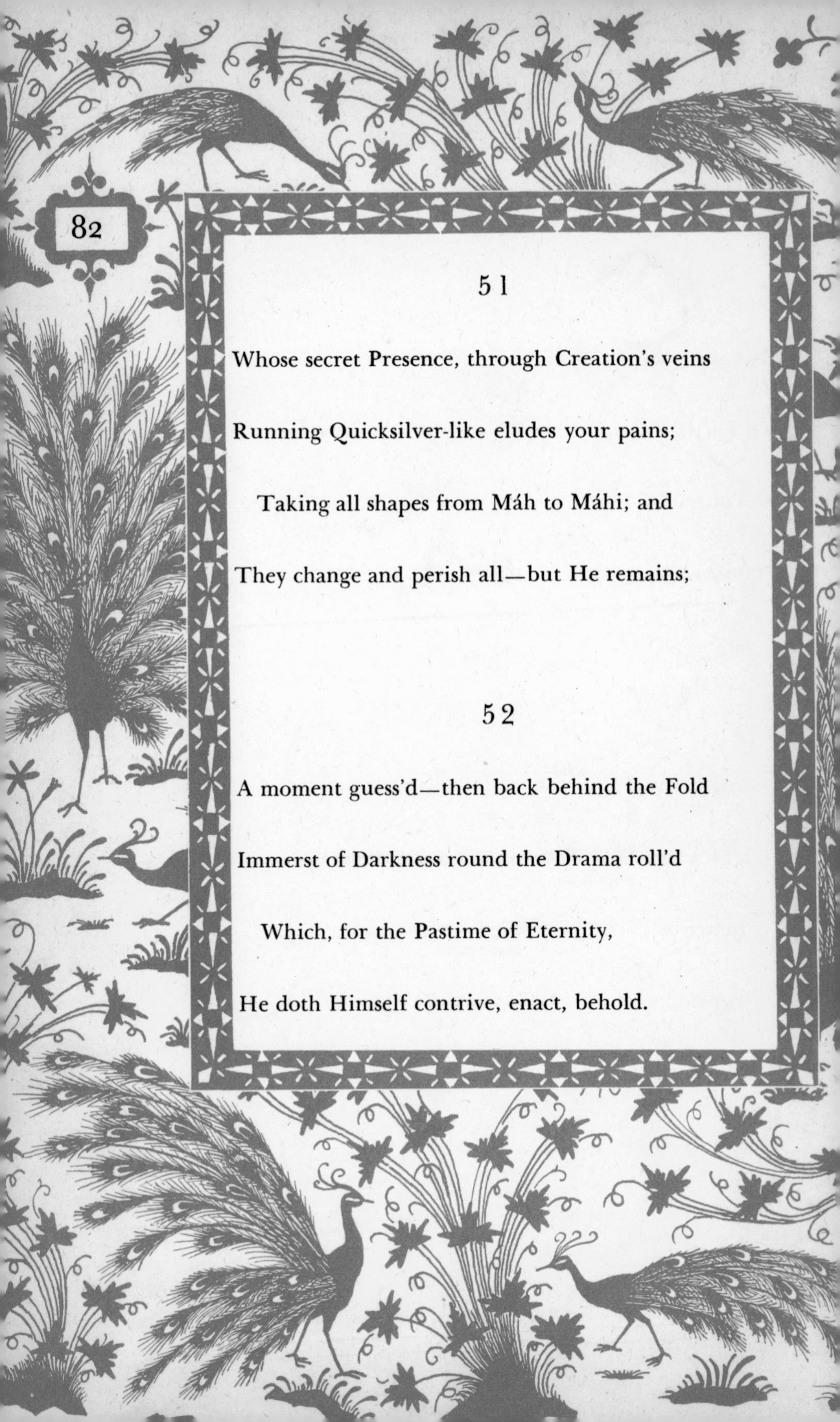

51

Whose secret Presence, through Creation's veins
Running Quicksilver-like eludes your pains;
Taking all shapes from Máh to Máhi; and
They change and perish all—but He remains;

52

A moment guess'd—then back behind the Fold
Immerst of Darkness round the Drama roll'd
Which, for the Pastime of Eternity,
He doth Himself contrive, enact, behold.

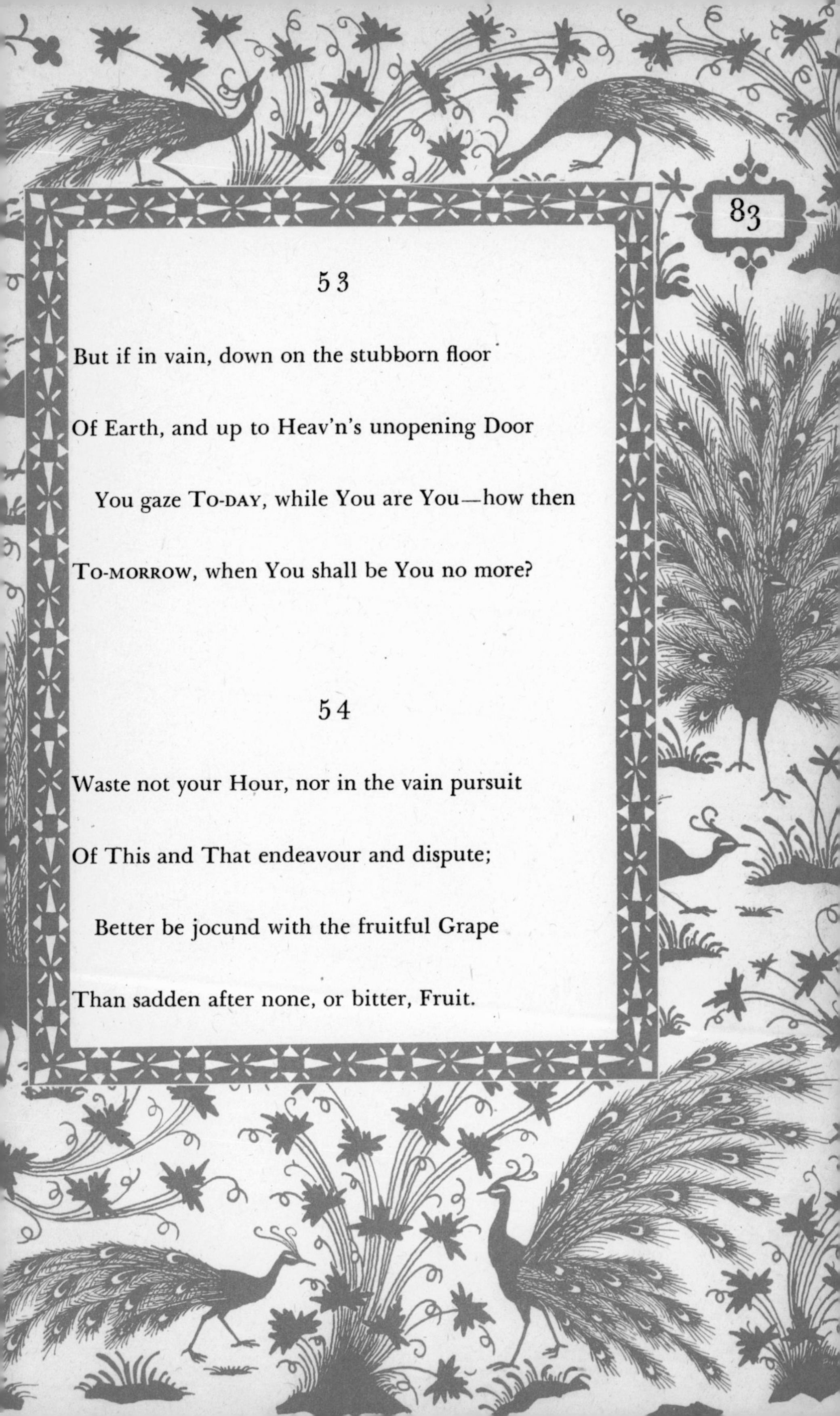

53

But if in vain, down on the stubborn floor
Of Earth, and up to Heav'n's unopening Door
  You gaze To-day, while You are You—how then
To-morrow, when You shall be You no more?

54

Waste not your Hour, nor in the vain pursuit
Of This and That endeavour and dispute;
  Better be jocund with the fruitful Grape
Than sadden after none, or bitter, Fruit.

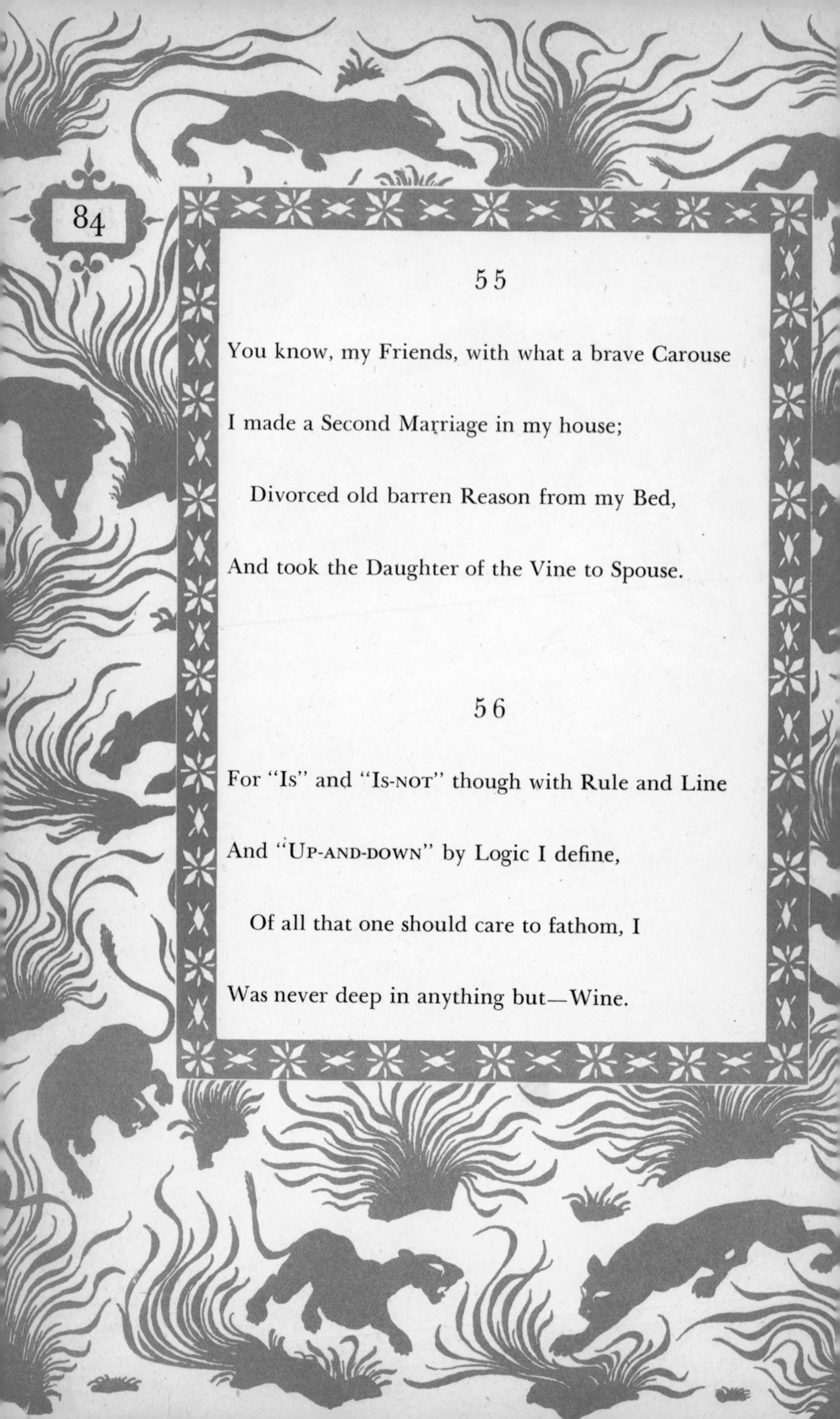

55

You know, my Friends, with what a brave Carouse
I made a Second Marriage in my house;
   Divorced old barren Reason from my Bed,
And took the Daughter of the Vine to Spouse.

56

For "Is" and "Is-not" though with Rule and Line
And "Up-and-down" by Logic I define,
   Of all that one should care to fathom, I
Was never deep in anything but—Wine.

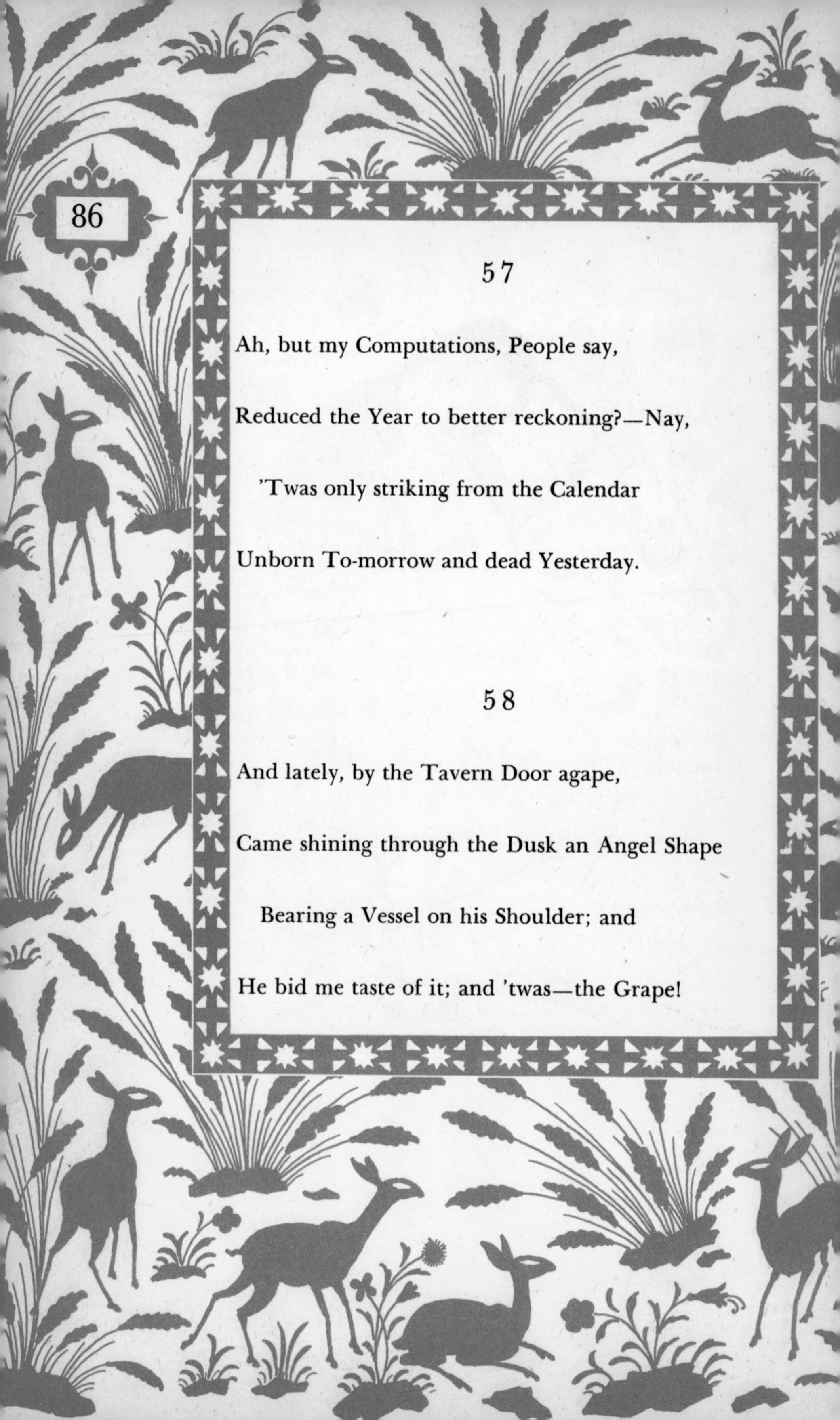

57

Ah, but my Computations, People say,
Reduced the Year to better reckoning?—Nay,
'Twas only striking from the Calendar
Unborn To-morrow and dead Yesterday.

58

And lately, by the Tavern Door agape,
Came shining through the Dusk an Angel Shape
Bearing a Vessel on his Shoulder; and
He bid me taste of it; and 'twas—the Grape!

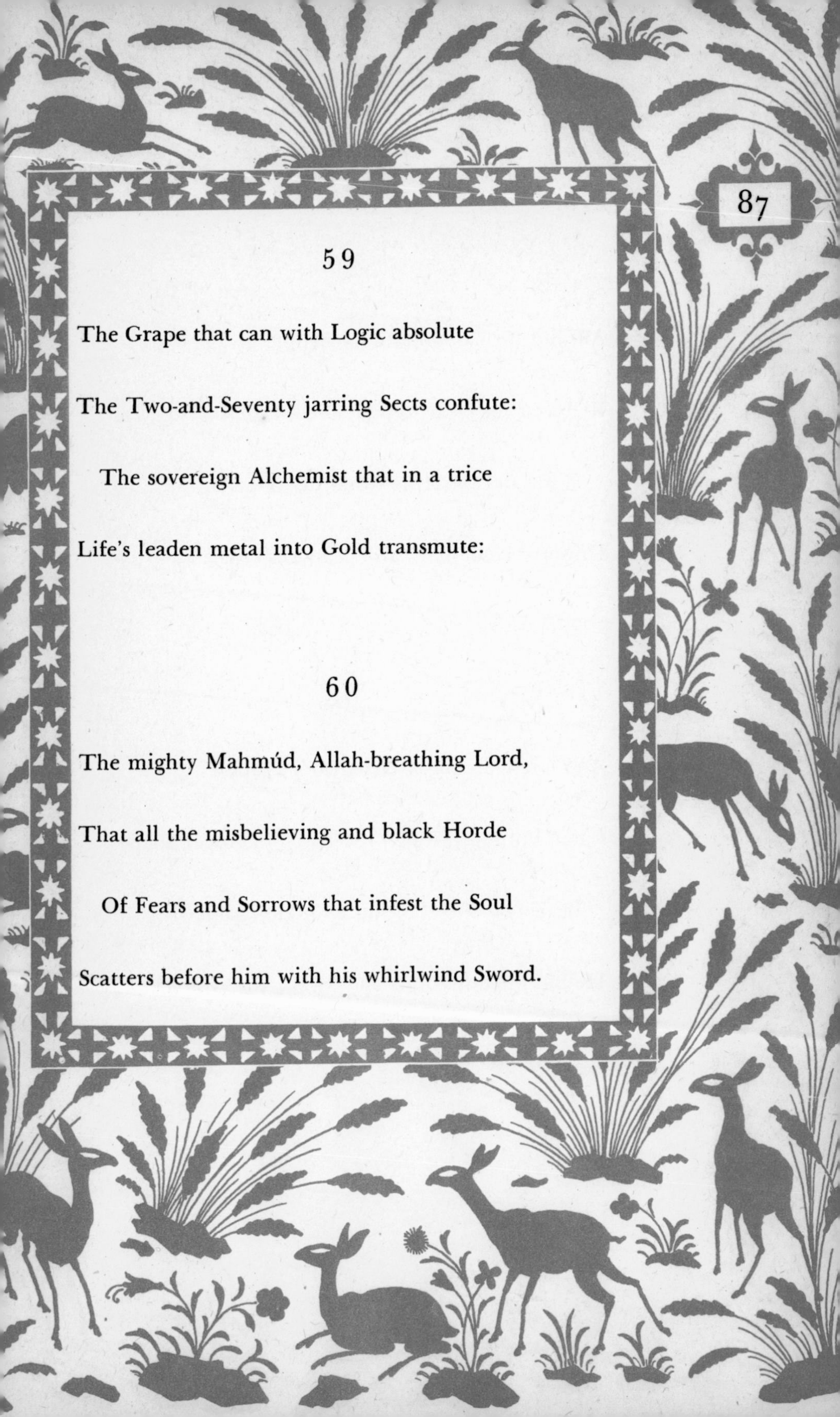

59

The Grape that can with Logic absolute
The Two-and-Seventy jarring Sects confute:
   The sovereign Alchemist that in a trice
Life's leaden metal into Gold transmute:

60

The mighty Mahmúd, Allah-breathing Lord,
That all the misbelieving and black Horde
   Of Fears and Sorrows that infest the Soul
Scatters before him with his whirlwind Sword.

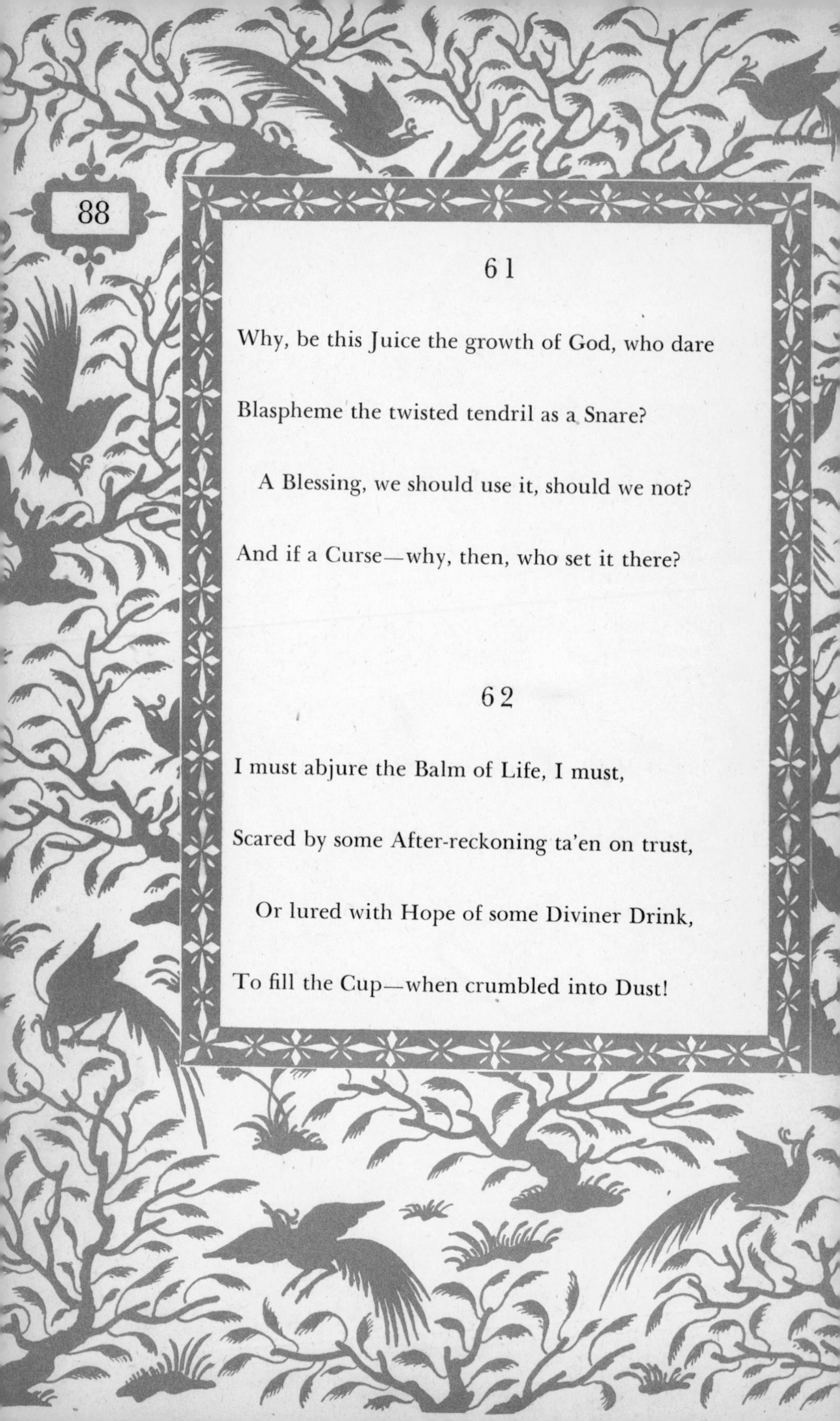

61

Why, be this Juice the growth of God, who dare
Blaspheme the twisted tendril as a Snare?
A Blessing, we should use it, should we not?
And if a Curse—why, then, who set it there?

62

I must abjure the Balm of Life, I must,
Scared by some After-reckoning ta'en on trust,
Or lured with Hope of some Diviner Drink,
To fill the Cup—when crumbled into Dust!

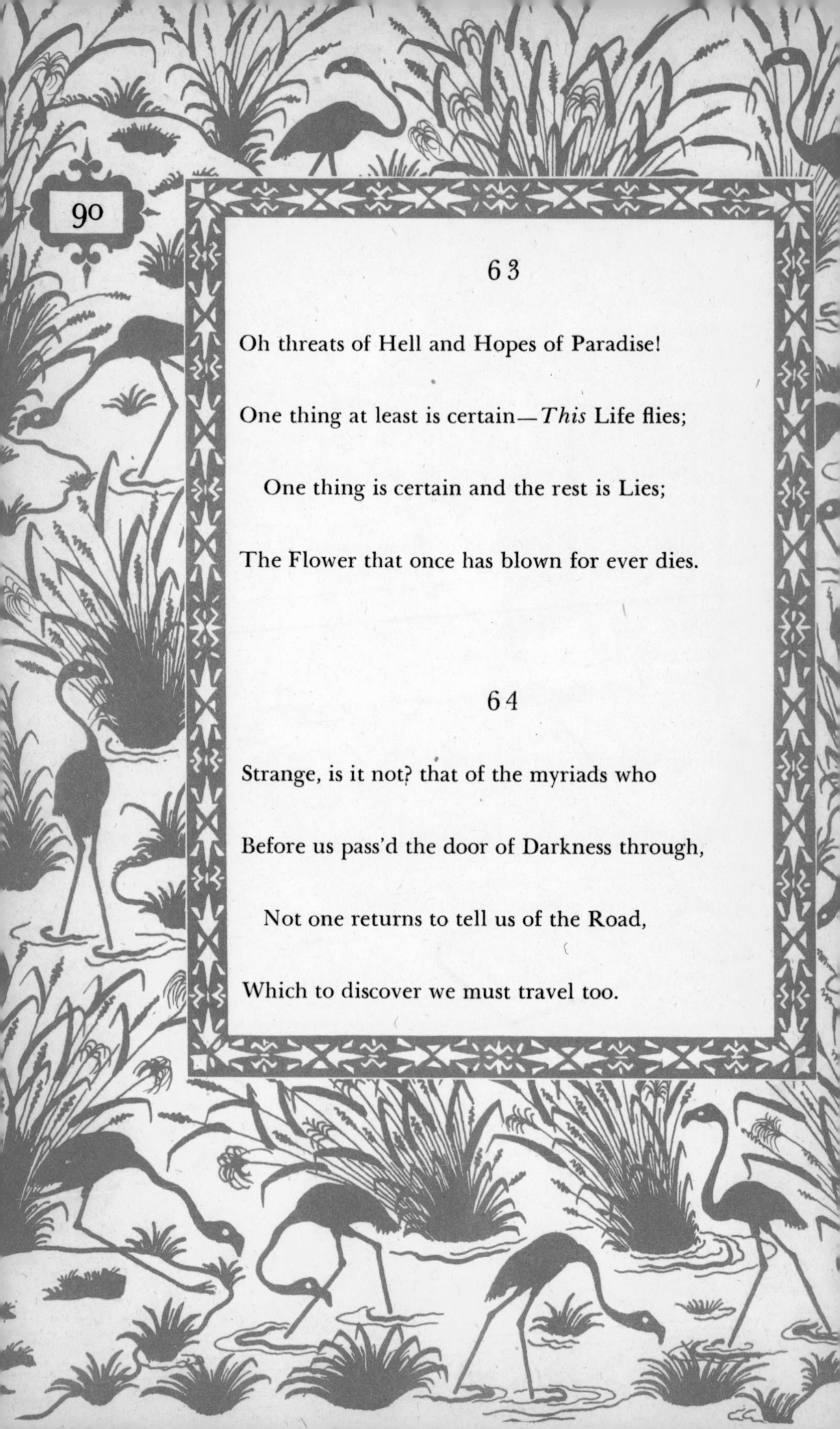

63

Oh threats of Hell and Hopes of Paradise!
One thing at least is certain—*This* Life flies;
One thing is certain and the rest is Lies;
The Flower that once has blown for ever dies.

64

Strange, is it not? that of the myriads who
Before us pass'd the door of Darkness through,
Not one returns to tell us of the Road,
Which to discover we must travel too.

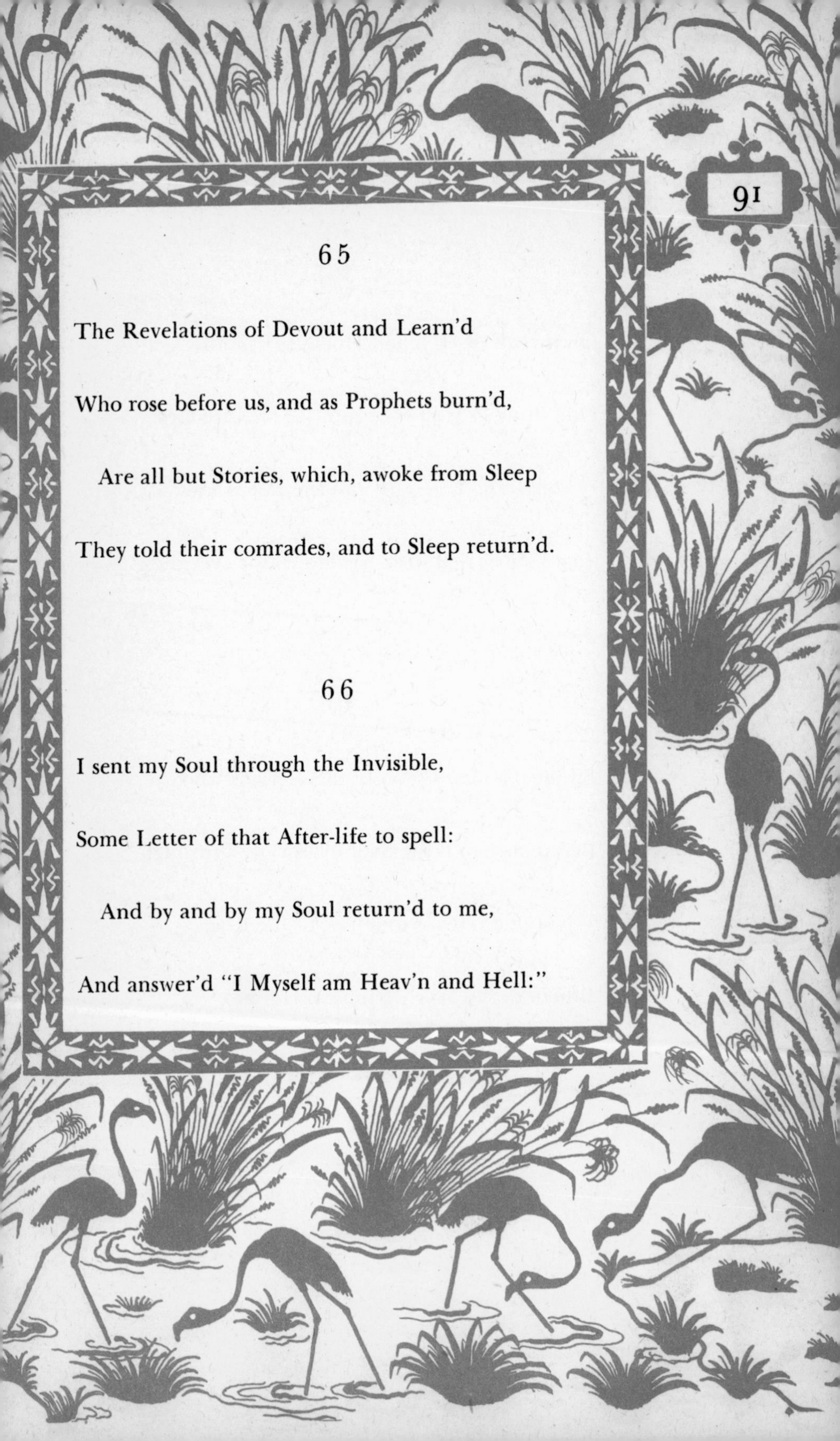

65

The Revelations of Devout and Learn'd
Who rose before us, and as Prophets burn'd,
Are all but Stories, which, awoke from Sleep
They told their comrades, and to Sleep return'd.

66

I sent my Soul through the Invisible,
Some Letter of that After-life to spell:
And by and by my Soul return'd to me,
And answer'd "I Myself am Heav'n and Hell:"

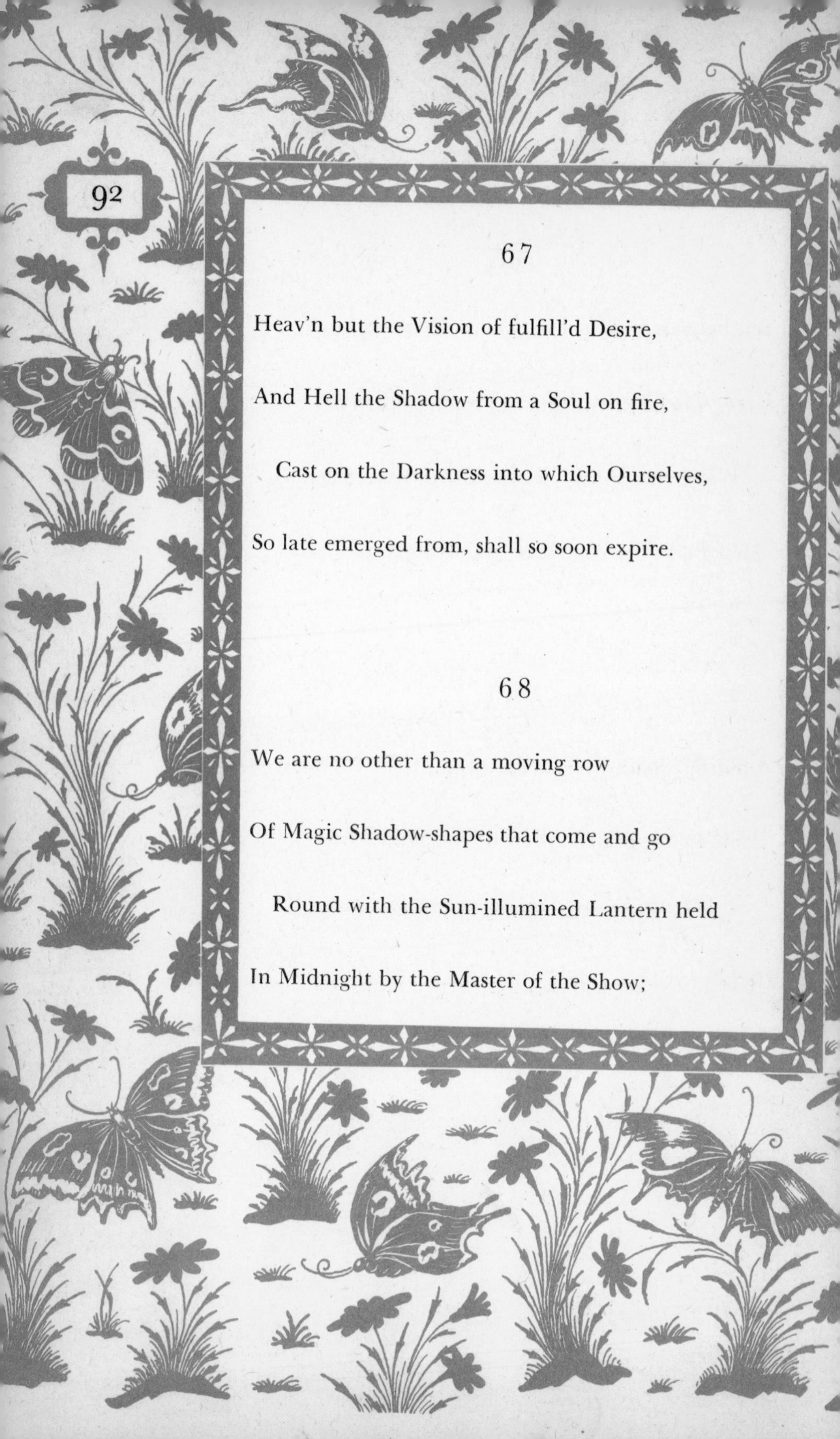

67

Heav'n but the Vision of fulfill'd Desire,
And Hell the Shadow from a Soul on fire,
Cast on the Darkness into which Ourselves,
So late emerged from, shall so soon expire.

68

We are no other than a moving row
Of Magic Shadow-shapes that come and go
Round with the Sun-illumined Lantern held
In Midnight by the Master of the Show;

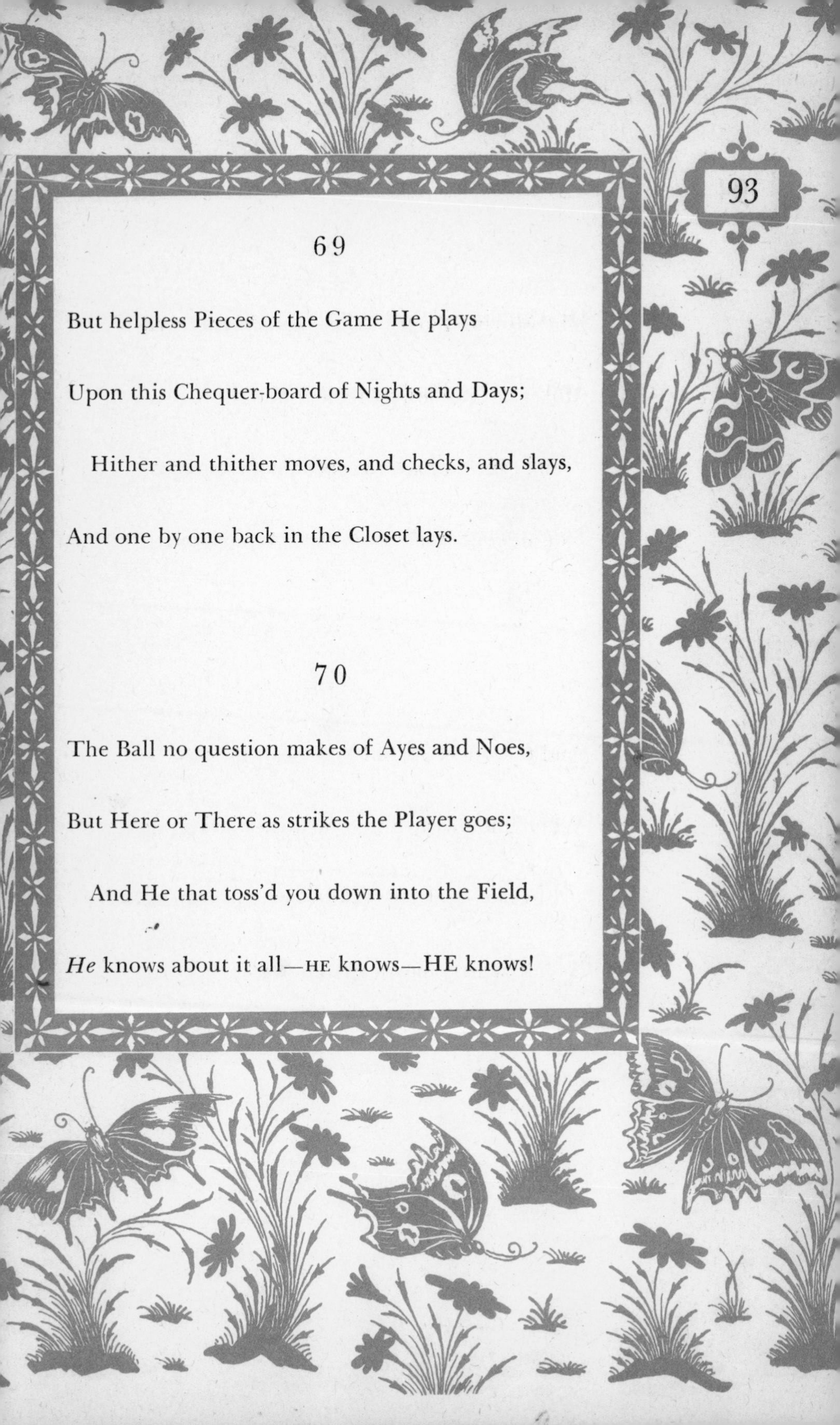

69

But helpless Pieces of the Game He plays
Upon this Chequer-board of Nights and Days;
Hither and thither moves, and checks, and slays,
And one by one back in the Closet lays.

70

The Ball no question makes of Ayes and Noes,
But Here or There as strikes the Player goes;
And He that toss'd you down into the Field,
He knows about it all—HE knows—HE knows!

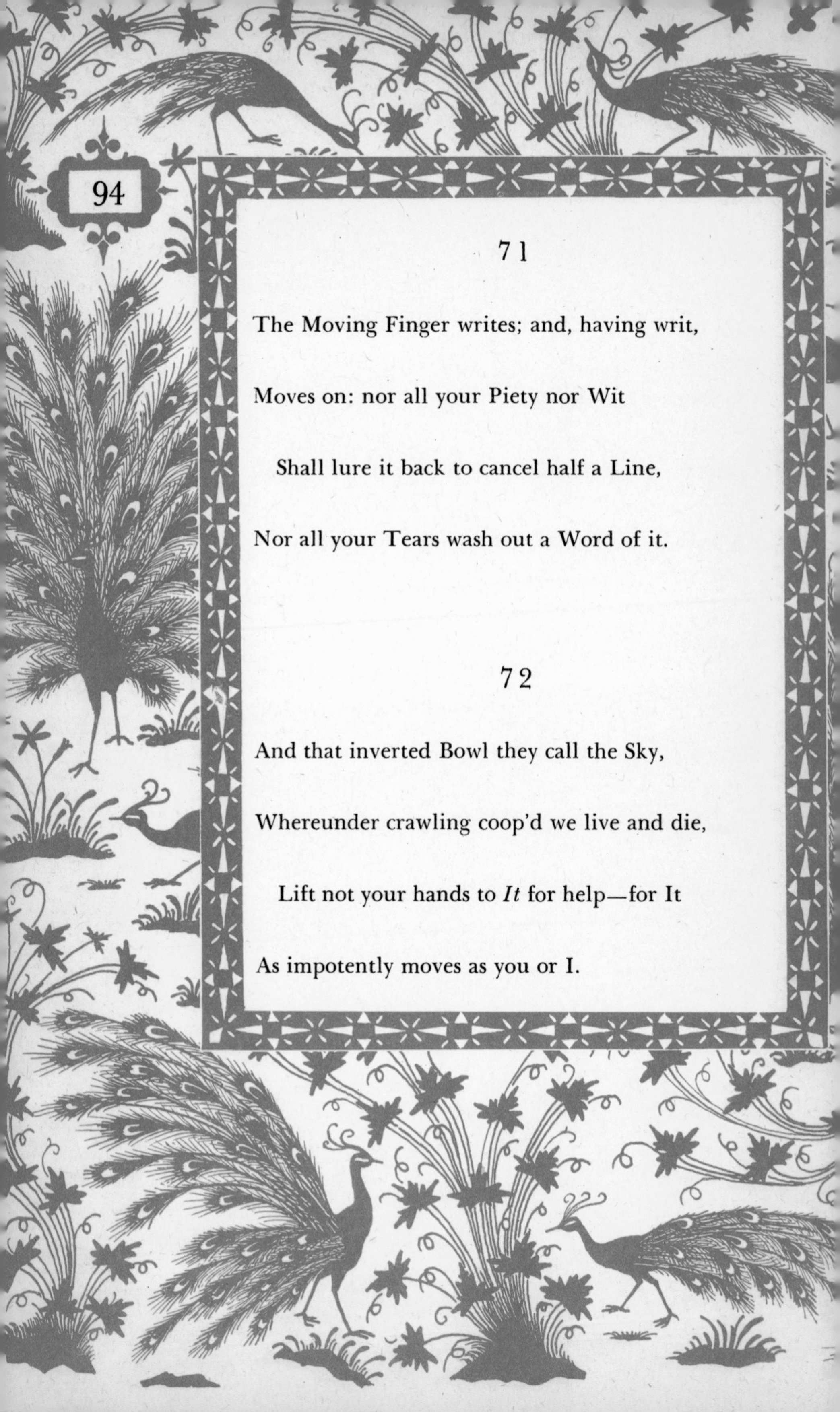

71

The Moving Finger writes; and, having writ,
Moves on: nor all your Piety nor Wit
  Shall lure it back to cancel half a Line,
Nor all your Tears wash out a Word of it.

72

And that inverted Bowl they call the Sky,
Whereunder crawling coop'd we live and die,
  Lift not your hands to *It* for help—for It
As impotently moves as you or I.

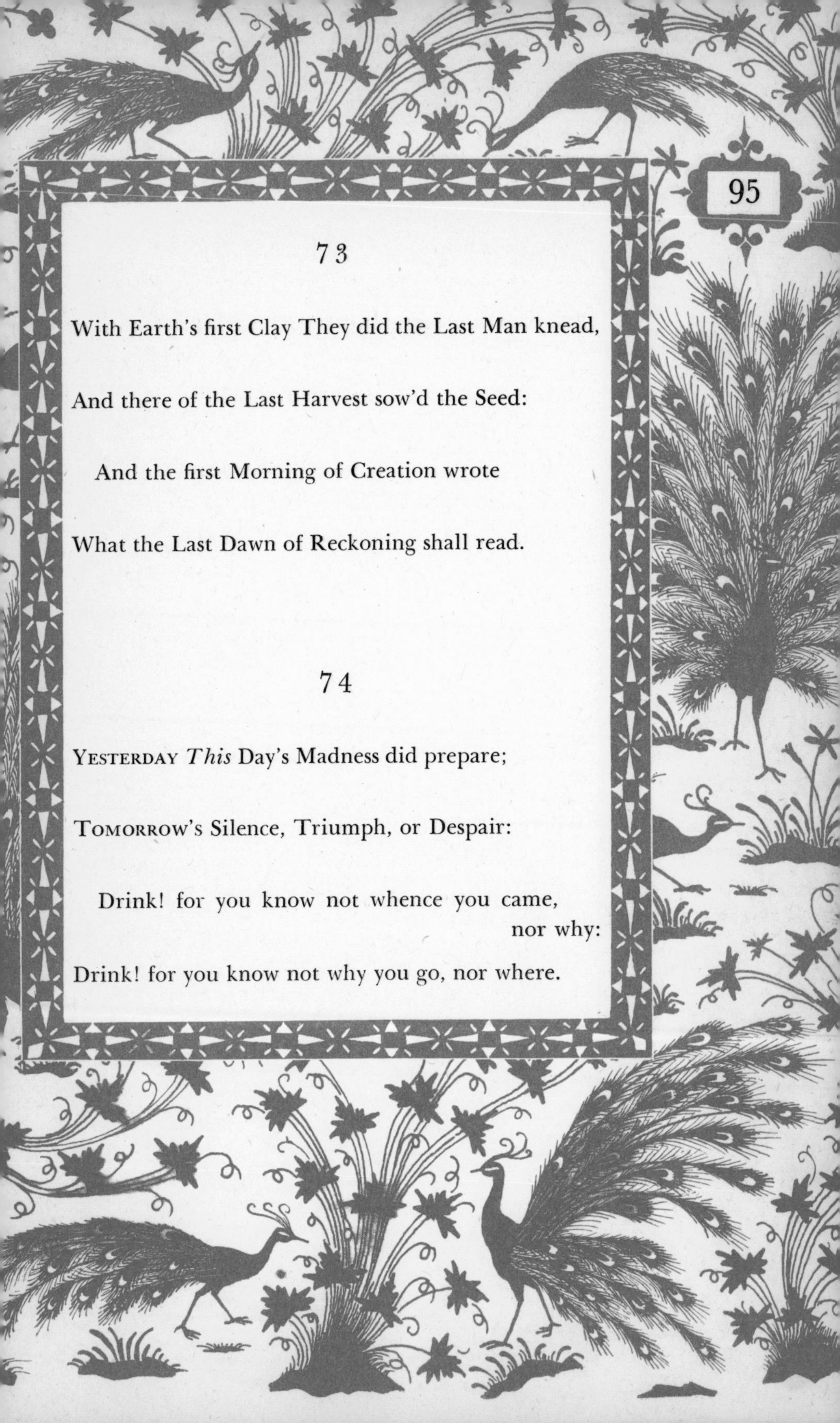

73

With Earth's first Clay They did the Last Man knead,
And there of the Last Harvest sow'd the Seed:
  And the first Morning of Creation wrote
What the Last Dawn of Reckoning shall read.

74

YESTERDAY *This* Day's Madness did prepare;
TOMORROW'S Silence, Triumph, or Despair:
  Drink! for you know not whence you came, nor why:
Drink! for you know not why you go, nor where.

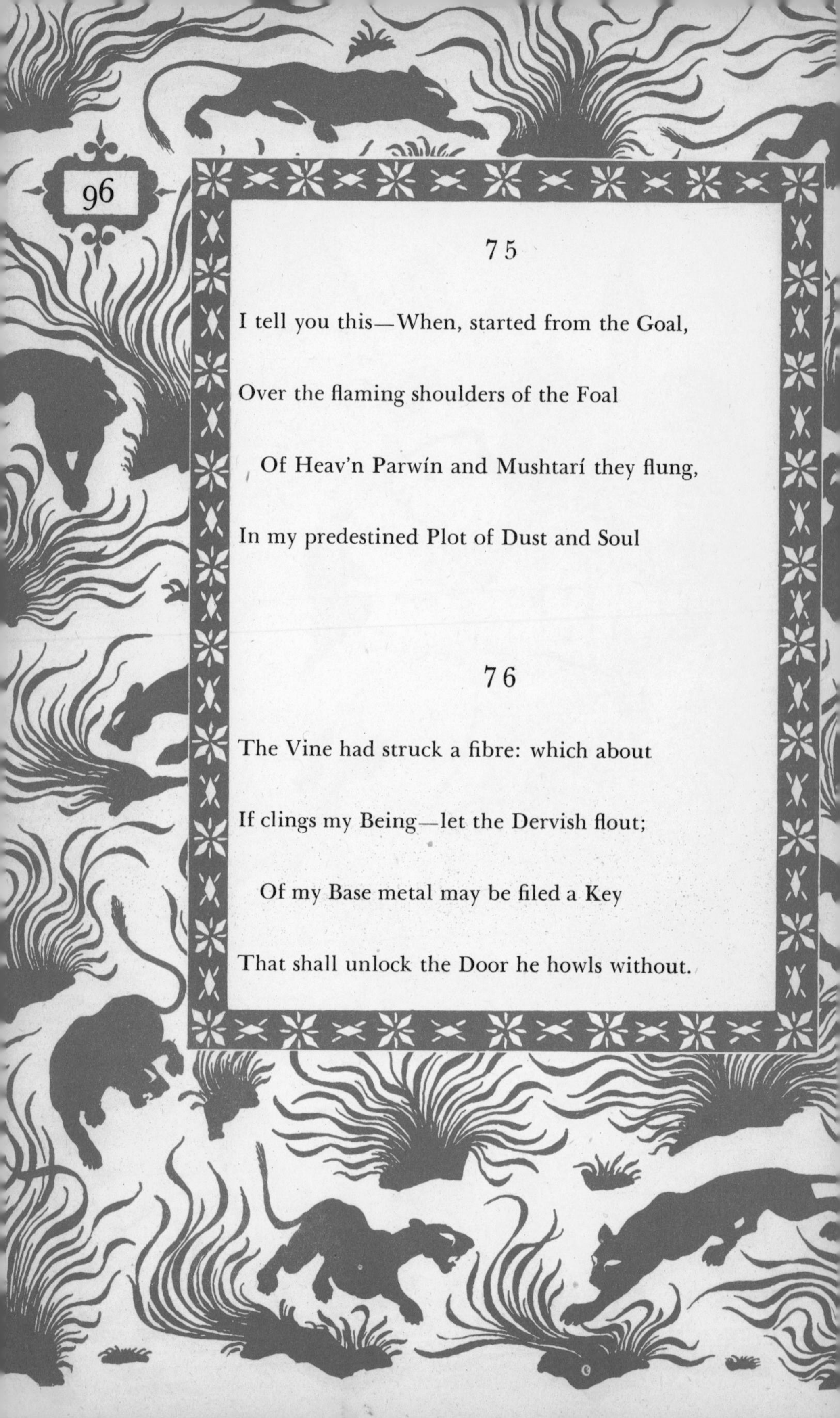

75

I tell you this—When, started from the Goal,
Over the flaming shoulders of the Foal
Of Heav'n Parwín and Mushtarí they flung,
In my predestined Plot of Dust and Soul

76

The Vine had struck a fibre: which about
If clings my Being—let the Dervish flout;
Of my Base metal may be filed a Key
That shall unlock the Door he howls without.

M. Sayah

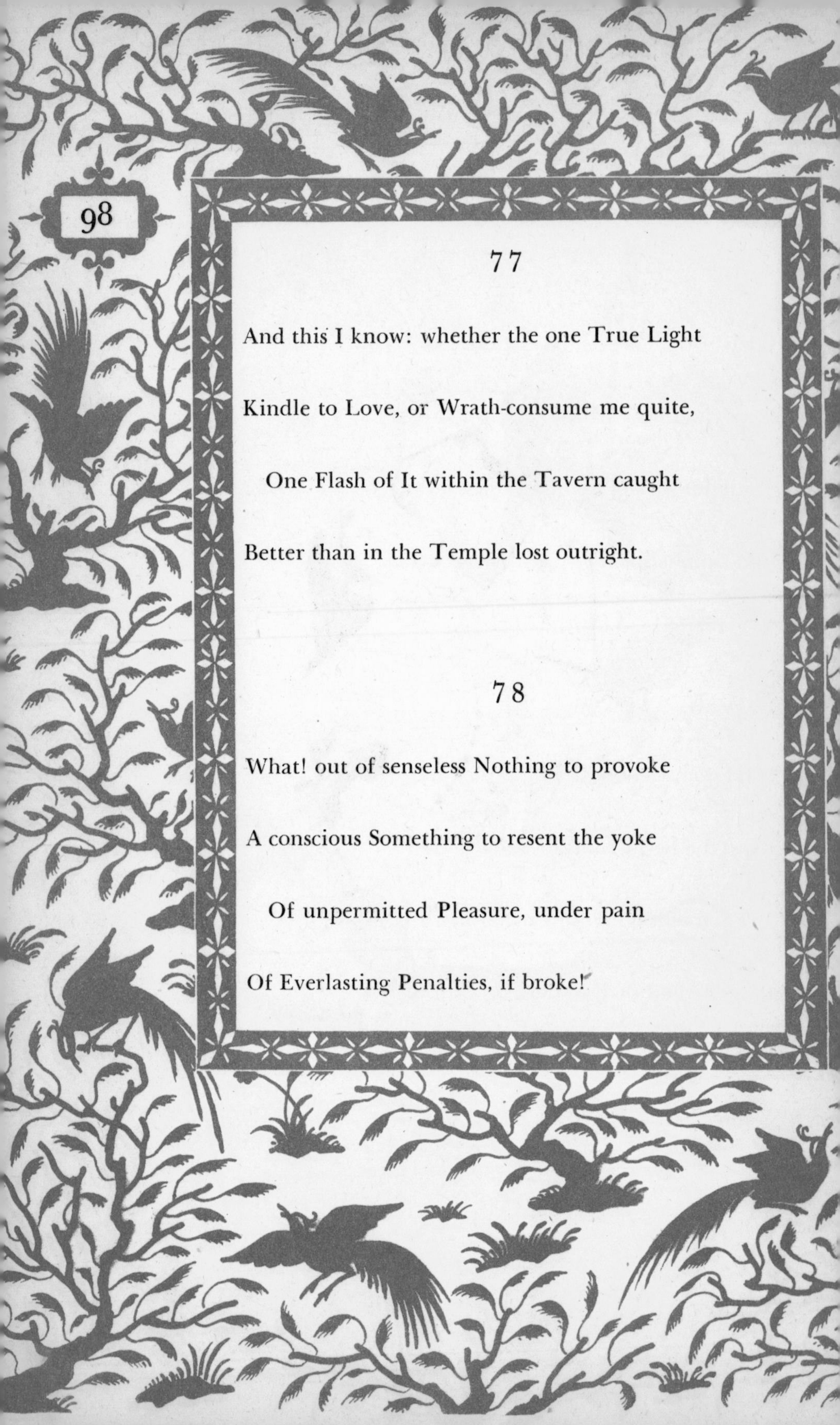

77

And this I know: whether the one True Light
Kindle to Love, or Wrath-consume me quite,
One Flash of It within the Tavern caught
Better than in the Temple lost outright.

78

What! out of senseless Nothing to provoke
A conscious Something to resent the yoke
Of unpermitted Pleasure, under pain
Of Everlasting Penalties, if broke!

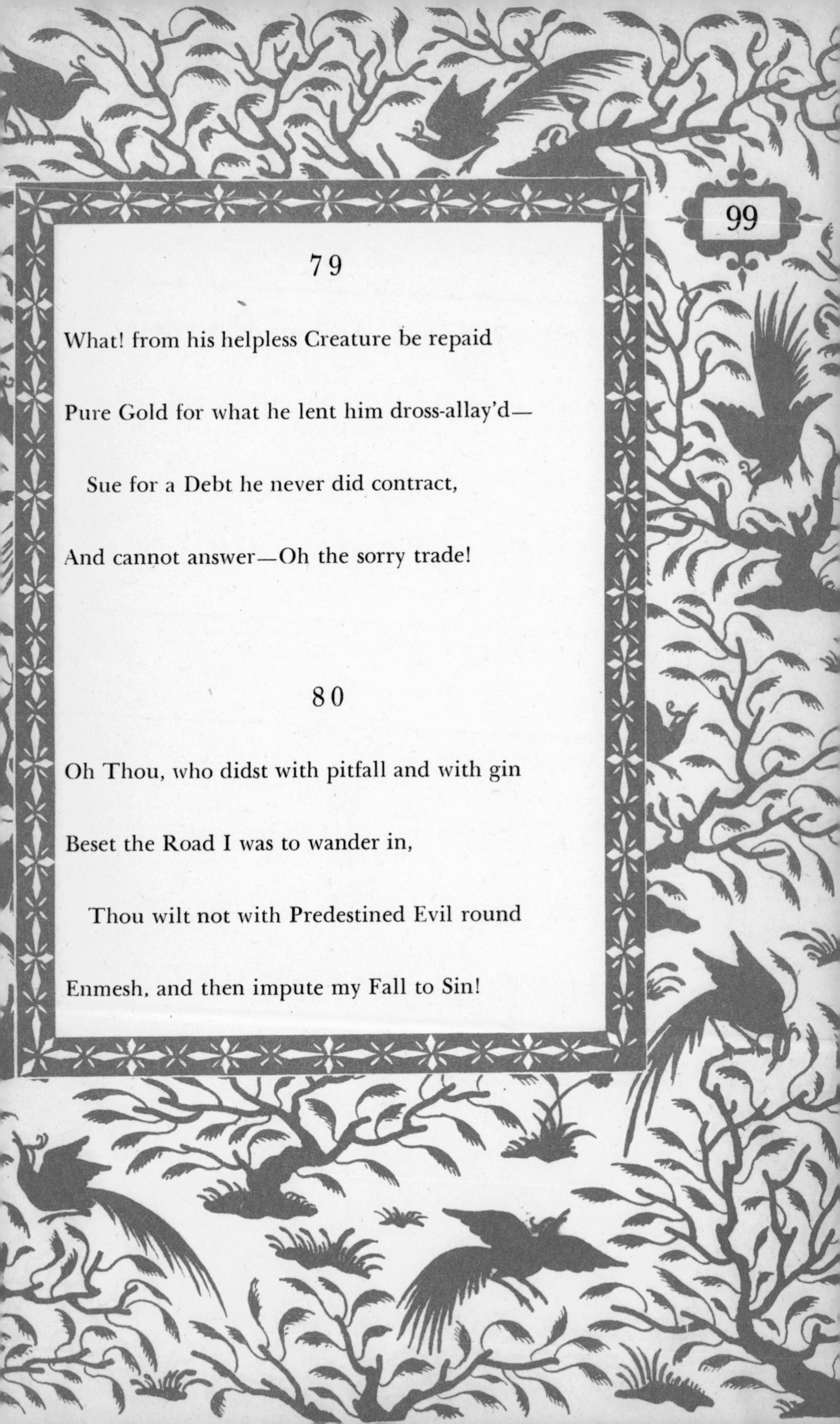

79

What! from his helpless Creature be repaid
Pure Gold for what he lent him dross-allay'd—
Sue for a Debt he never did contract,
And cannot answer—Oh the sorry trade!

80

Oh Thou, who didst with pitfall and with gin
Beset the Road I was to wander in,
Thou wilt not with Predestined Evil round
Enmesh, and then impute my Fall to Sin!

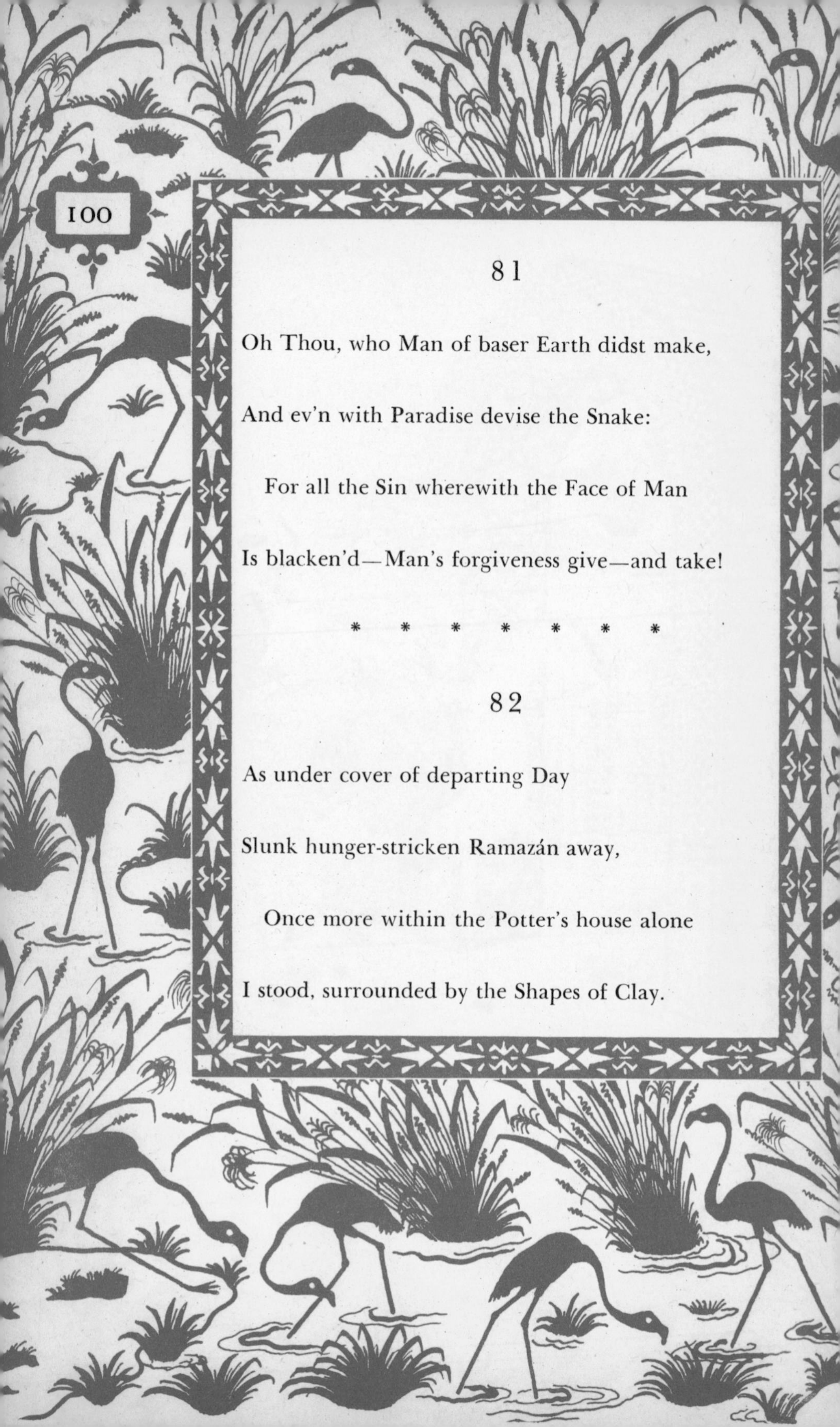

81

Oh Thou, who Man of baser Earth didst make,

And ev'n with Paradise devise the Snake:

For all the Sin wherewith the Face of Man

Is blacken'd—Man's forgiveness give—and take!

* * * * * * *

82

As under cover of departing Day

Slunk hunger-stricken Ramazán away,

Once more within the Potter's house alone

I stood, surrounded by the Shapes of Clay.

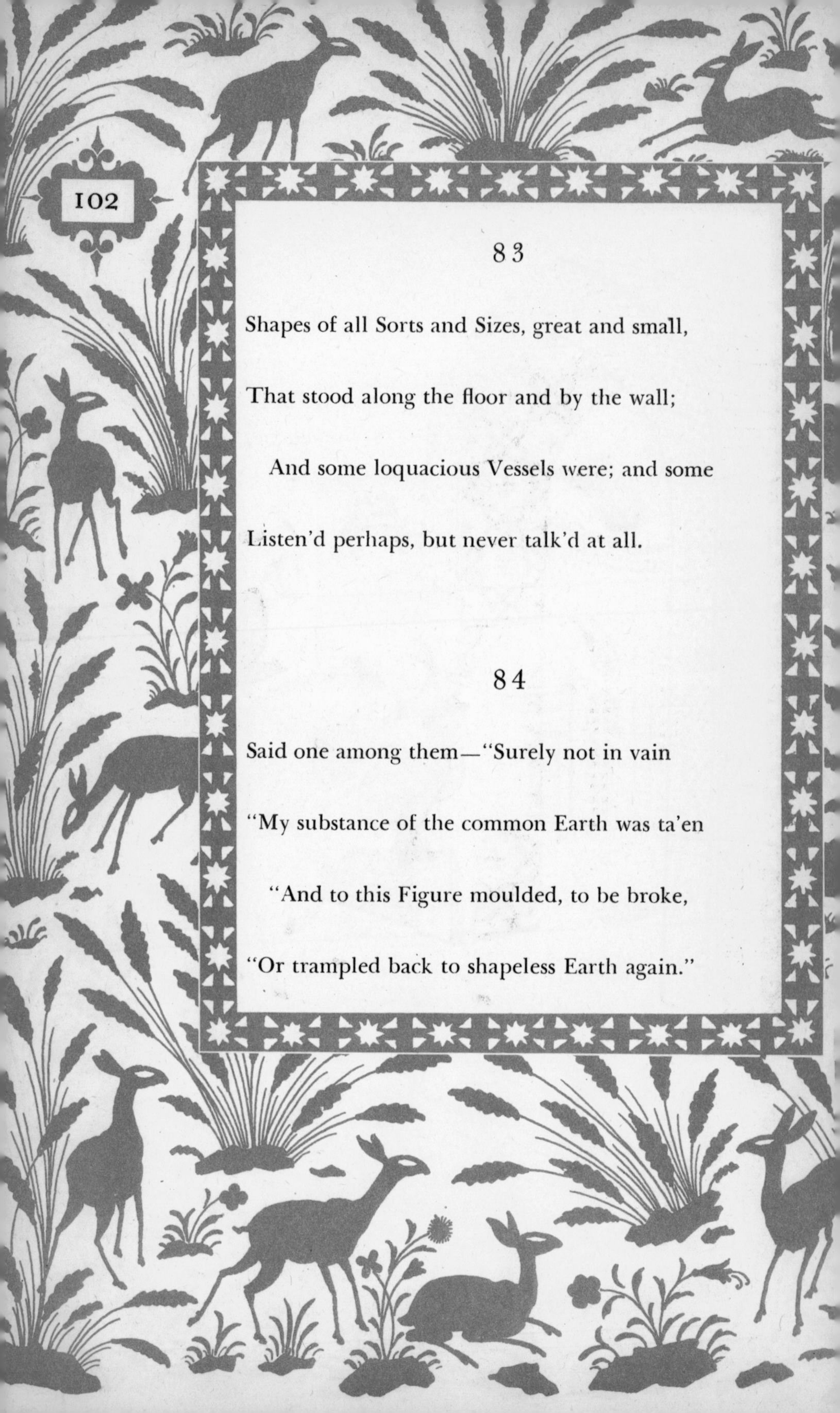

83

Shapes of all Sorts and Sizes, great and small,
That stood along the floor and by the wall;
    And some loquacious Vessels were; and some
Listen'd perhaps, but never talk'd at all.

84

Said one among them—"Surely not in vain
"My substance of the common Earth was ta'en
    "And to this Figure moulded, to be broke,
"Or trampled back to shapeless Earth again."

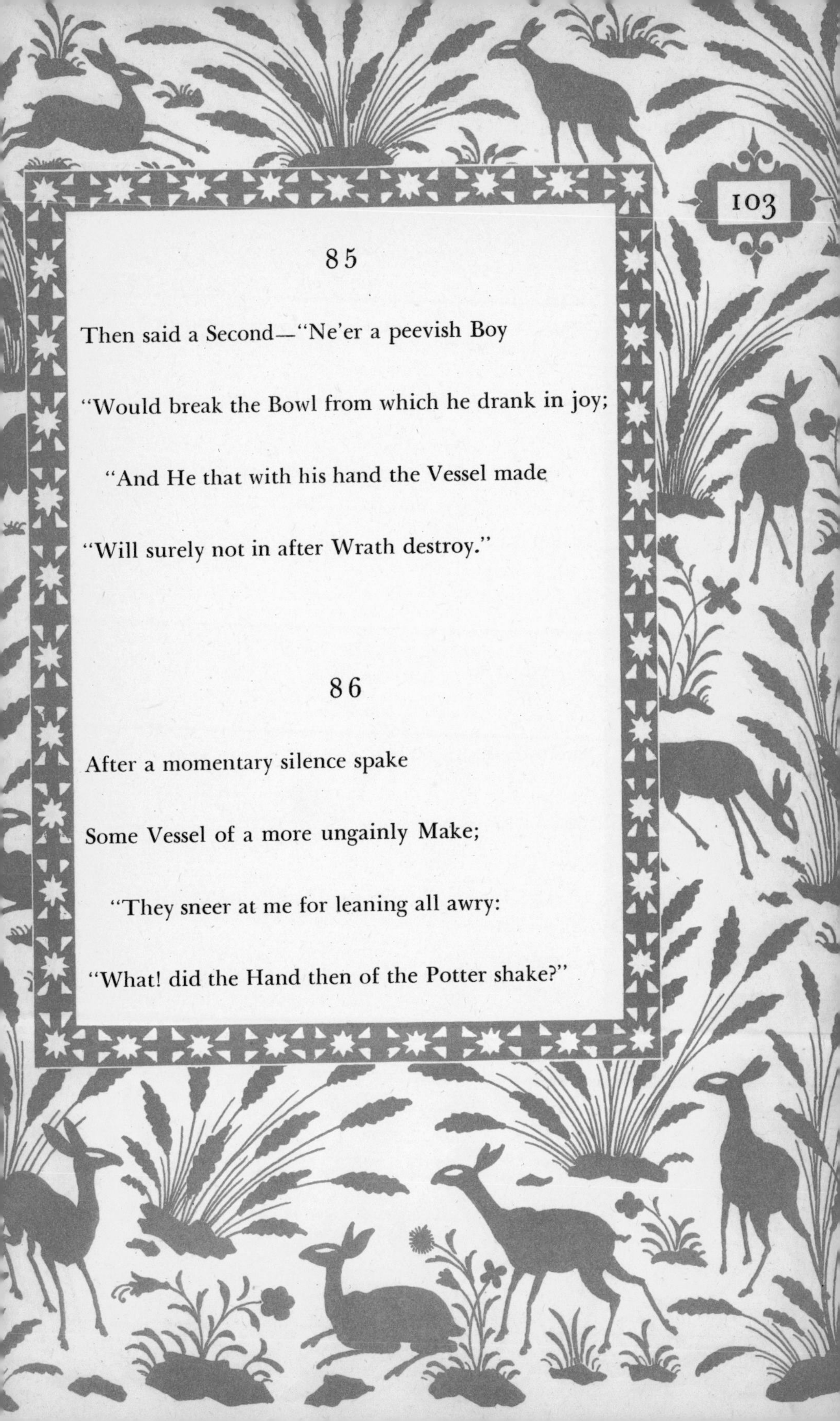

85

Then said a Second—"Ne'er a peevish Boy
"Would break the Bowl from which he drank in joy;
"And He that with his hand the Vessel made
"Will surely not in after Wrath destroy."

86

After a momentary silence spake
Some Vessel of a more ungainly Make;
"They sneer at me for leaning all awry:
"What! did the Hand then of the Potter shake?"

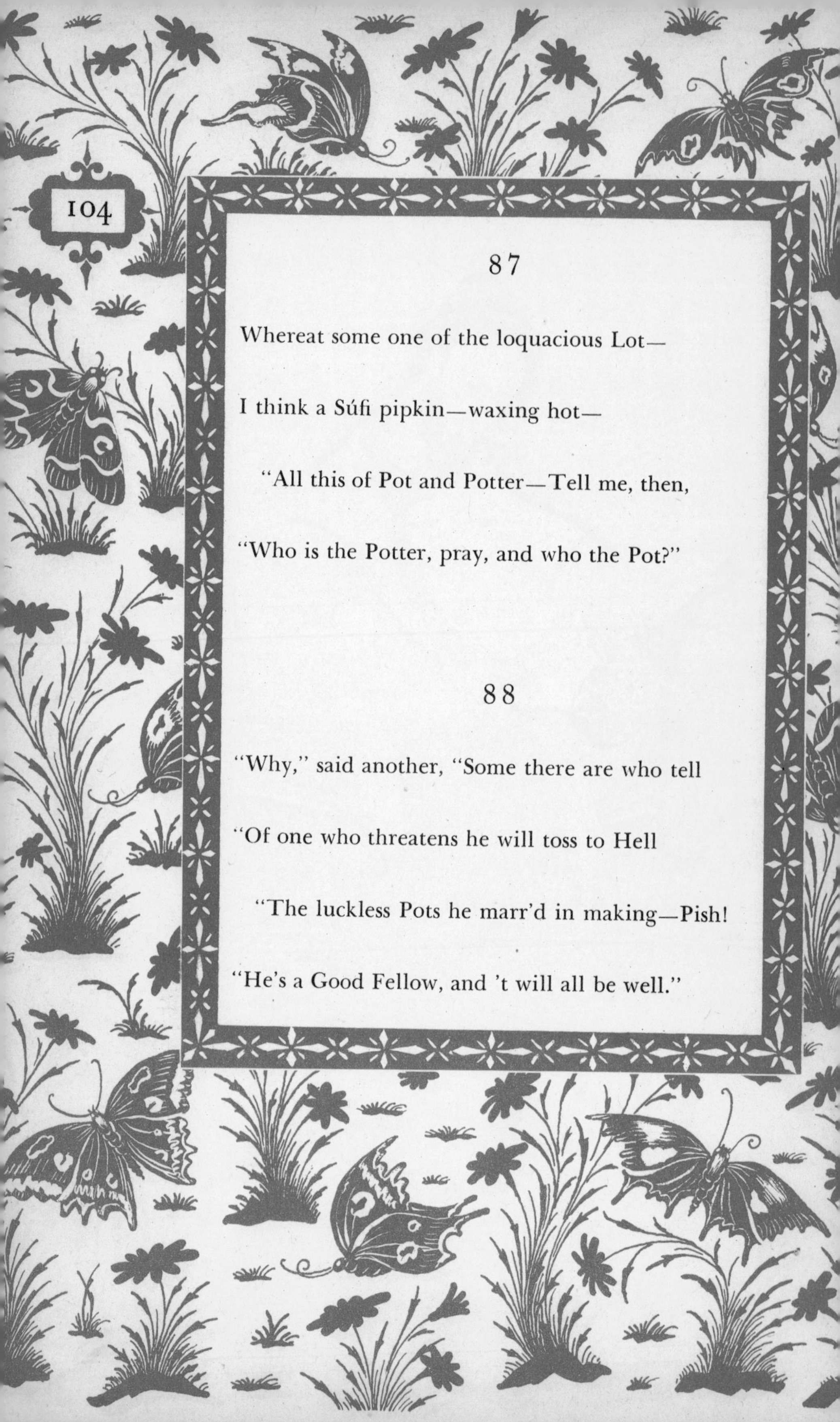

87

Whereat some one of the loquacious Lot—
I think a Súfi pipkin—waxing hot—
"All this of Pot and Potter—Tell me, then,
"Who is the Potter, pray, and who the Pot?"

88

"Why," said another, "Some there are who tell
"Of one who threatens he will toss to Hell
"The luckless Pots he marr'd in making—Pish!
"He's a Good Fellow, and 't will all be well."

M. Sayab

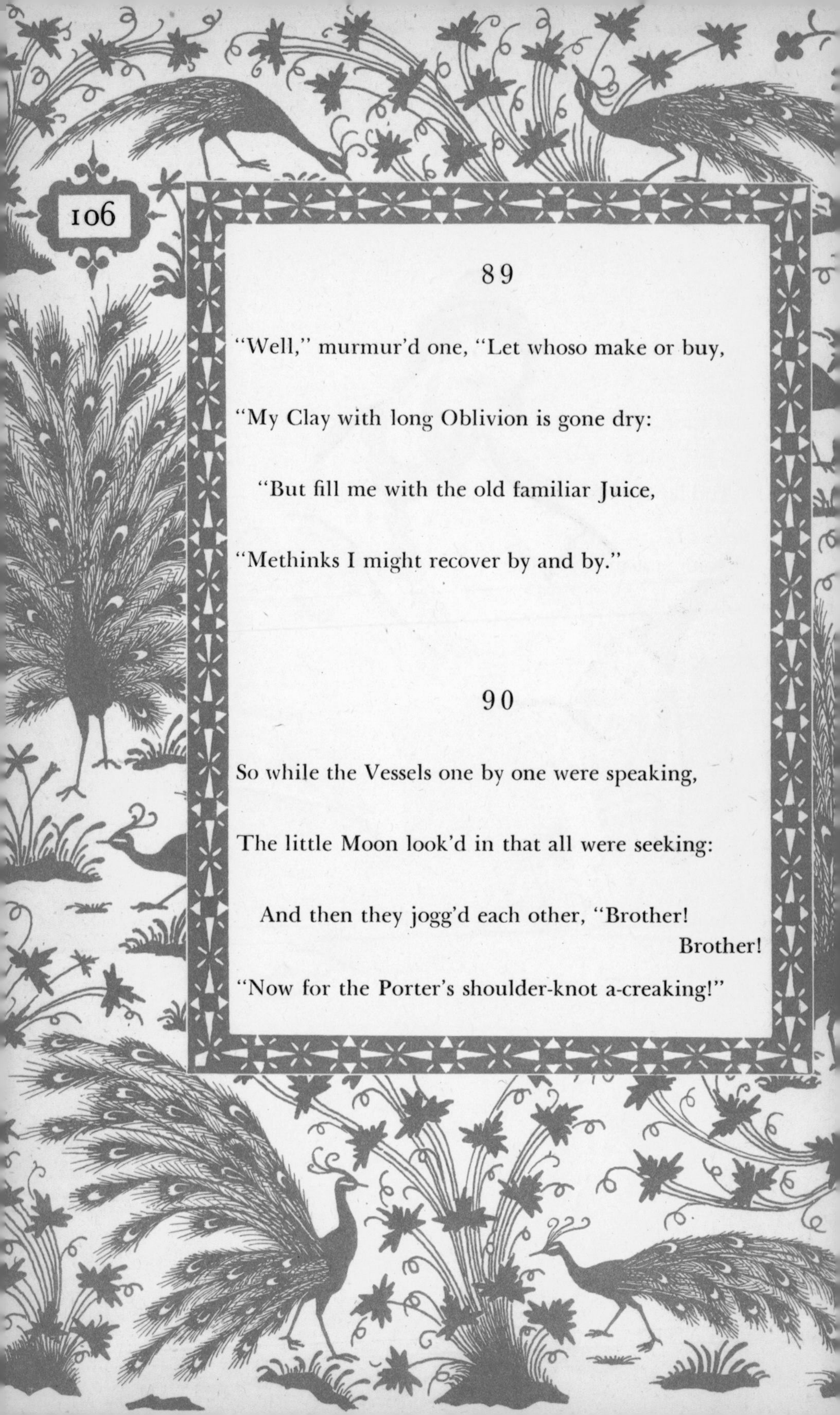

89

"Well," murmur'd one, "Let whoso make or buy,
"My Clay with long Oblivion is gone dry:
"But fill me with the old familiar Juice,
"Methinks I might recover by and by."

90

So while the Vessels one by one were speaking,
The little Moon look'd in that all were seeking:
And then they jogg'd each other, "Brother! Brother!
"Now for the Porter's shoulder-knot a-creaking!"

91

Ah, with the Grape my fading life provide,
And wash the Body whence the Life has died,
And lay me, shrouded in the living Leaf,
By some not unfrequented Garden-side.

92

That ev'n my buried Ashes such a snare
Of Vintage shall fling up into the Air
As not a True-believer passing by
But shall be overtaken unaware.

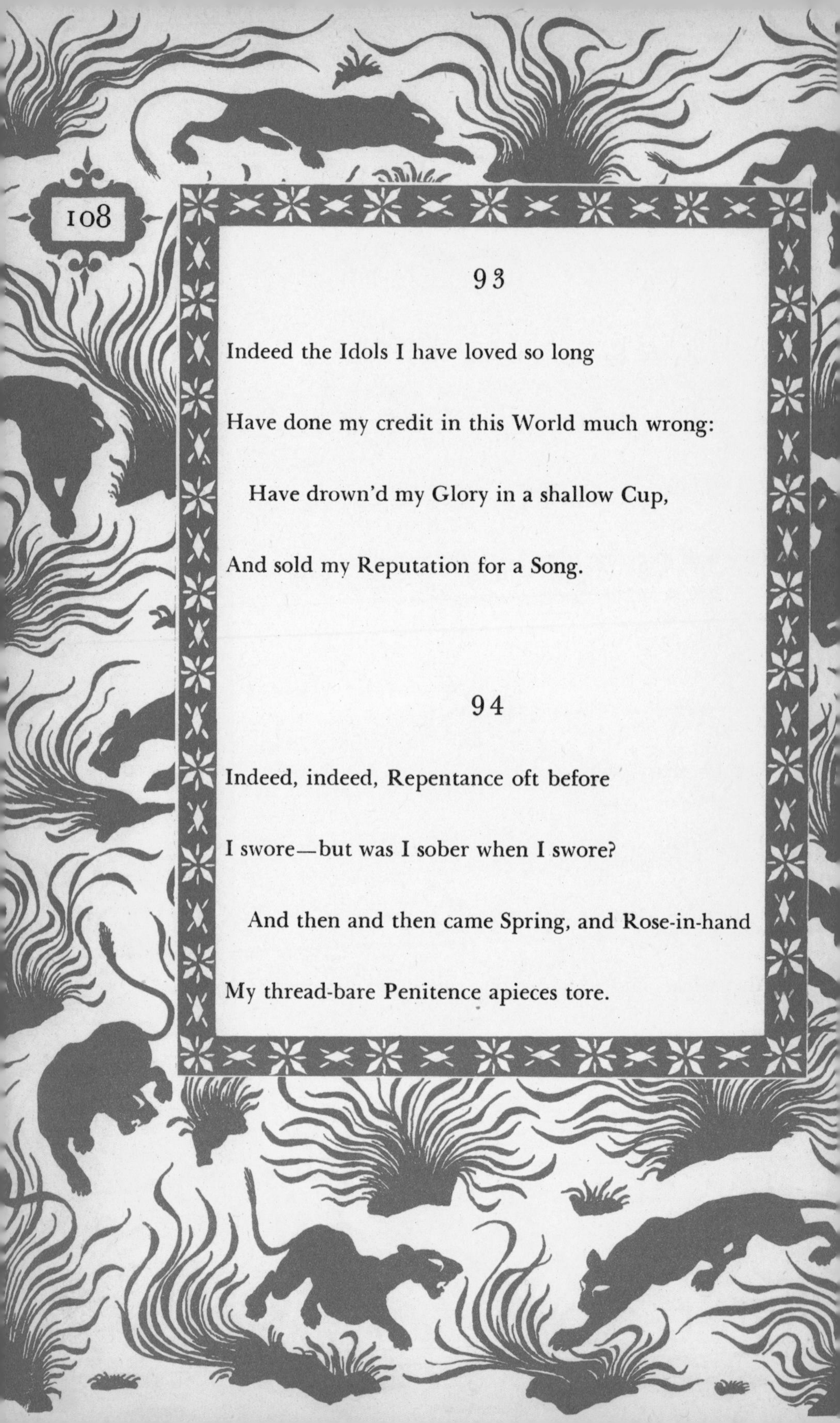

93

Indeed the Idols I have loved so long
Have done my credit in this World much wrong:
Have drown'd my Glory in a shallow Cup,
And sold my Reputation for a Song.

94

Indeed, indeed, Repentance oft before
I swore—but was I sober when I swore?
And then and then came Spring, and Rose-in-hand
My thread-bare Penitence apieces tore.

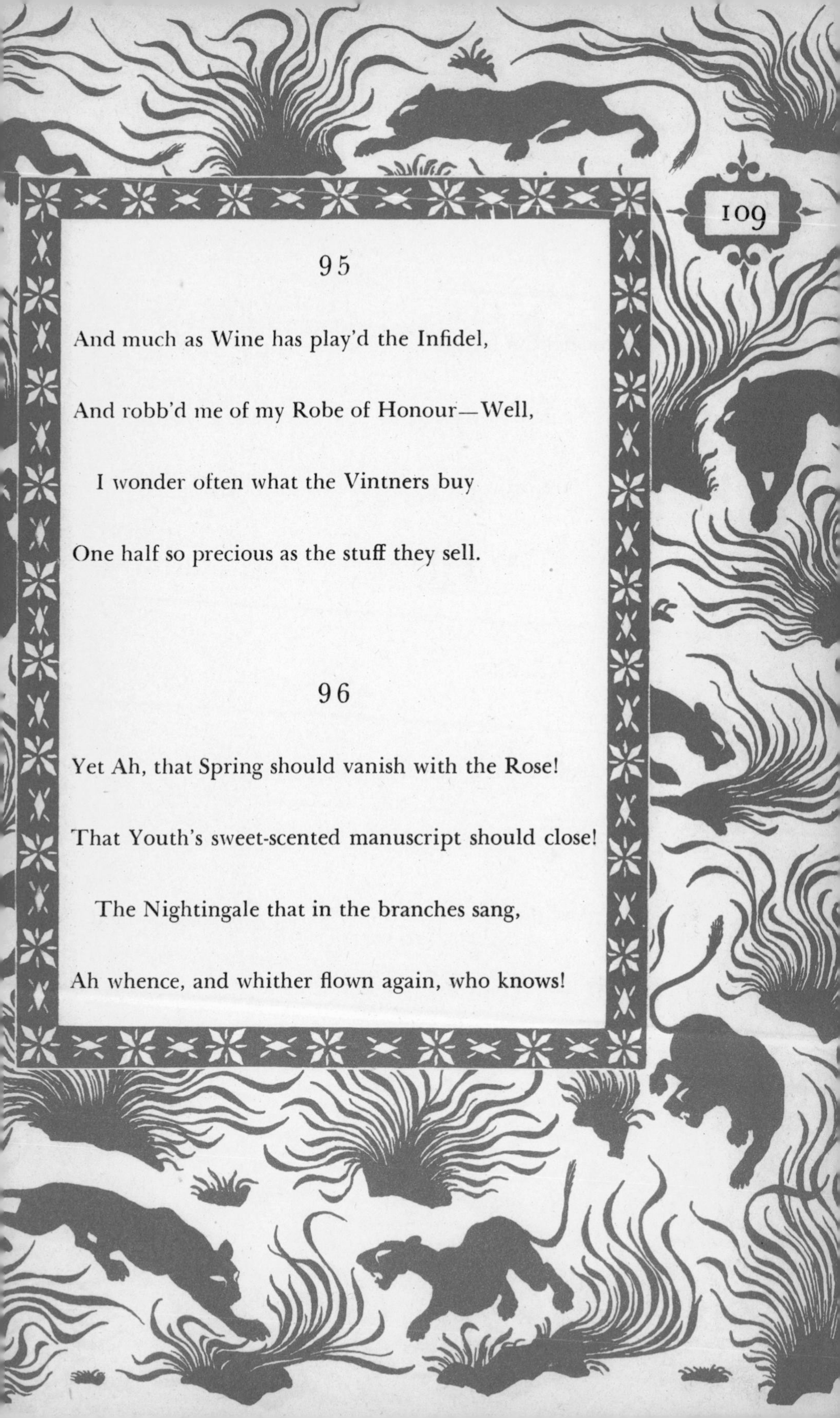

95

And much as Wine has play'd the Infidel,
And robb'd me of my Robe of Honour—Well,
   I wonder often what the Vintners buy
One half so precious as the stuff they sell.

96

Yet Ah, that Spring should vanish with the Rose!
That Youth's sweet-scented manuscript should close!
   The Nightingale that in the branches sang,
Ah whence, and whither flown again, who knows!

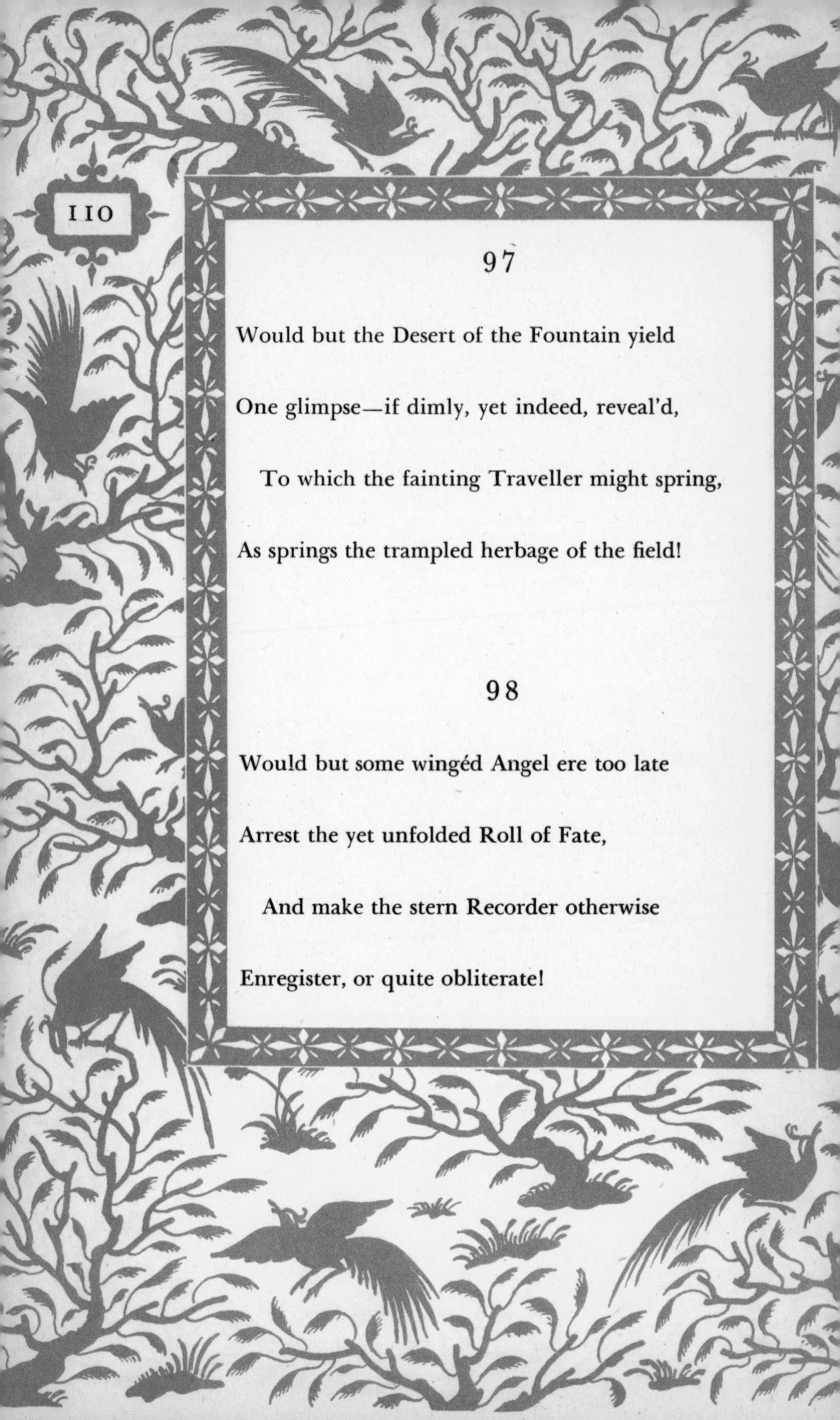

97

Would but the Desert of the Fountain yield
One glimpse—if dimly, yet indeed, reveal'd,
To which the fainting Traveller might spring,
As springs the trampled herbage of the field!

98

Would but some wingéd Angel ere too late
Arrest the yet unfolded Roll of Fate,
And make the stern Recorder otherwise
Enregister, or quite obliterate!

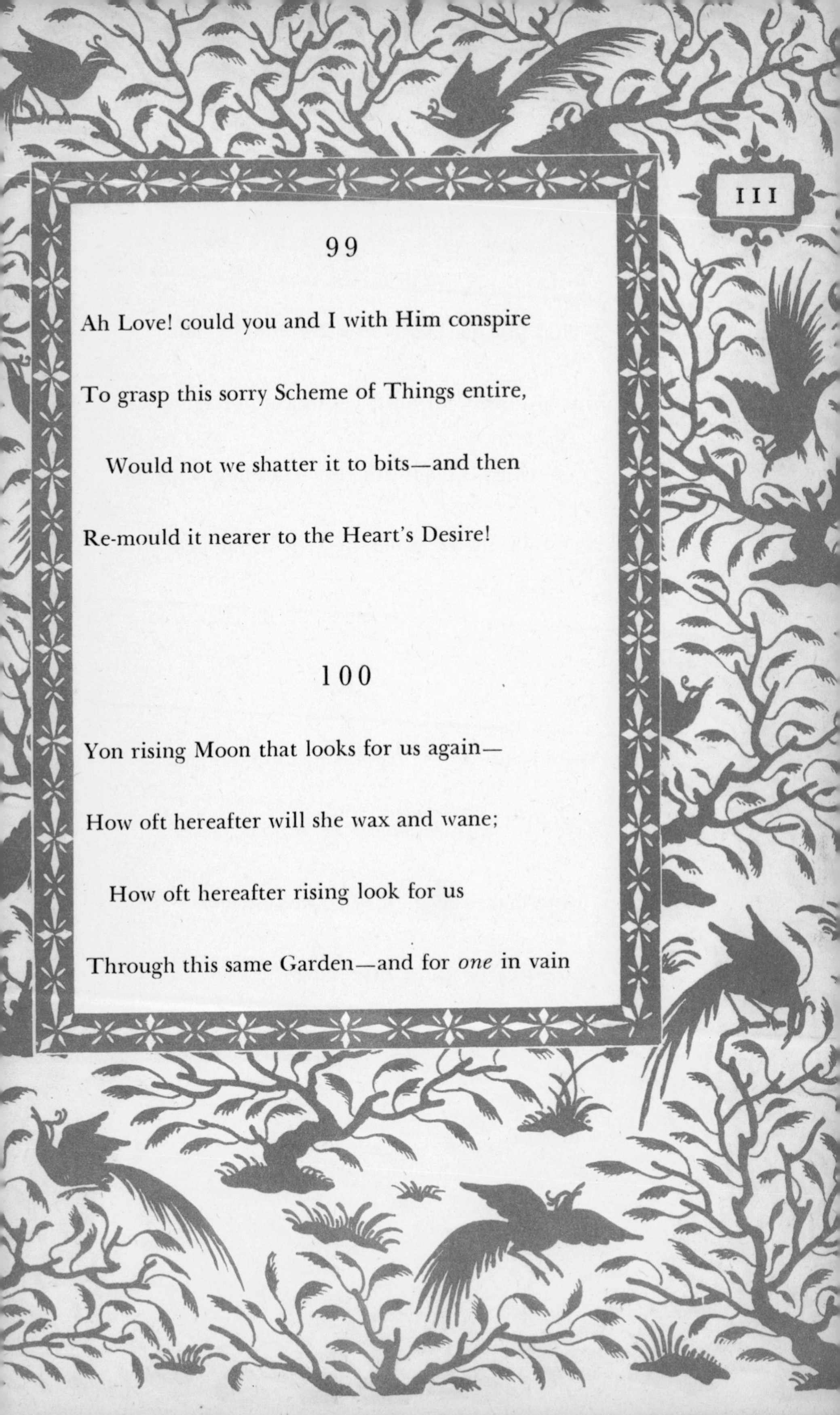

99

Ah Love! could you and I with Him conspire
To grasp this sorry Scheme of Things entire,
  Would not we shatter it to bits—and then
Re-mould it nearer to the Heart's Desire!

100

Yon rising Moon that looks for us again—
How oft hereafter will she wax and wane;
  How oft hereafter rising look for us
Through this same Garden—and for *one* in vain

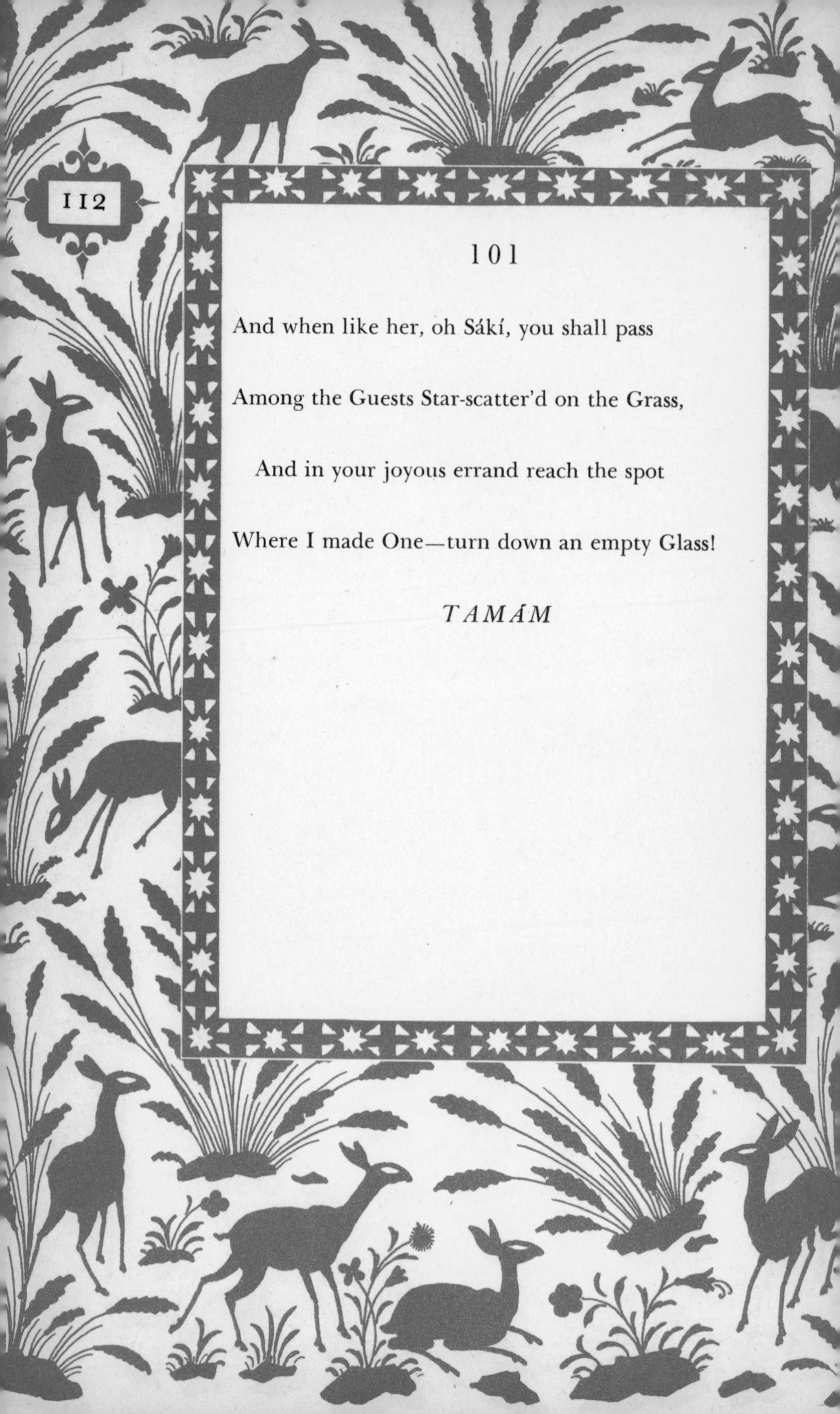

101

And when like her, oh Sákí, you shall pass
Among the Guests Star-scatter'd on the Grass,
And in your joyous errand reach the spot
Where I made One—turn down an empty Glass!

TAMÁM

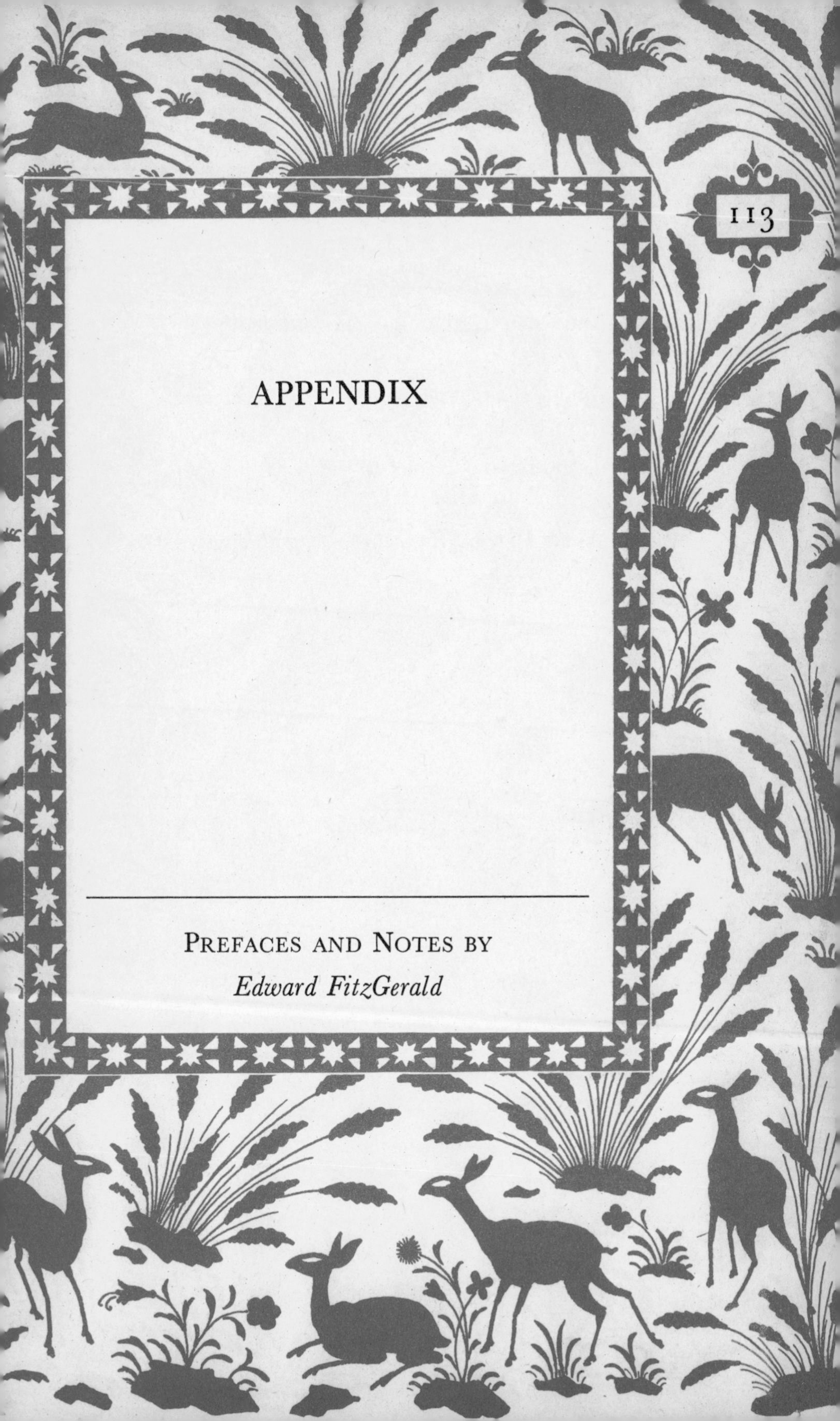

APPENDIX

PREFACES AND NOTES BY

Edward FitzGerald

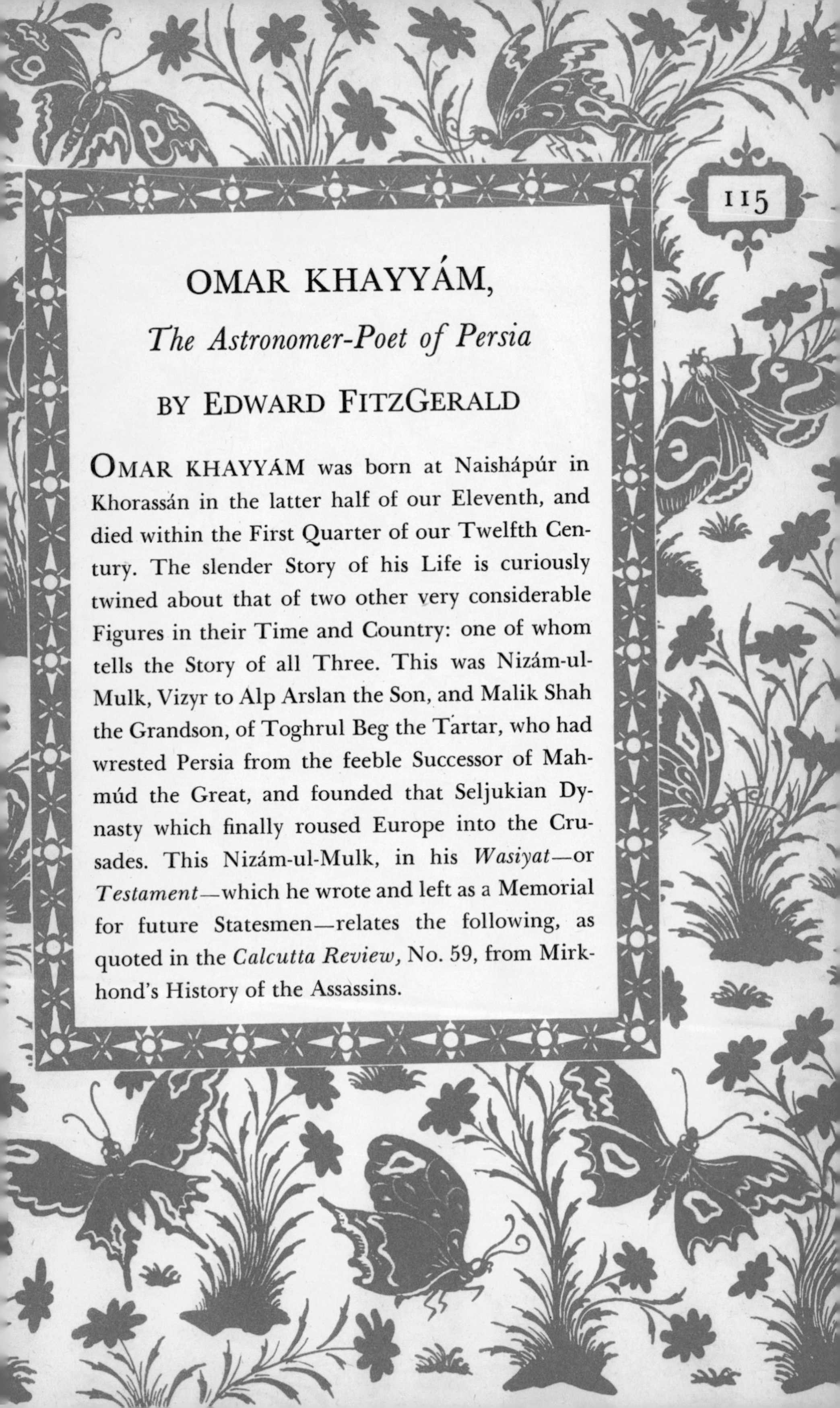

OMAR KHAYYÁM,

The Astronomer-Poet of Persia

BY EDWARD FITZGERALD

OMAR KHAYYÁM was born at Naishápúr in Khorassán in the latter half of our Eleventh, and died within the First Quarter of our Twelfth Century. The slender Story of his Life is curiously twined about that of two other very considerable Figures in their Time and Country: one of whom tells the Story of all Three. This was Nizám-ul-Mulk, Vizyr to Alp Arslan the Son, and Malik Shah the Grandson, of Toghrul Beg the Tartar, who had wrested Persia from the feeble Successor of Mahmúd the Great, and founded that Seljukian Dynasty which finally roused Europe into the Crusades. This Nizám-ul-Mulk, in his *Wasiyat*—or *Testament*—which he wrote and left as a Memorial for future Statesmen—relates the following, as quoted in the *Calcutta Review,* No. 59, from Mirkhond's History of the Assassins.

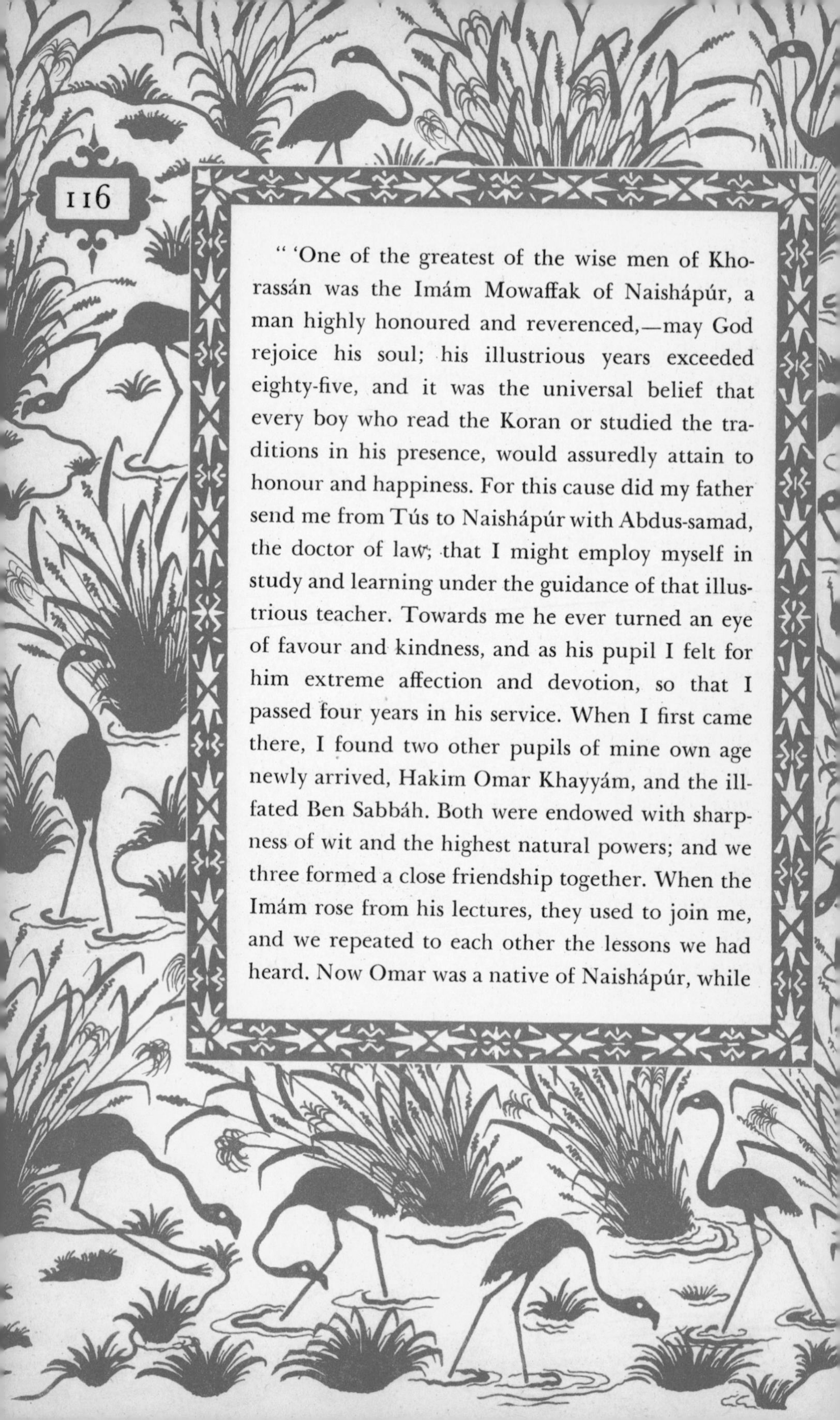

" 'One of the greatest of the wise men of Khorassán was the Imám Mowaffak of Naishápúr, a man highly honoured and reverenced,—may God rejoice his soul; his illustrious years exceeded eighty-five, and it was the universal belief that every boy who read the Koran or studied the traditions in his presence, would assuredly attain to honour and happiness. For this cause did my father send me from Tús to Naishápúr with Abdus-samad, the doctor of law, that I might employ myself in study and learning under the guidance of that illustrious teacher. Towards me he ever turned an eye of favour and kindness, and as his pupil I felt for him extreme affection and devotion, so that I passed four years in his service. When I first came there, I found two other pupils of mine own age newly arrived, Hakim Omar Khayyám, and the ill-fated Ben Sabbáh. Both were endowed with sharpness of wit and the highest natural powers; and we three formed a close friendship together. When the Imám rose from his lectures, they used to join me, and we repeated to each other the lessons we had heard. Now Omar was a native of Naishápúr, while

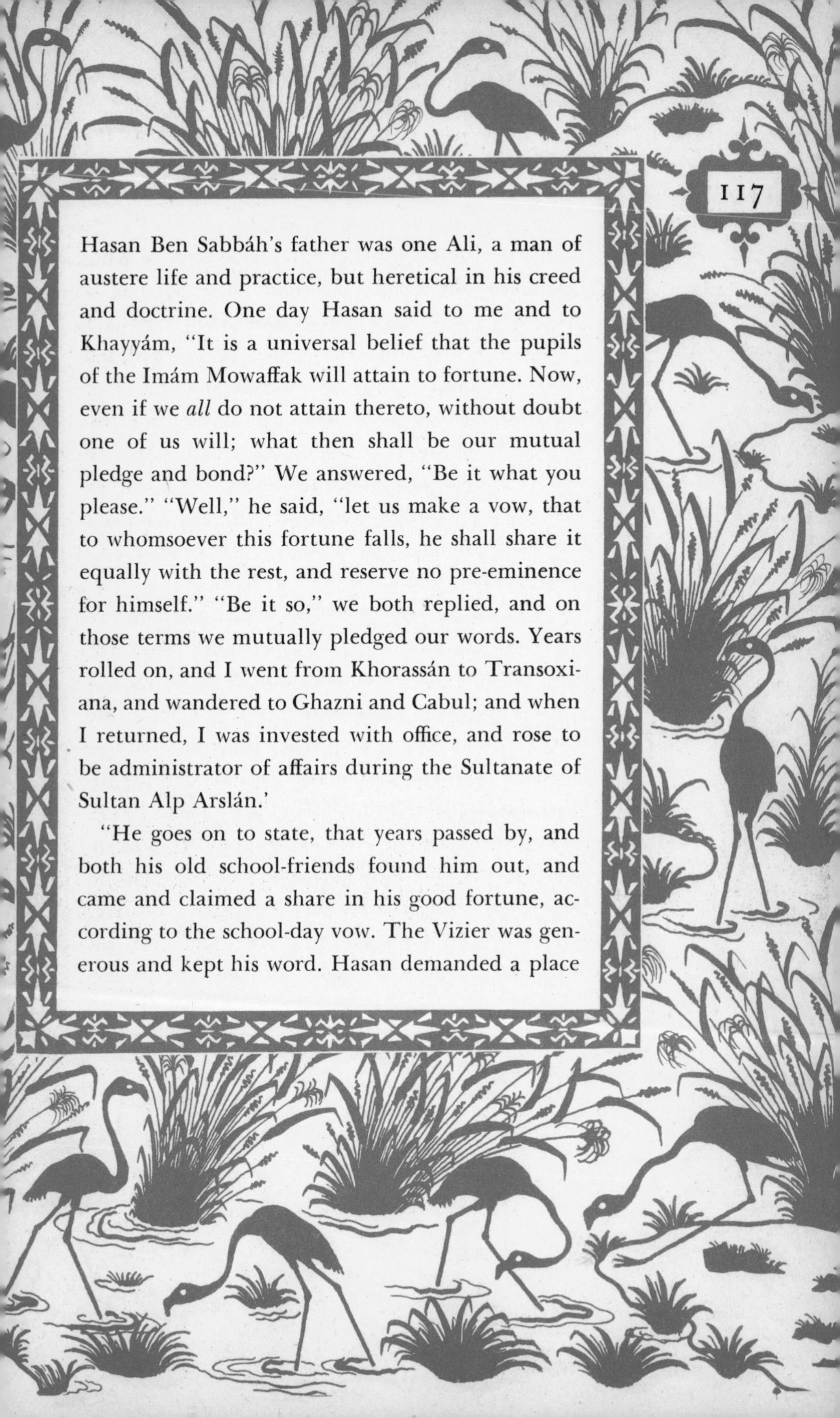

Hasan Ben Sabbáh's father was one Ali, a man of austere life and practice, but heretical in his creed and doctrine. One day Hasan said to me and to Khayyám, "It is a universal belief that the pupils of the Imám Mowaffak will attain to fortune. Now, even if we *all* do not attain thereto, without doubt one of us will; what then shall be our mutual pledge and bond?" We answered, "Be it what you please." "Well," he said, "let us make a vow, that to whomsoever this fortune falls, he shall share it equally with the rest, and reserve no pre-eminence for himself." "Be it so," we both replied, and on those terms we mutually pledged our words. Years rolled on, and I went from Khorassán to Transoxiana, and wandered to Ghazni and Cabul; and when I returned, I was invested with office, and rose to be administrator of affairs during the Sultanate of Sultan Alp Arslán.'

"He goes on to state, that years passed by, and both his old school-friends found him out, and came and claimed a share in his good fortune, according to the school-day vow. The Vizier was generous and kept his word. Hasan demanded a place

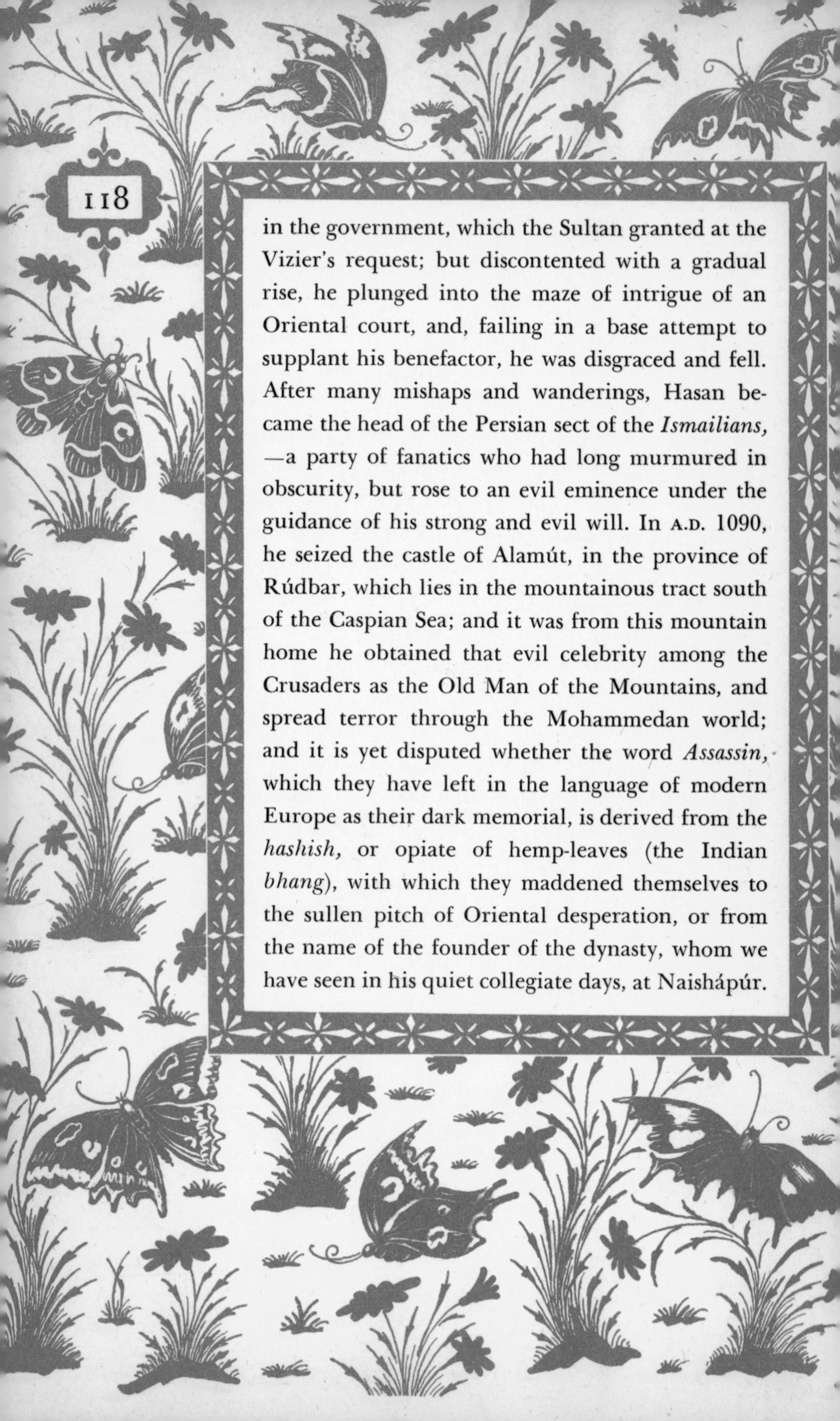

in the government, which the Sultan granted at the Vizier's request; but discontented with a gradual rise, he plunged into the maze of intrigue of an Oriental court, and, failing in a base attempt to supplant his benefactor, he was disgraced and fell. After many mishaps and wanderings, Hasan became the head of the Persian sect of the *Ismailians,* —a party of fanatics who had long murmured in obscurity, but rose to an evil eminence under the guidance of his strong and evil will. In A.D. 1090, he seized the castle of Alamút, in the province of Rúdbar, which lies in the mountainous tract south of the Caspian Sea; and it was from this mountain home he obtained that evil celebrity among the Crusaders as the Old Man of the Mountains, and spread terror through the Mohammedan world; and it is yet disputed whether the word *Assassin,* which they have left in the language of modern Europe as their dark memorial, is derived from the *hashish,* or opiate of hemp-leaves (the Indian *bhang*), with which they maddened themselves to the sullen pitch of Oriental desperation, or from the name of the founder of the dynasty, whom we have seen in his quiet collegiate days, at Naishápúr.

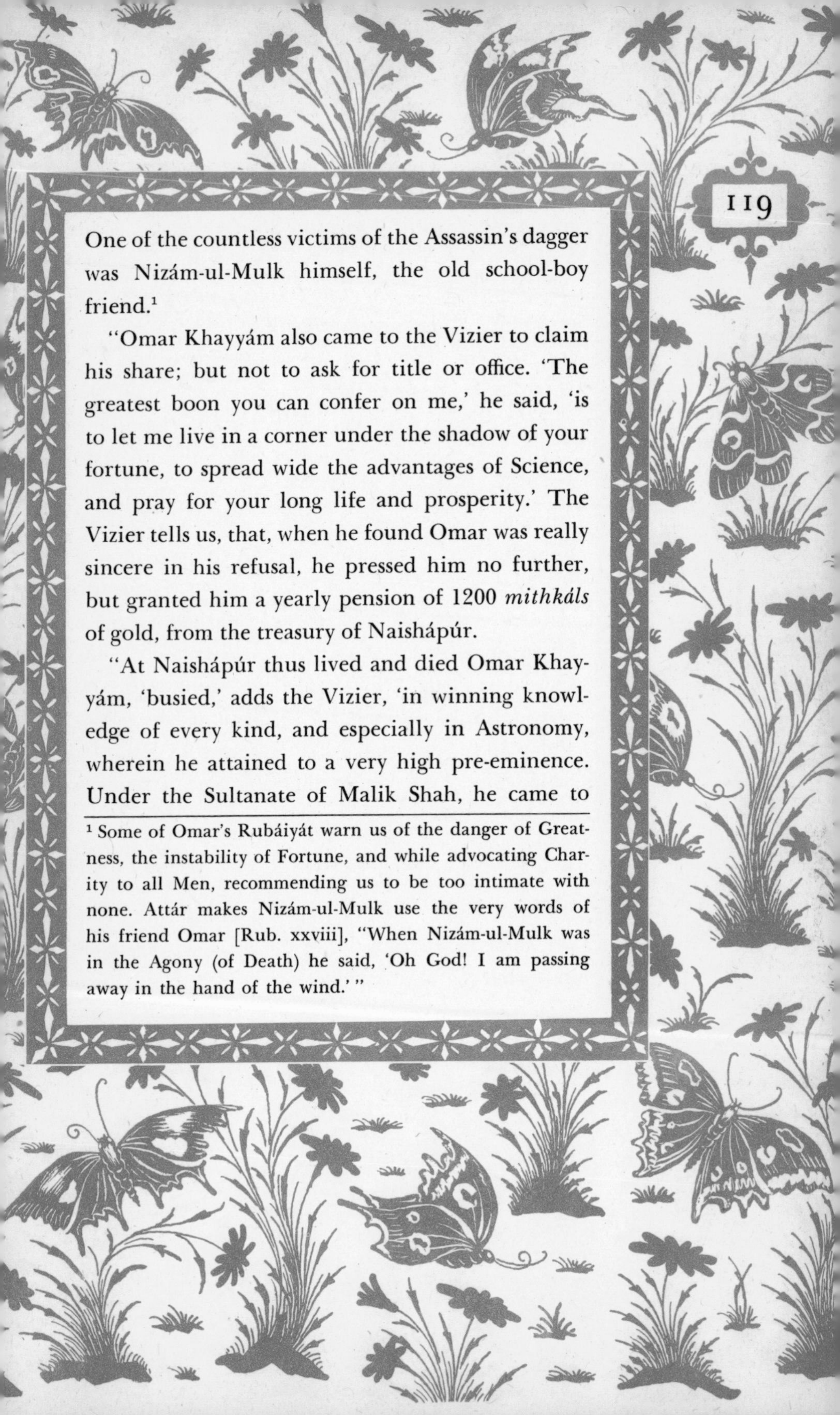

One of the countless victims of the Assassin's dagger was Nizám-ul-Mulk himself, the old school-boy friend.[1]

"Omar Khayyám also came to the Vizier to claim his share; but not to ask for title or office. 'The greatest boon you can confer on me,' he said, 'is to let me live in a corner under the shadow of your fortune, to spread wide the advantages of Science, and pray for your long life and prosperity.' The Vizier tells us, that, when he found Omar was really sincere in his refusal, he pressed him no further, but granted him a yearly pension of 1200 *mithkáls* of gold, from the treasury of Naishápúr.

"At Naishápúr thus lived and died Omar Khayyám, 'busied,' adds the Vizier, 'in winning knowledge of every kind, and especially in Astronomy, wherein he attained to a very high pre-eminence. Under the Sultanate of Malik Shah, he came to

[1] Some of Omar's Rubáiyát warn us of the danger of Greatness, the instability of Fortune, and while advocating Charity to all Men, recommending us to be too intimate with none. Attár makes Nizám-ul-Mulk use the very words of his friend Omar [Rub. xxviii], "When Nizám-ul-Mulk was in the Agony (of Death) he said, 'Oh God! I am passing away in the hand of the wind.' "

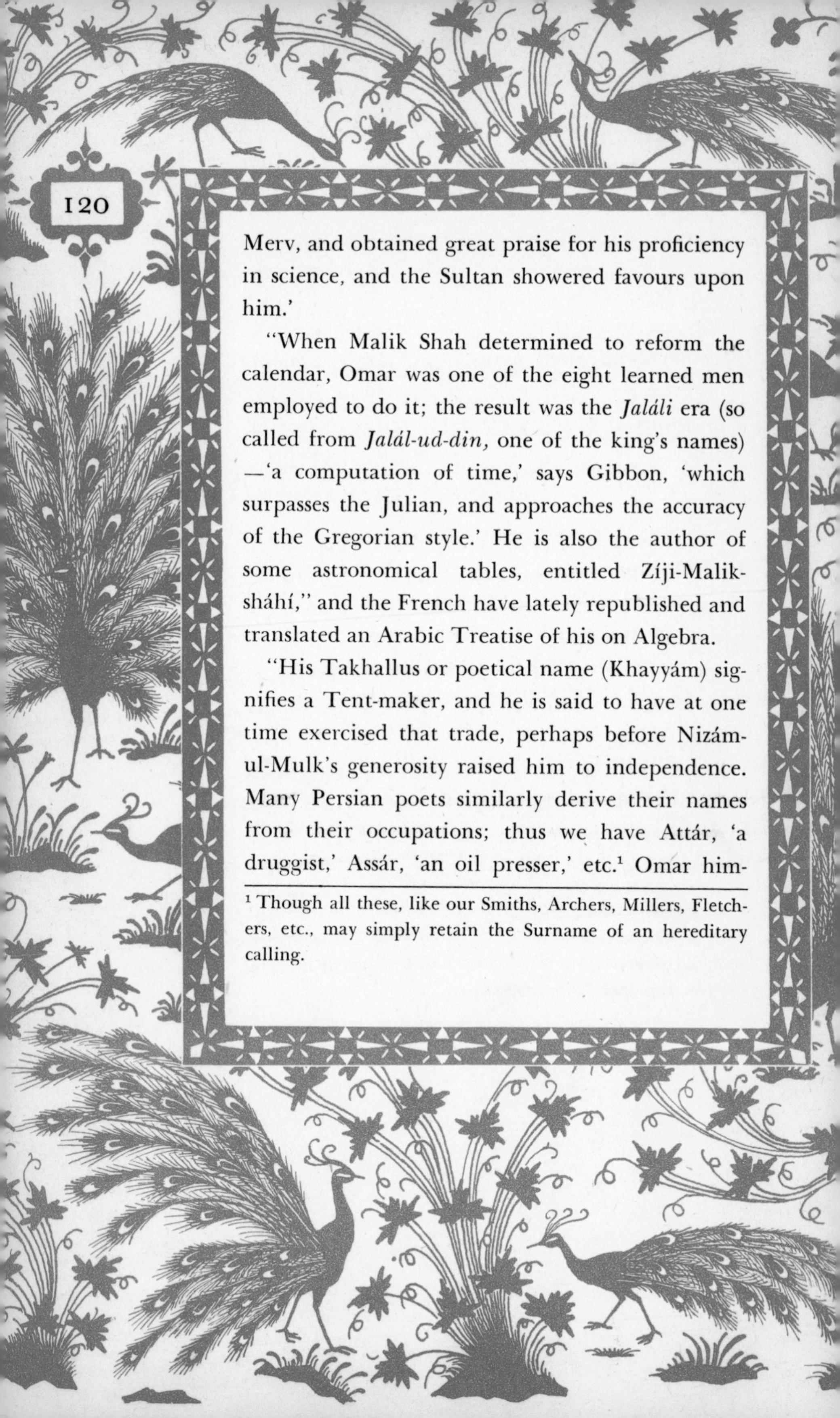

Merv, and obtained great praise for his proficiency in science, and the Sultan showered favours upon him.'

"When Malik Shah determined to reform the calendar, Omar was one of the eight learned men employed to do it; the result was the *Jaláli* era (so called from *Jalál-ud-din,* one of the king's names) —'a computation of time,' says Gibbon, 'which surpasses the Julian, and approaches the accuracy of the Gregorian style.' He is also the author of some astronomical tables, entitled Zíji-Malik-sháhí," and the French have lately republished and translated an Arabic Treatise of his on Algebra.

"His Takhallus or poetical name (Khayyám) signifies a Tent-maker, and he is said to have at one time exercised that trade, perhaps before Nizám-ul-Mulk's generosity raised him to independence. Many Persian poets similarly derive their names from their occupations; thus we have Attár, 'a druggist,' Assár, 'an oil presser,' etc.[1] Omar him-

[1] Though all these, like our Smiths, Archers, Millers, Fletchers, etc., may simply retain the Surname of an hereditary calling.

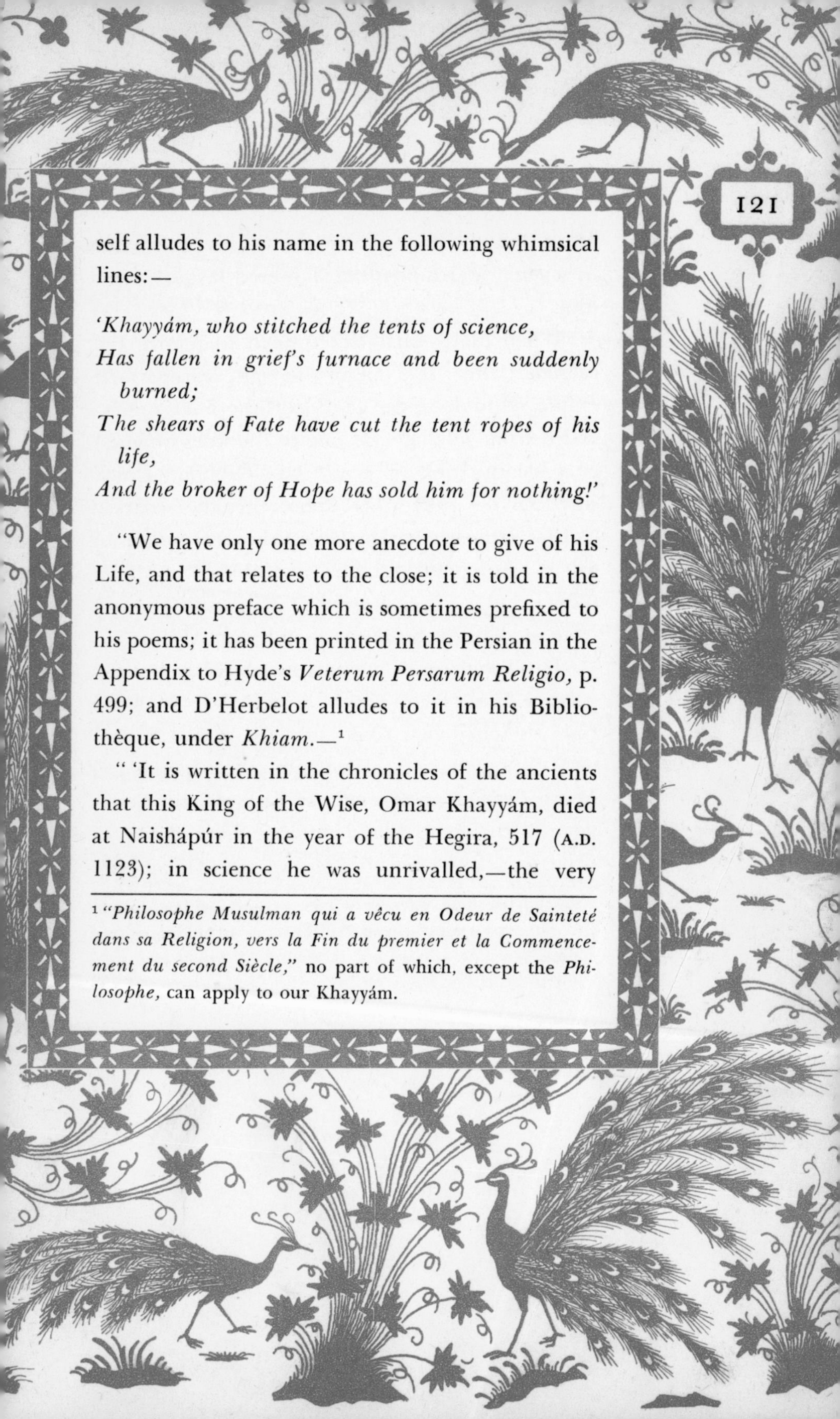

self alludes to his name in the following whimsical lines:—

'Khayyám, who stitched the tents of science,
Has fallen in grief's furnace and been suddenly burned;
The shears of Fate have cut the tent ropes of his life,
And the broker of Hope has sold him for nothing!'

"We have only one more anecdote to give of his Life, and that relates to the close; it is told in the anonymous preface which is sometimes prefixed to his poems; it has been printed in the Persian in the Appendix to Hyde's *Veterum Persarum Religio,* p. 499; and D'Herbelot alludes to it in his Bibliothèque, under *Khiam.*—[1]

" 'It is written in the chronicles of the ancients that this King of the Wise, Omar Khayyám, died at Naishápúr in the year of the Hegira, 517 (A.D. 1123); in science he was unrivalled,—the very

[1] *"Philosophe Musulman qui a vêcu en Odeur de Sainteté dans sa Religion, vers la Fin du premier et la Commencement du second Siècle,"* no part of which, except the *Philosophe,* can apply to our Khayyám.

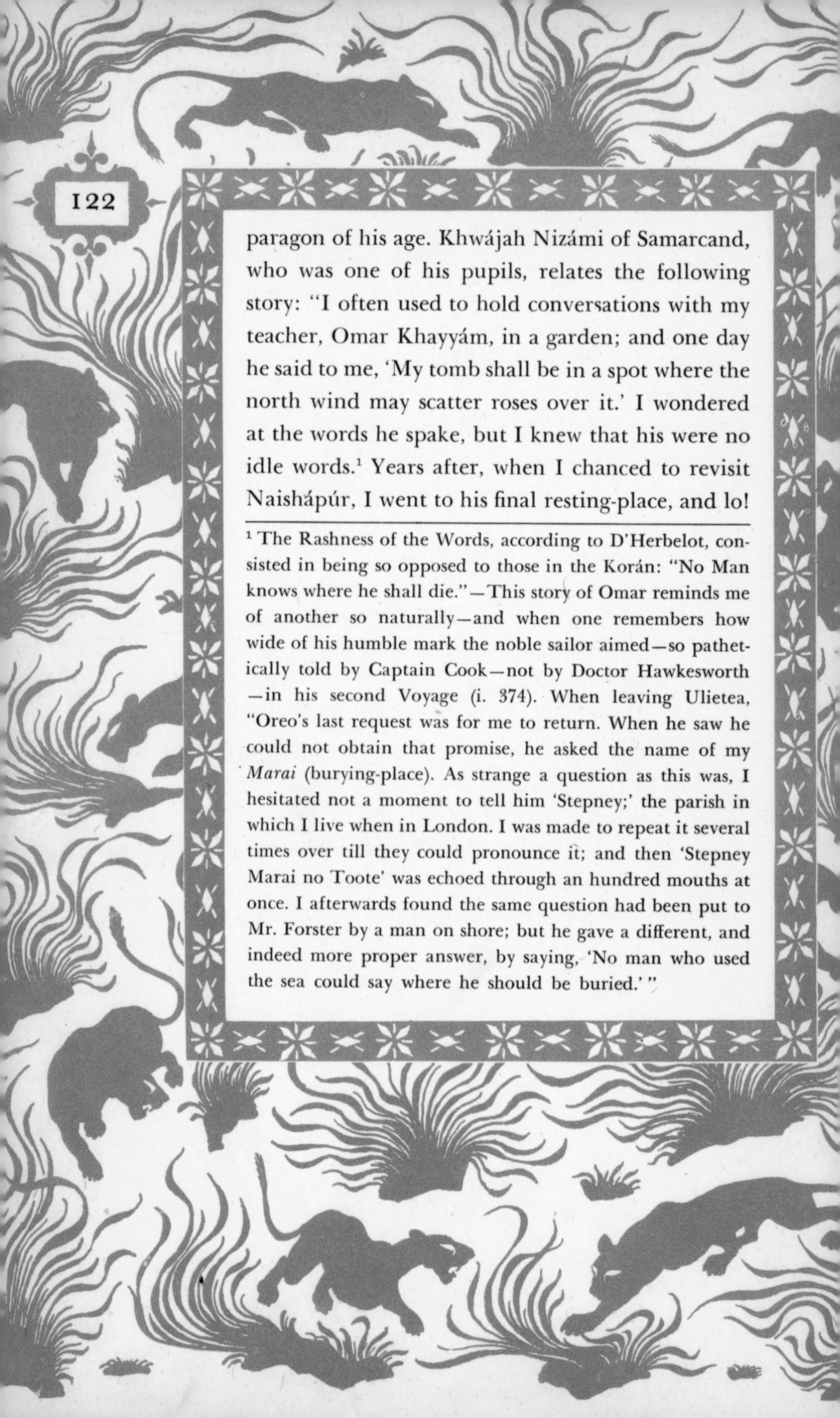

paragon of his age. Khwájah Nizámi of Samarcand, who was one of his pupils, relates the following story: "I often used to hold conversations with my teacher, Omar Khayyám, in a garden; and one day he said to me, 'My tomb shall be in a spot where the north wind may scatter roses over it.' I wondered at the words he spake, but I knew that his were no idle words.[1] Years after, when I chanced to revisit Naishápúr, I went to his final resting-place, and lo!

[1] The Rashness of the Words, according to D'Herbelot, consisted in being so opposed to those in the Korán: "No Man knows where he shall die."—This story of Omar reminds me of another so naturally—and when one remembers how wide of his humble mark the noble sailor aimed—so pathetically told by Captain Cook—not by Doctor Hawkesworth—in his second Voyage (i. 374). When leaving Ulietea, "Oreo's last request was for me to return. When he saw he could not obtain that promise, he asked the name of my *Marai* (burying-place). As strange a question as this was, I hesitated not a moment to tell him 'Stepney;' the parish in which I live when in London. I was made to repeat it several times over till they could pronounce it; and then 'Stepney Marai no Toote' was echoed through an hundred mouths at once. I afterwards found the same question had been put to Mr. Forster by a man on shore; but he gave a different, and indeed more proper answer, by saying, 'No man who used the sea could say where he should be buried.'"

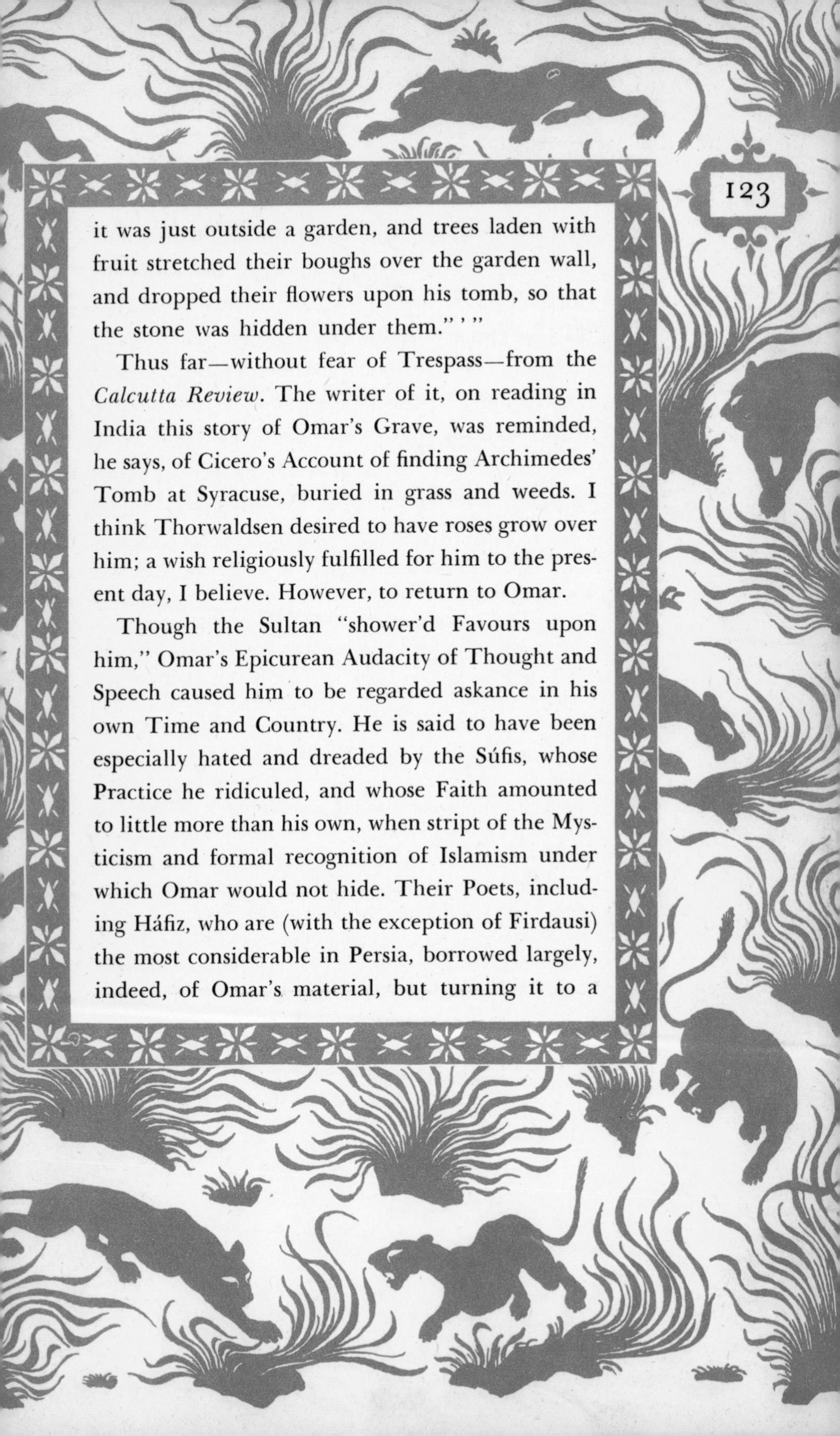

it was just outside a garden, and trees laden with fruit stretched their boughs over the garden wall, and dropped their flowers upon his tomb, so that the stone was hidden under them." ' "

Thus far—without fear of Trespass—from the *Calcutta Review*. The writer of it, on reading in India this story of Omar's Grave, was reminded, he says, of Cicero's Account of finding Archimedes' Tomb at Syracuse, buried in grass and weeds. I think Thorwaldsen desired to have roses grow over him; a wish religiously fulfilled for him to the present day, I believe. However, to return to Omar.

Though the Sultan "shower'd Favours upon him," Omar's Epicurean Audacity of Thought and Speech caused him to be regarded askance in his own Time and Country. He is said to have been especially hated and dreaded by the Súfis, whose Practice he ridiculed, and whose Faith amounted to little more than his own, when stript of the Mysticism and formal recognition of Islamism under which Omar would not hide. Their Poets, including Háfiz, who are (with the exception of Firdausi) the most considerable in Persia, borrowed largely, indeed, of Omar's material, but turning it to a

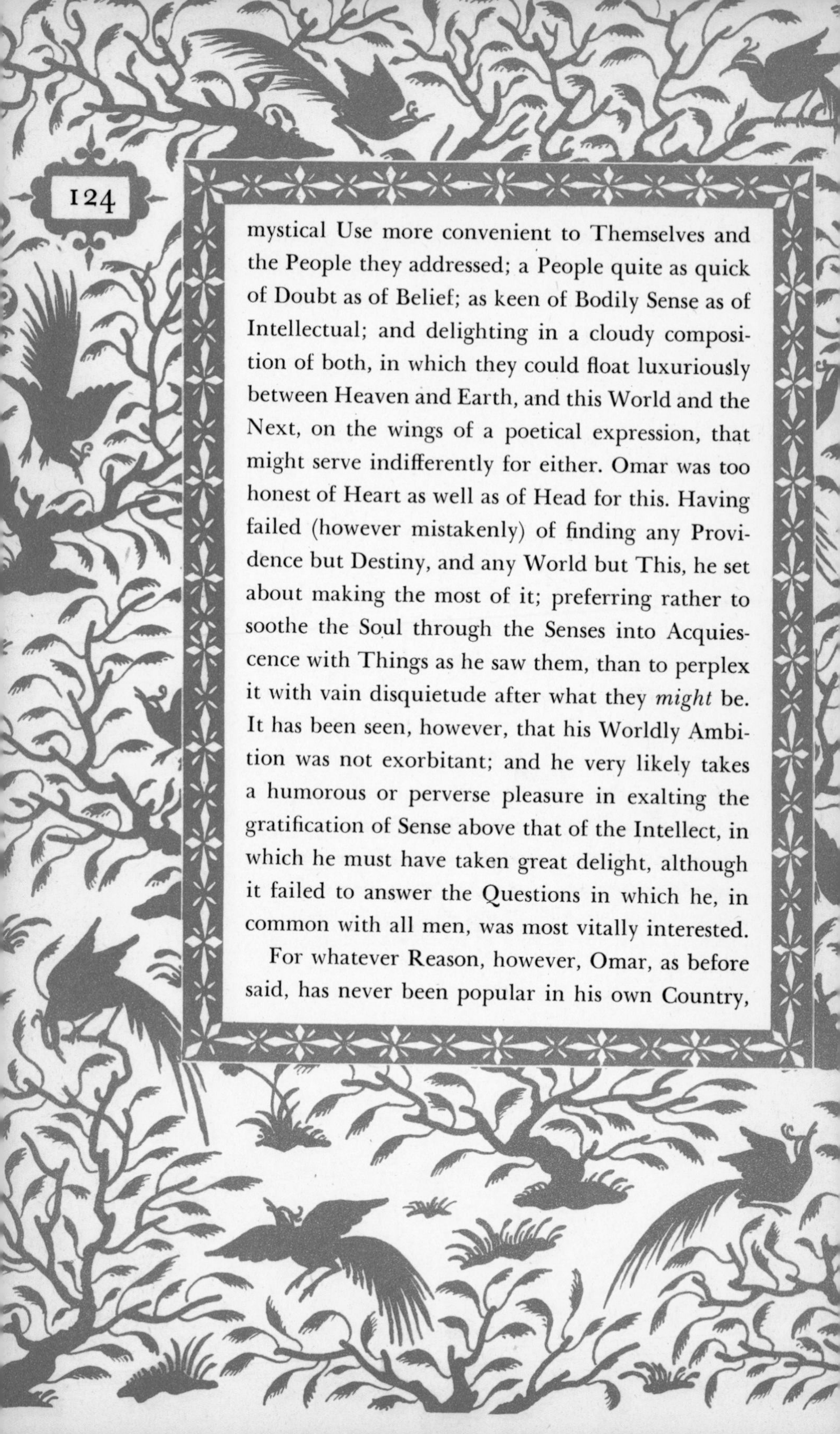

mystical Use more convenient to Themselves and the People they addressed; a People quite as quick of Doubt as of Belief; as keen of Bodily Sense as of Intellectual; and delighting in a cloudy composition of both, in which they could float luxuriously between Heaven and Earth, and this World and the Next, on the wings of a poetical expression, that might serve indifferently for either. Omar was too honest of Heart as well as of Head for this. Having failed (however mistakenly) of finding any Providence but Destiny, and any World but This, he set about making the most of it; preferring rather to soothe the Soul through the Senses into Acquiescence with Things as he saw them, than to perplex it with vain disquietude after what they *might* be. It has been seen, however, that his Worldly Ambition was not exorbitant; and he very likely takes a humorous or perverse pleasure in exalting the gratification of Sense above that of the Intellect, in which he must have taken great delight, although it failed to answer the Questions in which he, in common with all men, was most vitally interested.

For whatever Reason, however, Omar, as before said, has never been popular in his own Country,

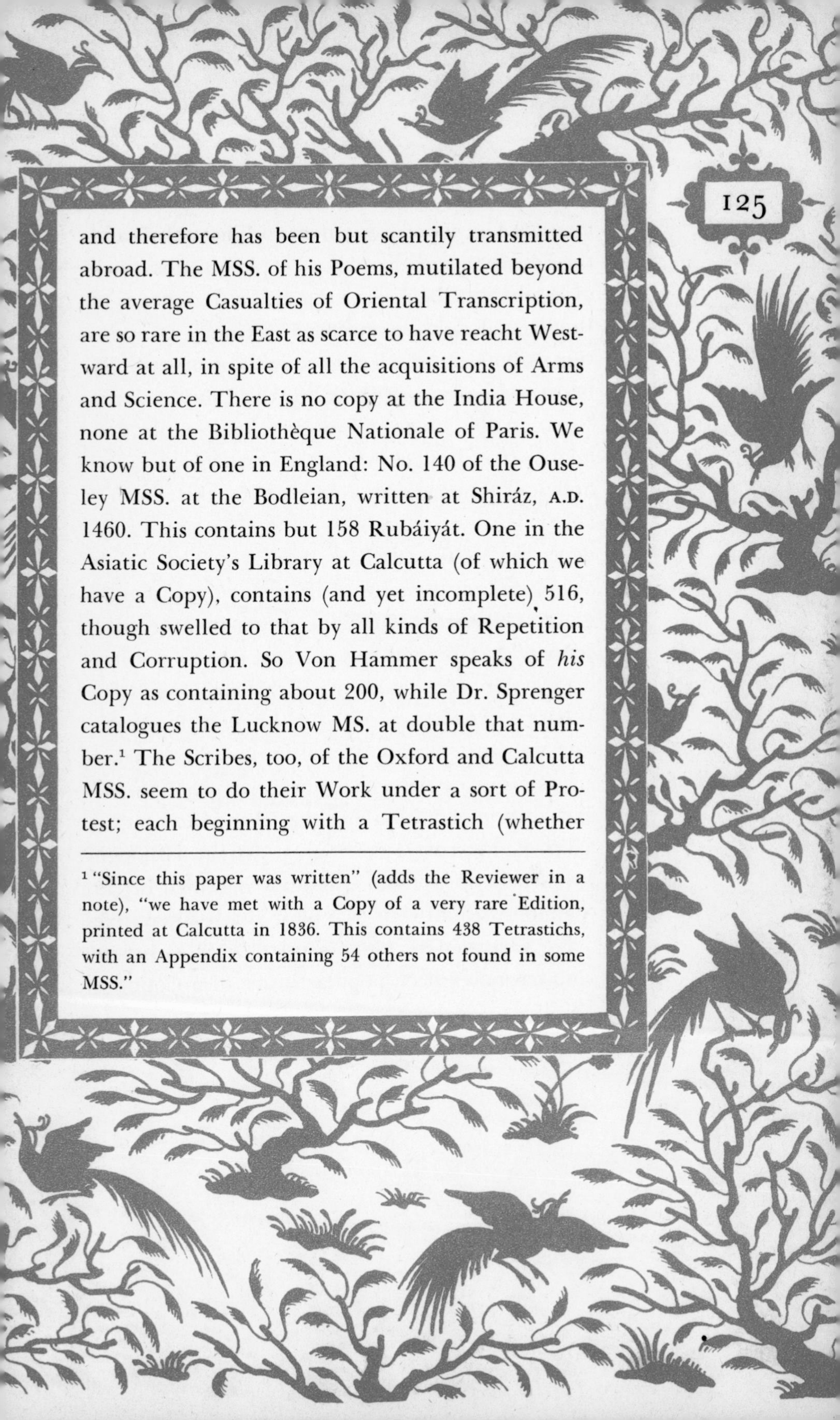

and therefore has been but scantily transmitted abroad. The MSS. of his Poems, mutilated beyond the average Casualties of Oriental Transcription, are so rare in the East as scarce to have reacht Westward at all, in spite of all the acquisitions of Arms and Science. There is no copy at the India House, none at the Bibliothèque Nationale of Paris. We know but of one in England: No. 140 of the Ouseley MSS. at the Bodleian, written at Shiráz, A.D. 1460. This contains but 158 Rubáiyát. One in the Asiatic Society's Library at Calcutta (of which we have a Copy), contains (and yet incomplete) 516, though swelled to that by all kinds of Repetition and Corruption. So Von Hammer speaks of *his* Copy as containing about 200, while Dr. Sprenger catalogues the Lucknow MS. at double that number.[1] The Scribes, too, of the Oxford and Calcutta MSS. seem to do their Work under a sort of Protest; each beginning with a Tetrastich (whether

[1] "Since this paper was written" (adds the Reviewer in a note), "we have met with a Copy of a very rare Edition, printed at Calcutta in 1836. This contains 438 Tetrastichs, with an Appendix containing 54 others not found in some MSS."

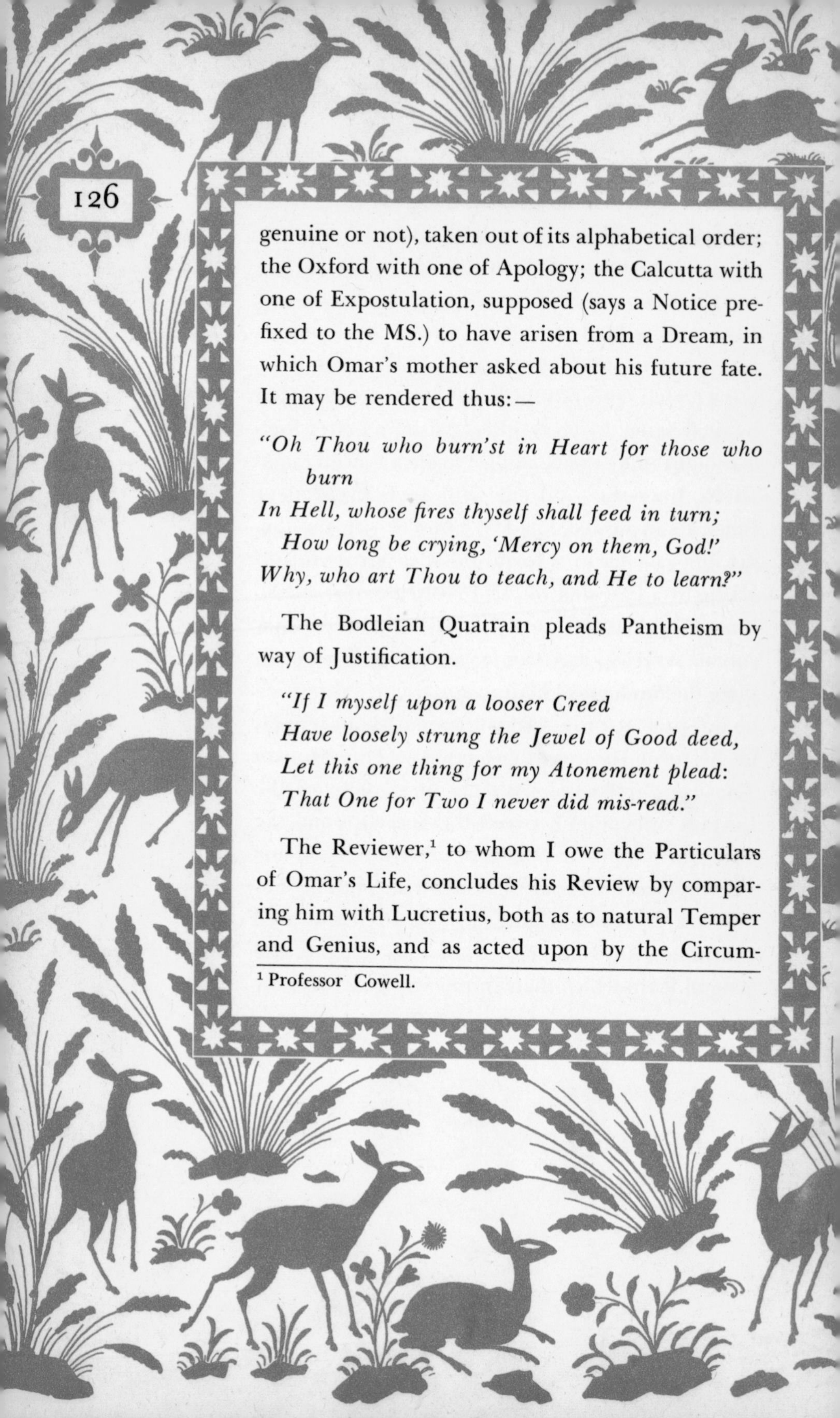

genuine or not), taken out of its alphabetical order; the Oxford with one of Apology; the Calcutta with one of Expostulation, supposed (says a Notice prefixed to the MS.) to have arisen from a Dream, in which Omar's mother asked about his future fate. It may be rendered thus:—

"Oh Thou who burn'st in Heart for those who burn
In Hell, whose fires thyself shall feed in turn;
How long be crying, 'Mercy on them, God!'
Why, who art Thou to teach, and He to learn?"

The Bodleian Quatrain pleads Pantheism by way of Justification.

"If I myself upon a looser Creed
Have loosely strung the Jewel of Good deed,
Let this one thing for my Atonement plead:
That One for Two I never did mis-read."

The Reviewer,[1] to whom I owe the Particulars of Omar's Life, concludes his Review by comparing him with Lucretius, both as to natural Temper and Genius, and as acted upon by the Circum-

[1] Professor Cowell.

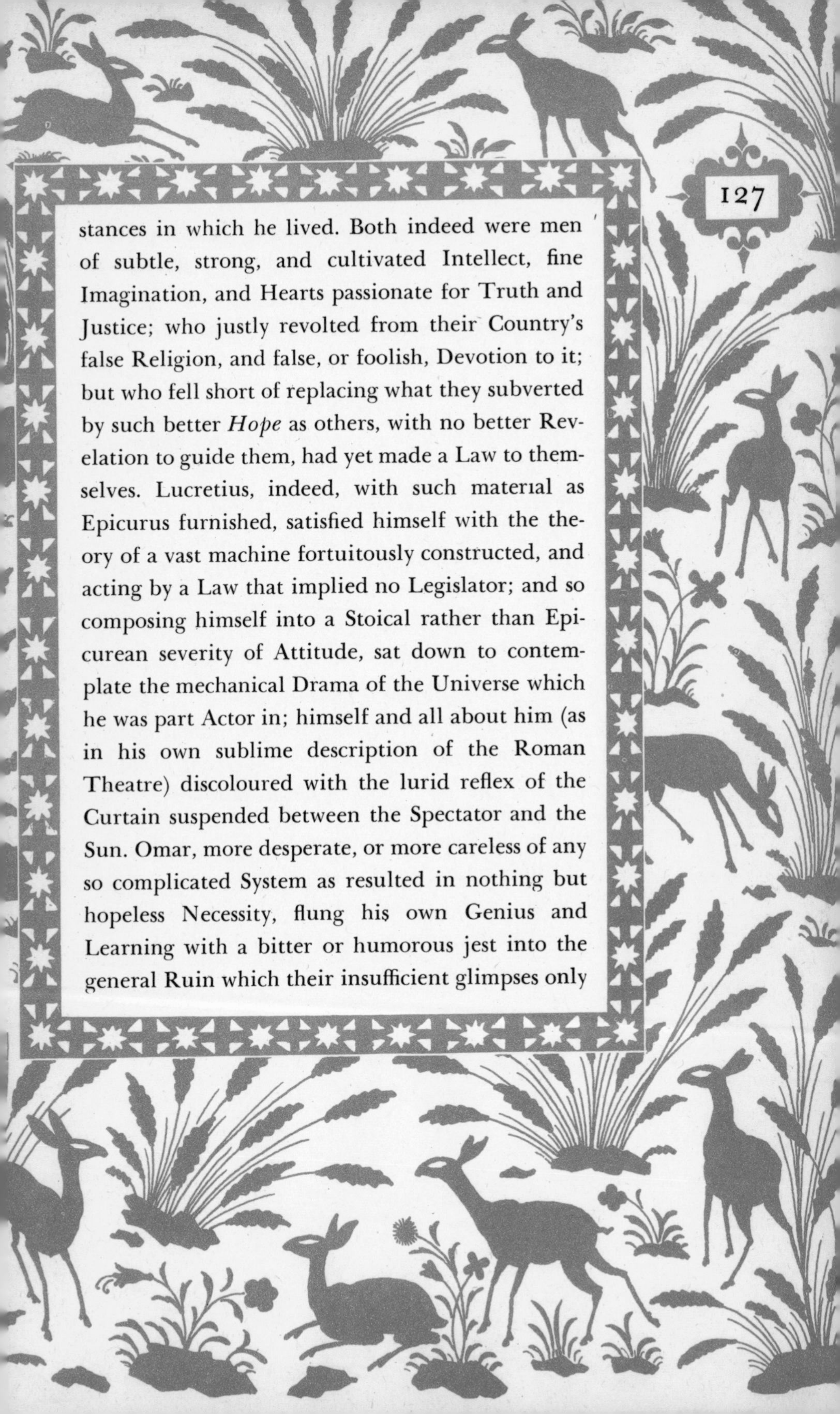

stances in which he lived. Both indeed were men of subtle, strong, and cultivated Intellect, fine Imagination, and Hearts passionate for Truth and Justice; who justly revolted from their Country's false Religion, and false, or foolish, Devotion to it; but who fell short of replacing what they subverted by such better *Hope* as others, with no better Revelation to guide them, had yet made a Law to themselves. Lucretius, indeed, with such material as Epicurus furnished, satisfied himself with the theory of a vast machine fortuitously constructed, and acting by a Law that implied no Legislator; and so composing himself into a Stoical rather than Epicurean severity of Attitude, sat down to contemplate the mechanical Drama of the Universe which he was part Actor in; himself and all about him (as in his own sublime description of the Roman Theatre) discoloured with the lurid reflex of the Curtain suspended between the Spectator and the Sun. Omar, more desperate, or more careless of any so complicated System as resulted in nothing but hopeless Necessity, flung his own Genius and Learning with a bitter or humorous jest into the general Ruin which their insufficient glimpses only

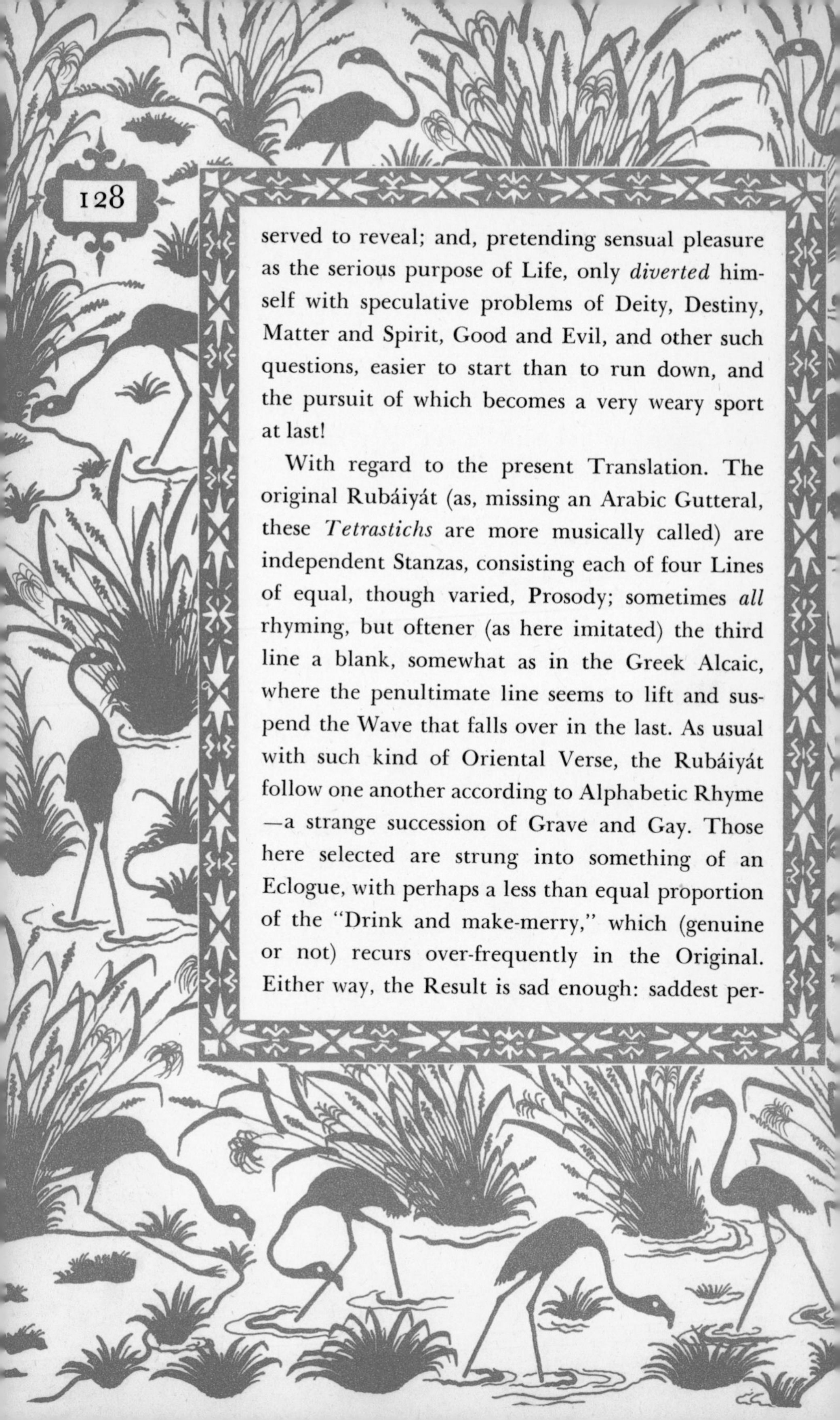

served to reveal; and, pretending sensual pleasure as the serious purpose of Life, only *diverted* himself with speculative problems of Deity, Destiny, Matter and Spirit, Good and Evil, and other such questions, easier to start than to run down, and the pursuit of which becomes a very weary sport at last!

With regard to the present Translation. The original Rubáiyát (as, missing an Arabic Gutteral, these *Tetrastichs* are more musically called) are independent Stanzas, consisting each of four Lines of equal, though varied, Prosody; sometimes *all* rhyming, but oftener (as here imitated) the third line a blank, somewhat as in the Greek Alcaic, where the penultimate line seems to lift and suspend the Wave that falls over in the last. As usual with such kind of Oriental Verse, the Rubáiyát follow one another according to Alphabetic Rhyme —a strange succession of Grave and Gay. Those here selected are strung into something of an Eclogue, with perhaps a less than equal proportion of the "Drink and make-merry," which (genuine or not) recurs over-frequently in the Original. Either way, the Result is sad enough: saddest per-

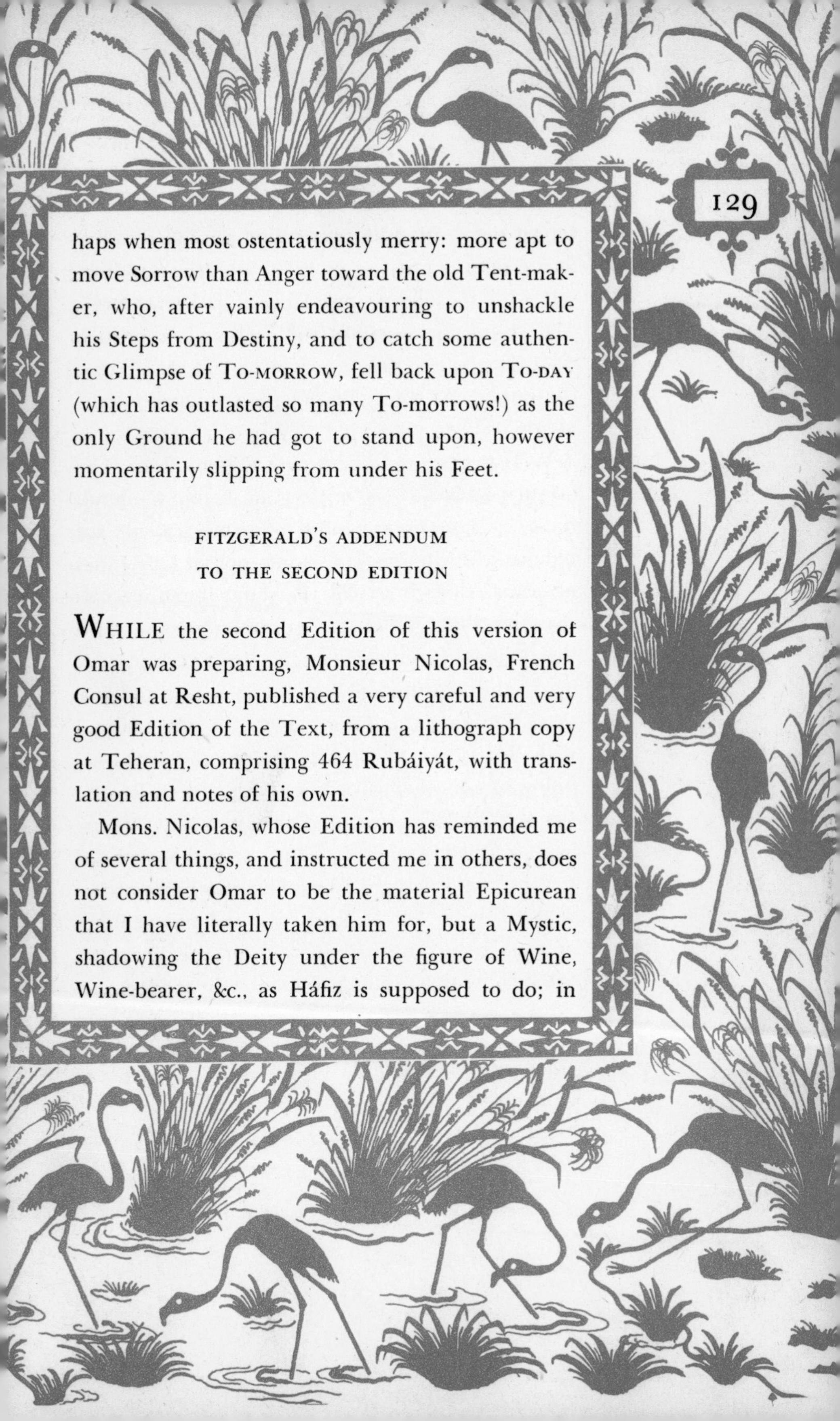

haps when most ostentatiously merry: more apt to move Sorrow than Anger toward the old Tent-maker, who, after vainly endeavouring to unshackle his Steps from Destiny, and to catch some authentic Glimpse of To-MORROW, fell back upon To-DAY (which has outlasted so many To-morrows!) as the only Ground he had got to stand upon, however momentarily slipping from under his Feet.

FITZGERALD'S ADDENDUM TO THE SECOND EDITION

WHILE the second Edition of this version of Omar was preparing, Monsieur Nicolas, French Consul at Resht, published a very careful and very good Edition of the Text, from a lithograph copy at Teheran, comprising 464 Rubáiyát, with translation and notes of his own.

Mons. Nicolas, whose Edition has reminded me of several things, and instructed me in others, does not consider Omar to be the material Epicurean that I have literally taken him for, but a Mystic, shadowing the Deity under the figure of Wine, Wine-bearer, &c., as Háfiz is supposed to do; in

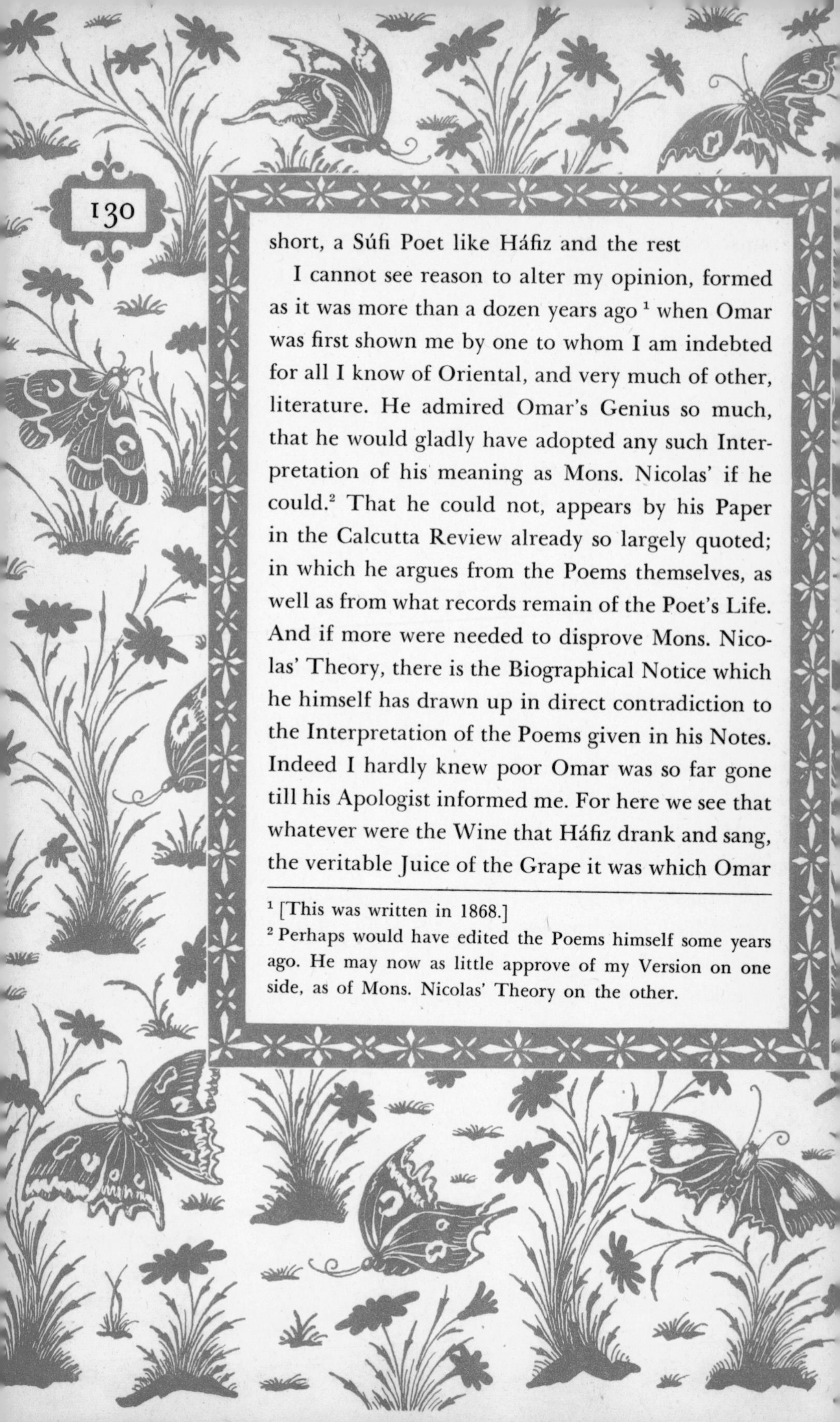

short, a Súfi Poet like Háfiz and the rest

I cannot see reason to alter my opinion, formed as it was more than a dozen years ago [1] when Omar was first shown me by one to whom I am indebted for all I know of Oriental, and very much of other, literature. He admired Omar's Genius so much, that he would gladly have adopted any such Interpretation of his meaning as Mons. Nicolas' if he could.[2] That he could not, appears by his Paper in the Calcutta Review already so largely quoted; in which he argues from the Poems themselves, as well as from what records remain of the Poet's Life. And if more were needed to disprove Mons. Nicolas' Theory, there is the Biographical Notice which he himself has drawn up in direct contradiction to the Interpretation of the Poems given in his Notes. Indeed I hardly knew poor Omar was so far gone till his Apologist informed me. For here we see that whatever were the Wine that Háfiz drank and sang, the veritable Juice of the Grape it was which Omar

---

[1] [This was written in 1868.]

[2] Perhaps would have edited the Poems himself some years ago. He may now as little approve of my Version on one side, as of Mons. Nicolas' Theory on the other.

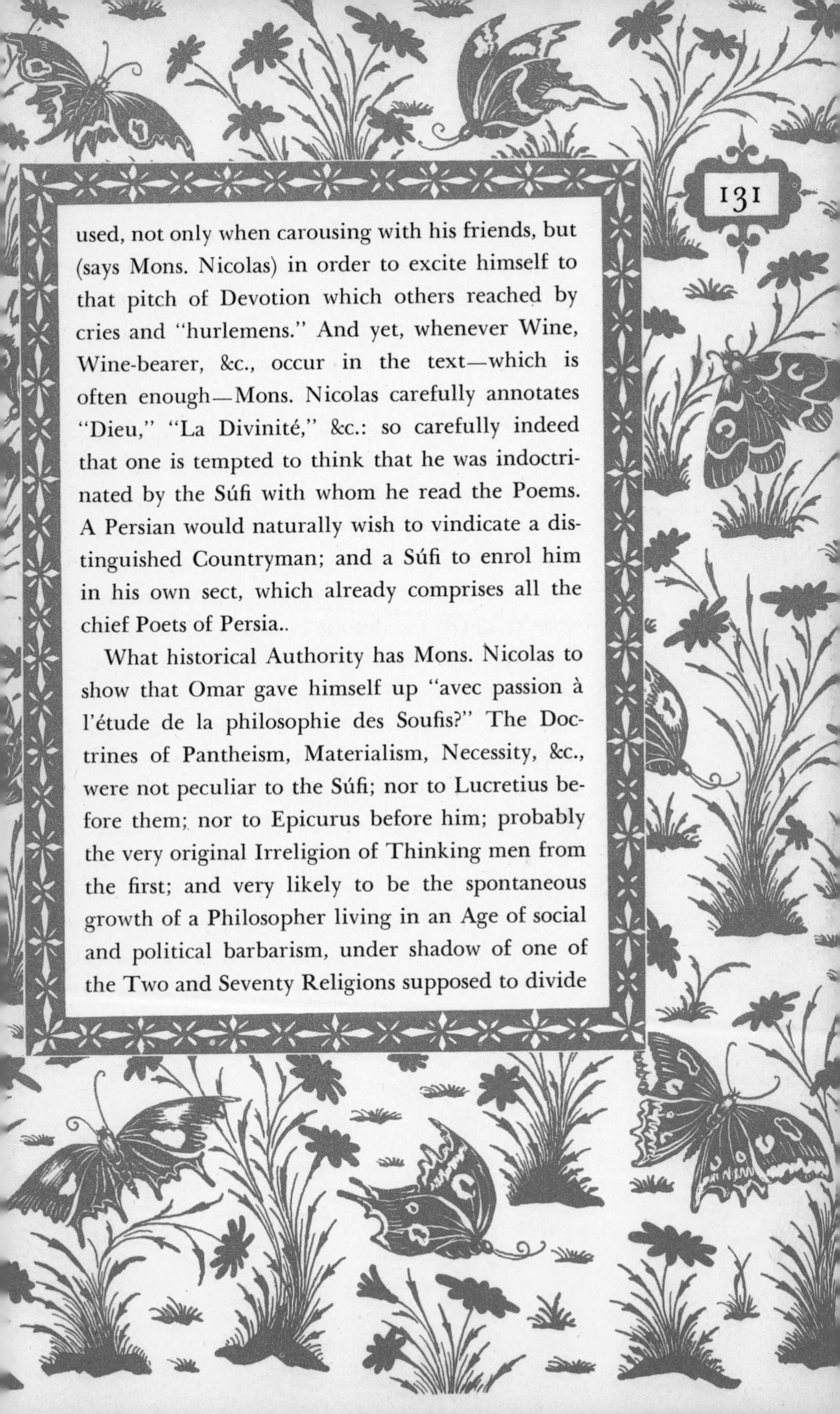

used, not only when carousing with his friends, but (says Mons. Nicolas) in order to excite himself to that pitch of Devotion which others reached by cries and "hurlemens." And yet, whenever Wine, Wine-bearer, &c., occur in the text—which is often enough—Mons. Nicolas carefully annotates "Dieu," "La Divinité," &c.: so carefully indeed that one is tempted to think that he was indoctrinated by the Súfi with whom he read the Poems. A Persian would naturally wish to vindicate a distinguished Countryman; and a Súfi to enrol him in his own sect, which already comprises all the chief Poets of Persia..

What historical Authority has Mons. Nicolas to show that Omar gave himself up "avec passion à l'étude de la philosophie des Soufis?" The Doctrines of Pantheism, Materialism, Necessity, &c., were not peculiar to the Súfi; nor to Lucretius before them; nor to Epicurus before him; probably the very original Irreligion of Thinking men from the first; and very likely to be the spontaneous growth of a Philosopher living in an Age of social and political barbarism, under shadow of one of the Two and Seventy Religions supposed to divide

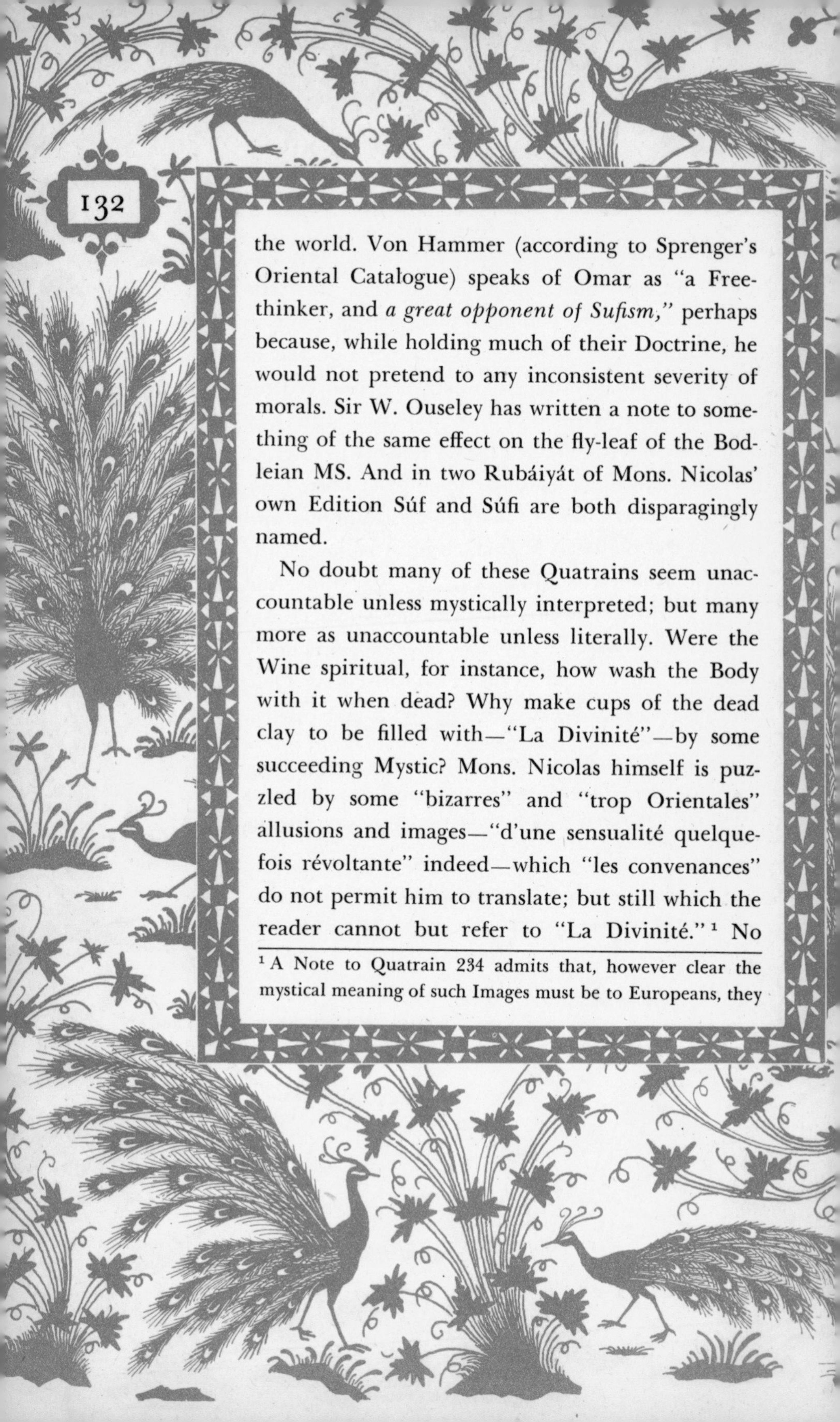

the world. Von Hammer (according to Sprenger's Oriental Catalogue) speaks of Omar as "a Free-thinker, and *a great opponent of Sufism,*" perhaps because, while holding much of their Doctrine, he would not pretend to any inconsistent severity of morals. Sir W. Ouseley has written a note to something of the same effect on the fly-leaf of the Bodleian MS. And in two Rubáiyát of Mons. Nicolas' own Edition Súf and Súfi are both disparagingly named.

No doubt many of these Quatrains seem unaccountable unless mystically interpreted; but many more as unaccountable unless literally. Were the Wine spiritual, for instance, how wash the Body with it when dead? Why make cups of the dead clay to be filled with—"La Divinité"—by some succeeding Mystic? Mons. Nicolas himself is puzzled by some "bizarres" and "trop Orientales" allusions and images—"d'une sensualité quelquefois révoltante" indeed—which "les convenances" do not permit him to translate; but still which the reader cannot but refer to "La Divinité."[1] No

[1] A Note to Quatrain 234 admits that, however clear the mystical meaning of such Images must be to Europeans, they

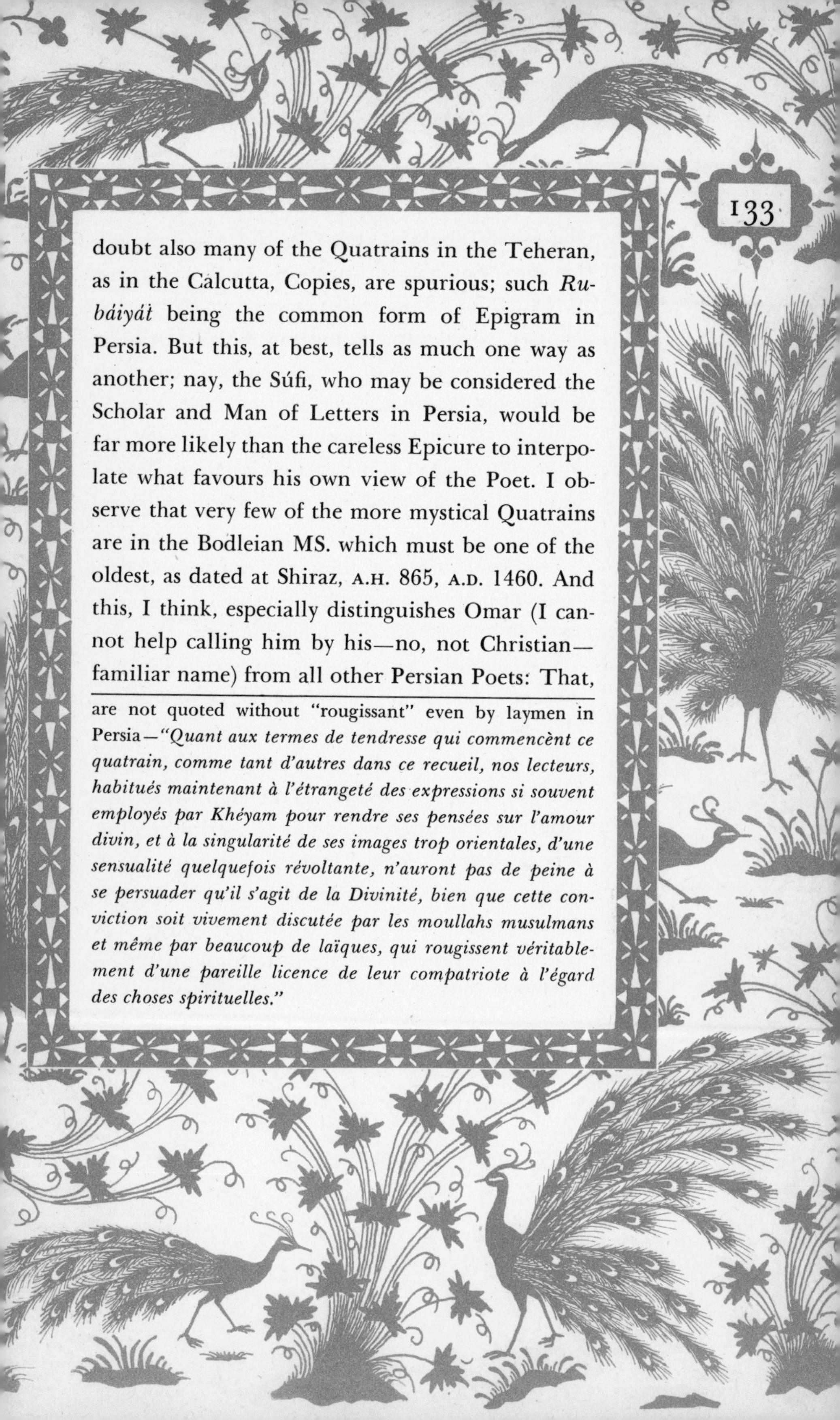

doubt also many of the Quatrains in the Teheran, as in the Calcutta, Copies, are spurious; such *Rubáiyát* being the common form of Epigram in Persia. But this, at best, tells as much one way as another; nay, the Súfi, who may be considered the Scholar and Man of Letters in Persia, would be far more likely than the careless Epicure to interpolate what favours his own view of the Poet. I observe that very few of the more mystical Quatrains are in the Bodleian MS. which must be one of the oldest, as dated at Shiraz, A.H. 865, A.D. 1460. And this, I think, especially distinguishes Omar (I cannot help calling him by his—no, not Christian—familiar name) from all other Persian Poets: That,

are not quoted without "rougissant" even by laymen in Persia—*"Quant aux termes de tendresse qui commencènt ce quatrain, comme tant d'autres dans ce recueil, nos lecteurs, habitués maintenant à l'étrangeté des expressions si souvent employés par Khéyam pour rendre ses pensées sur l'amour divin, et à la singularité de ses images trop orientales, d'une sensualité quelquefois révoltante, n'auront pas de peine à se persuader qu'il s'agit de la Divinité, bien que cette conviction soit vivement discutée par les moullahs musulmans et même par beaucoup de laïques, qui rougissent véritablement d'une pareille licence de leur compatriote à l'égard des choses spirituelles."*

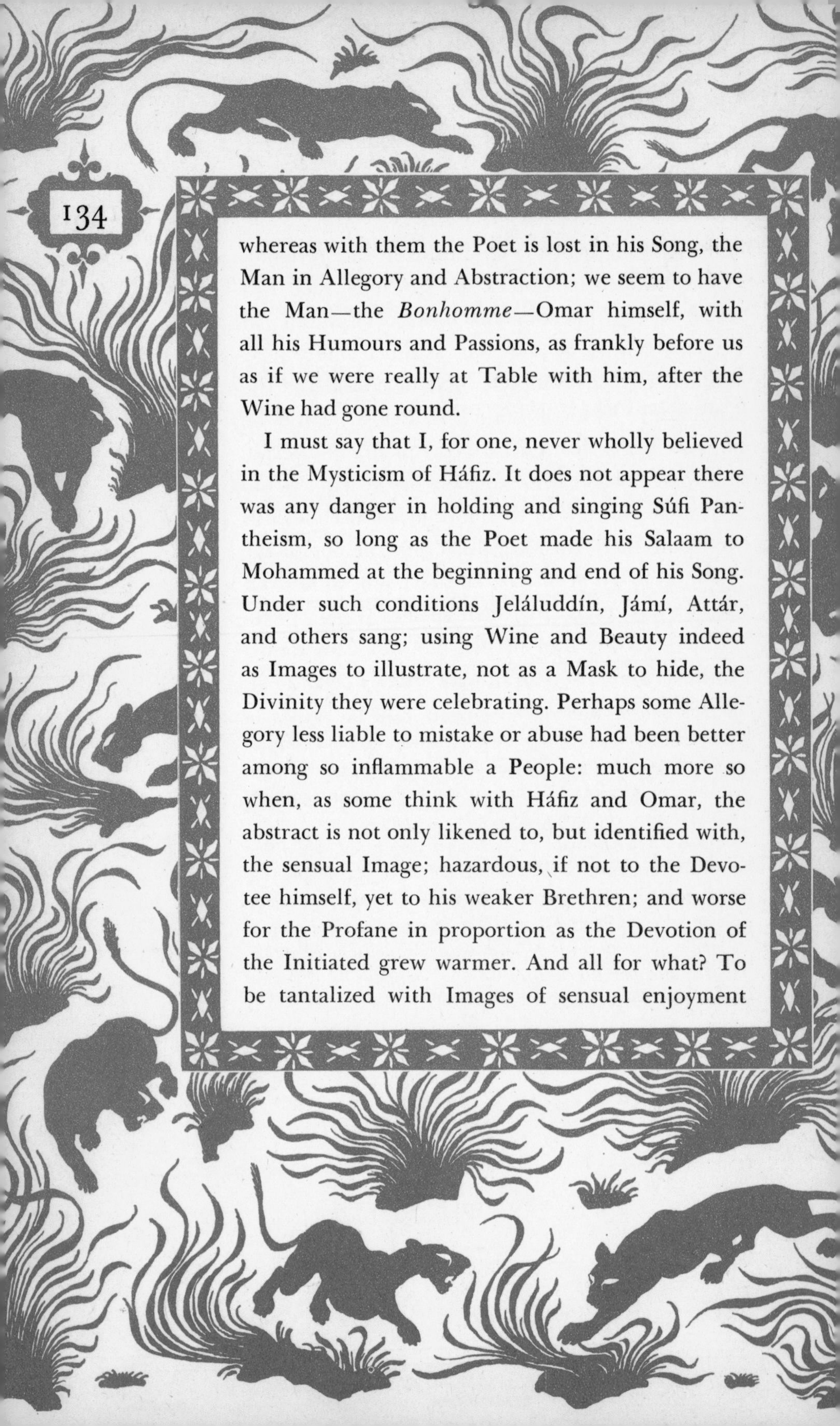

whereas with them the Poet is lost in his Song, the Man in Allegory and Abstraction; we seem to have the Man—the *Bonhomme*—Omar himself, with all his Humours and Passions, as frankly before us as if we were really at Table with him, after the Wine had gone round.

I must say that I, for one, never wholly believed in the Mysticism of Háfiz. It does not appear there was any danger in holding and singing Súfi Pantheism, so long as the Poet made his Salaam to Mohammed at the beginning and end of his Song. Under such conditions Jeláluddín, Jámí, Attár, and others sang; using Wine and Beauty indeed as Images to illustrate, not as a Mask to hide, the Divinity they were celebrating. Perhaps some Allegory less liable to mistake or abuse had been better among so inflammable a People: much more so when, as some think with Háfiz and Omar, the abstract is not only likened to, but identified with, the sensual Image; hazardous, if not to the Devotee himself, yet to his weaker Brethren; and worse for the Profane in proportion as the Devotion of the Initiated grew warmer. And all for what? To be tantalized with Images of sensual enjoyment

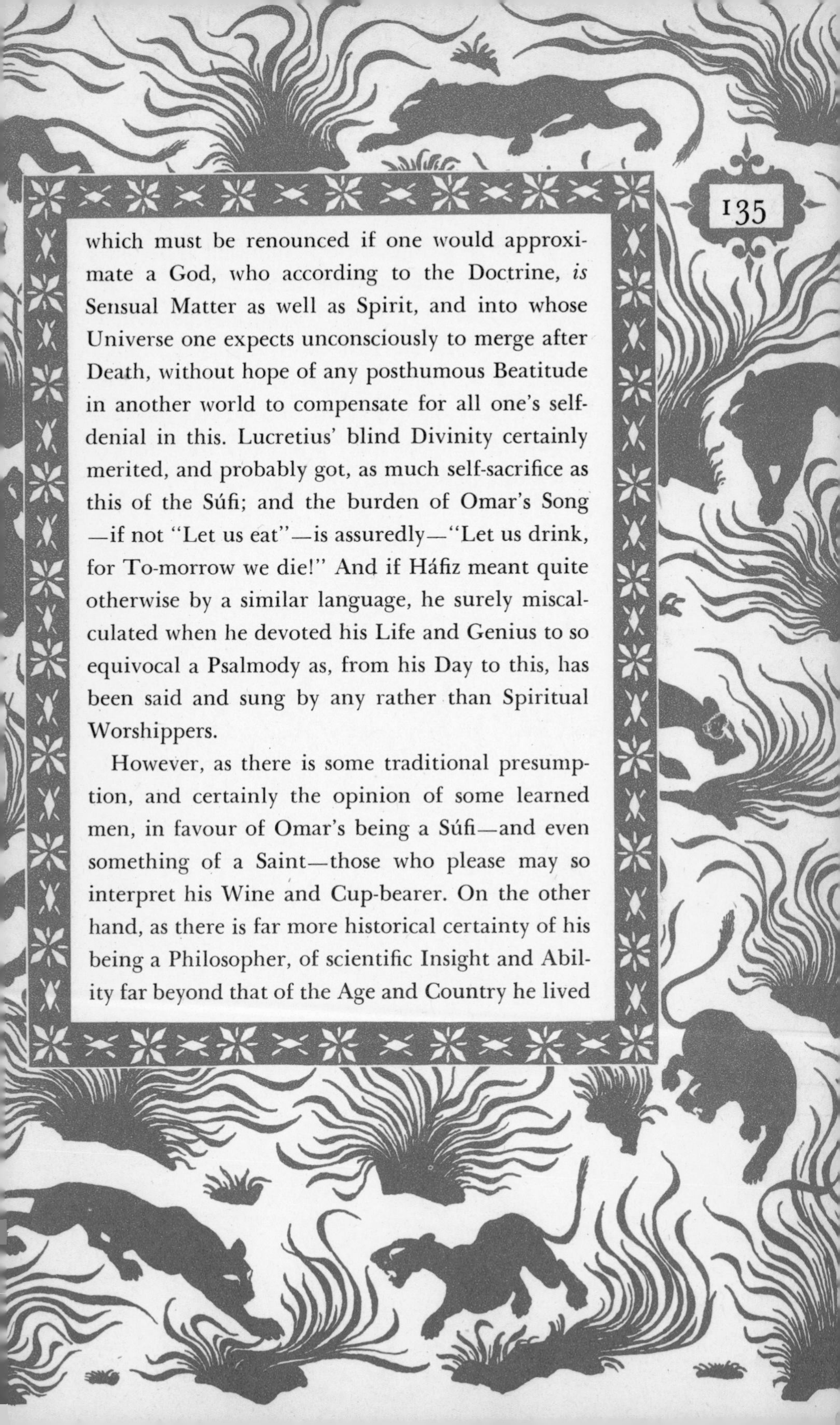

which must be renounced if one would approximate a God, who according to the Doctrine, *is* Sensual Matter as well as Spirit, and into whose Universe one expects unconsciously to merge after Death, without hope of any posthumous Beatitude in another world to compensate for all one's self-denial in this. Lucretius' blind Divinity certainly merited, and probably got, as much self-sacrifice as this of the Súfi; and the burden of Omar's Song —if not "Let us eat"—is assuredly—"Let us drink, for To-morrow we die!" And if Háfiz meant quite otherwise by a similar language, he surely miscalculated when he devoted his Life and Genius to so equivocal a Psalmody as, from his Day to this, has been said and sung by any rather than Spiritual Worshippers.

However, as there is some traditional presumption, and certainly the opinion of some learned men, in favour of Omar's being a Súfi—and even something of a Saint—those who please may so interpret his Wine and Cup-bearer. On the other hand, as there is far more historical certainty of his being a Philosopher, of scientific Insight and Ability far beyond that of the Age and Country he lived

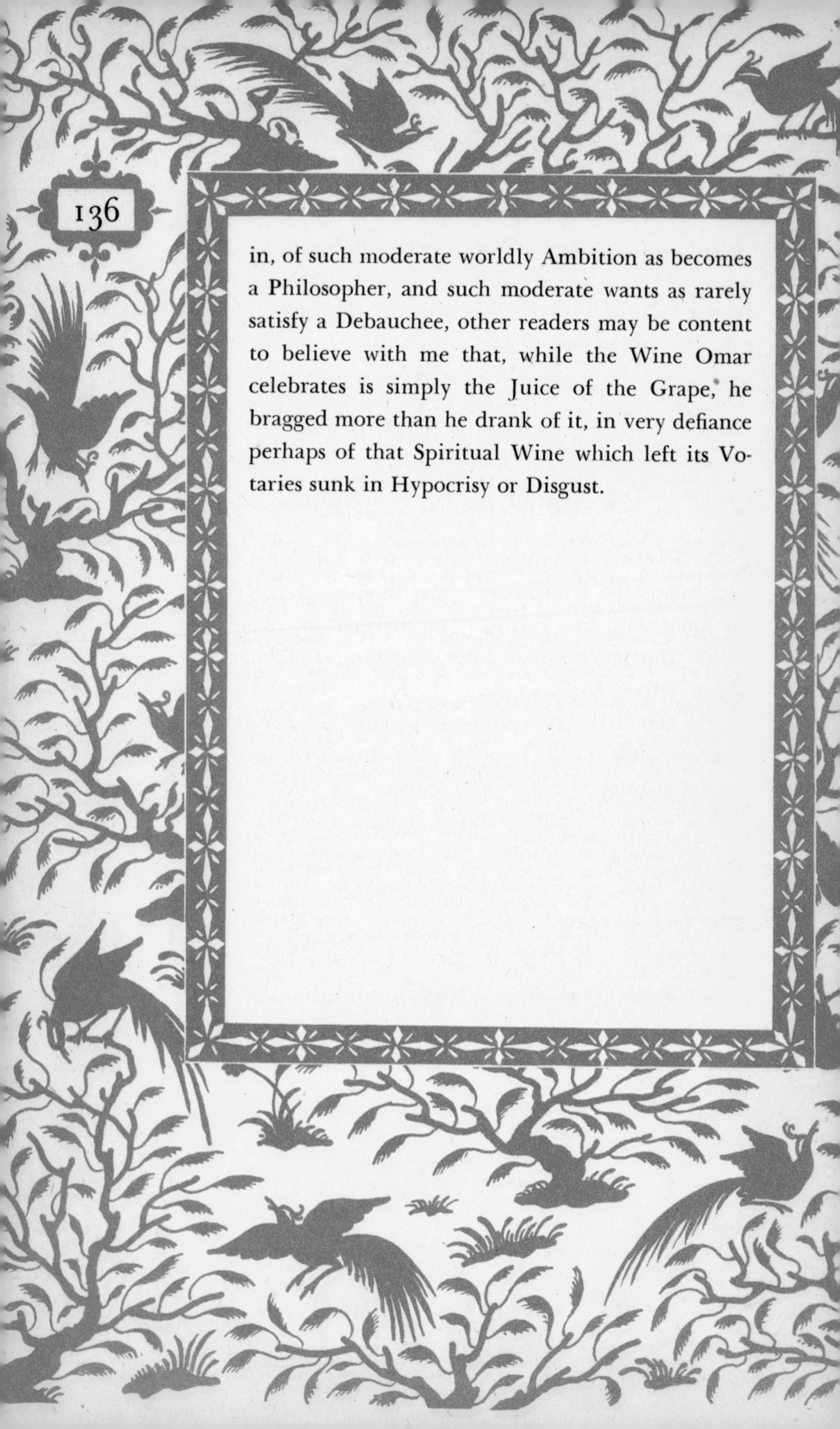

in, of such moderate worldly Ambition as becomes a Philosopher, and such moderate wants as rarely satisfy a Debauchee, other readers may be content to believe with me that, while the Wine Omar celebrates is simply the Juice of the Grape, he bragged more than he drank of it, in very defiance perhaps of that Spiritual Wine which left its Votaries sunk in Hypocrisy or Disgust.

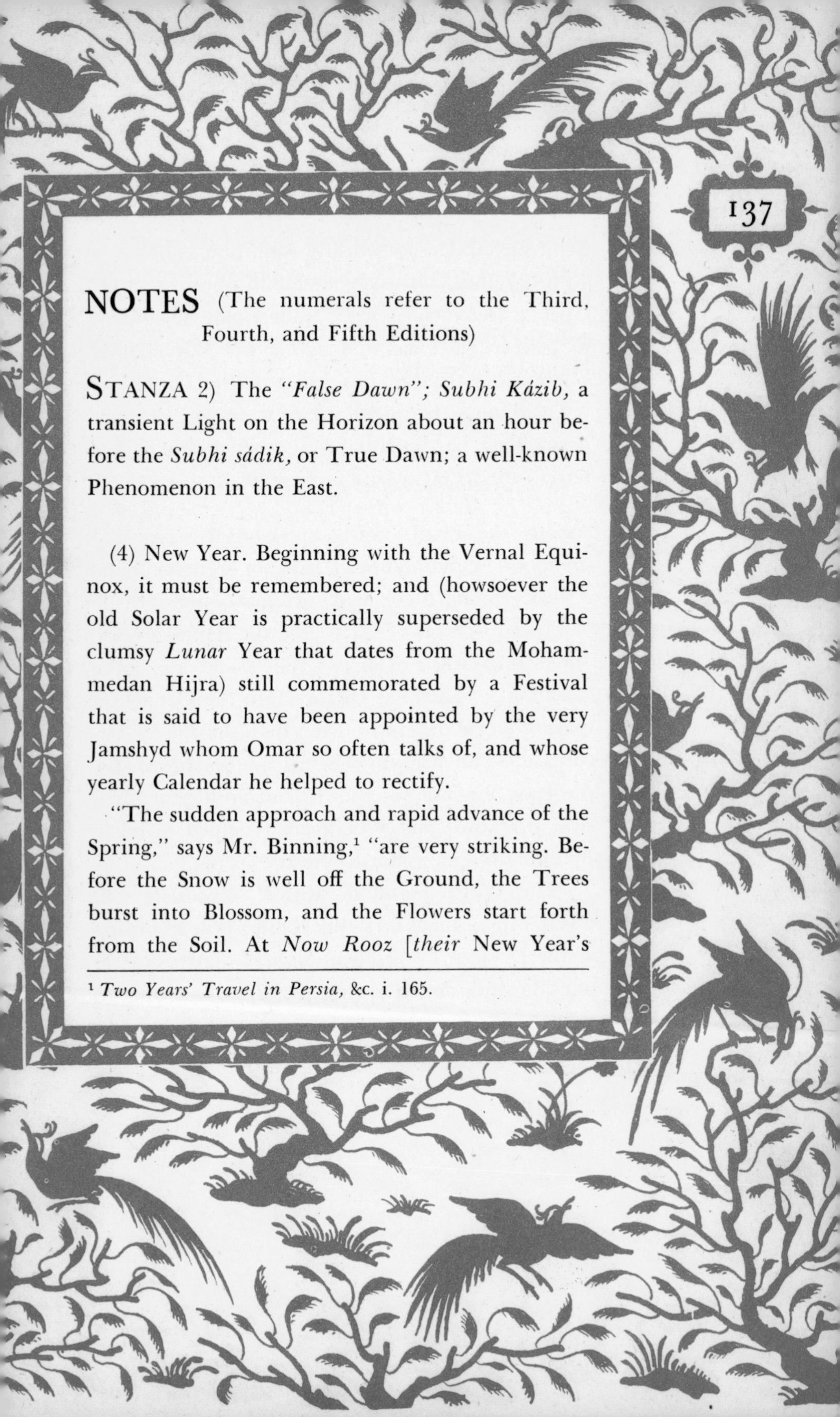

NOTES (The numerals refer to the Third, Fourth, and Fifth Editions)

STANZA 2) The *"False Dawn"; Subhi Kázib,* a transient Light on the Horizon about an hour before the *Subhi sádik,* or True Dawn; a well-known Phenomenon in the East.

(4) New Year. Beginning with the Vernal Equinox, it must be remembered; and (howsoever the old Solar Year is practically superseded by the clumsy *Lunar* Year that dates from the Mohammedan Hijra) still commemorated by a Festival that is said to have been appointed by the very Jamshyd whom Omar so often talks of, and whose yearly Calendar he helped to rectify.

"The sudden approach and rapid advance of the Spring," says Mr. Binning,[1] "are very striking. Before the Snow is well off the Ground, the Trees burst into Blossom, and the Flowers start forth from the Soil. At *Now Rooz* [*their* New Year's

[1] *Two Years' Travel in Persia,* &c. i. 165.

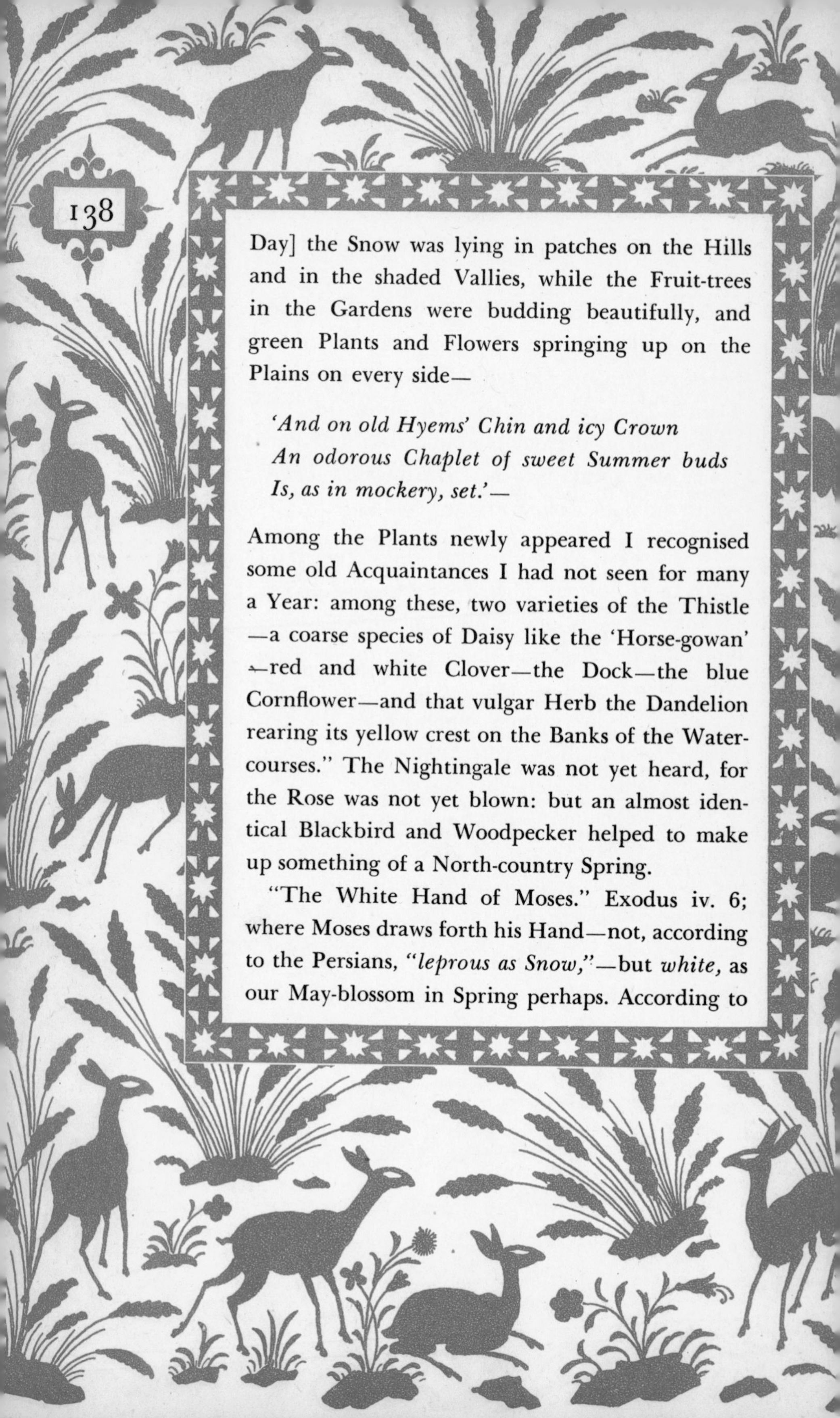

Day] the Snow was lying in patches on the Hills and in the shaded Vallies, while the Fruit-trees in the Gardens were budding beautifully, and green Plants and Flowers springing up on the Plains on every side—

'And on old Hyems' Chin and icy Crown
An odorous Chaplet of sweet Summer buds
Is, as in mockery, set.'—

Among the Plants newly appeared I recognised some old Acquaintances I had not seen for many a Year: among these, two varieties of the Thistle —a coarse species of Daisy like the 'Horse-gowan' —red and white Clover—the Dock—the blue Cornflower—and that vulgar Herb the Dandelion rearing its yellow crest on the Banks of the Water-courses." The Nightingale was not yet heard, for the Rose was not yet blown: but an almost identical Blackbird and Woodpecker helped to make up something of a North-country Spring.

"The White Hand of Moses." Exodus iv. 6; where Moses draws forth his Hand—not, according to the Persians, *"leprous as Snow,"*—but *white,* as our May-blossom in Spring perhaps. According to

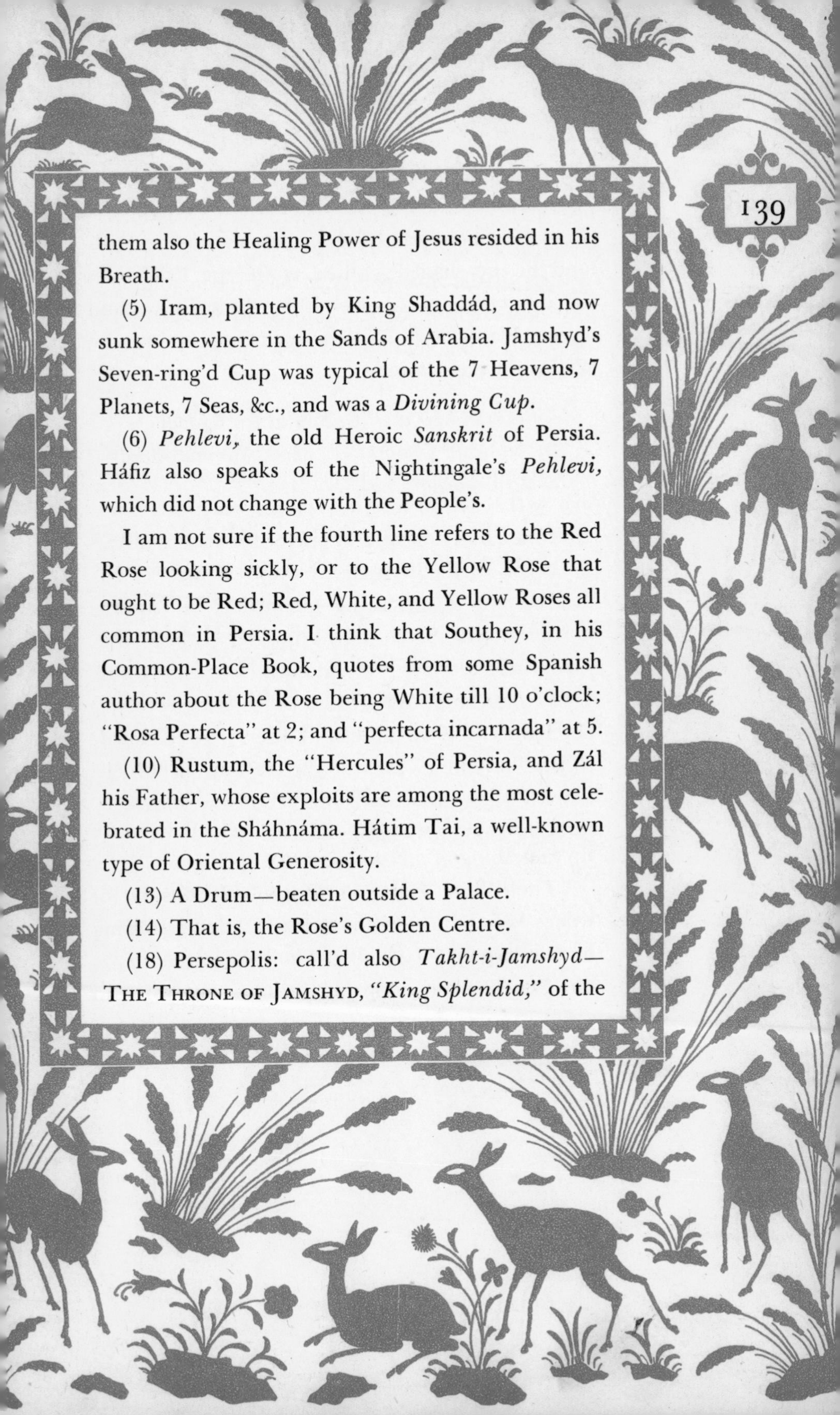

them also the Healing Power of Jesus resided in his Breath.

(5) Iram, planted by King Shaddád, and now sunk somewhere in the Sands of Arabia. Jamshyd's Seven-ring'd Cup was typical of the 7 Heavens, 7 Planets, 7 Seas, &c., and was a *Divining Cup*.

(6) *Pehlevi*, the old Heroic *Sanskrit* of Persia. Háfiz also speaks of the Nightingale's *Pehlevi*, which did not change with the People's.

I am not sure if the fourth line refers to the Red Rose looking sickly, or to the Yellow Rose that ought to be Red; Red, White, and Yellow Roses all common in Persia. I think that Southey, in his Common-Place Book, quotes from some Spanish author about the Rose being White till 10 o'clock; "Rosa Perfecta" at 2; and "perfecta incarnada" at 5.

(10) Rustum, the "Hercules" of Persia, and Zál his Father, whose exploits are among the most celebrated in the Sháhnáma. Hátim Tai, a well-known type of Oriental Generosity.

(13) A Drum—beaten outside a Palace.

(14) That is, the Rose's Golden Centre.

(18) Persepolis: call'd also *Takht-i-Jamshyd*—The Throne of Jamshyd, *"King Splendid,"* of the

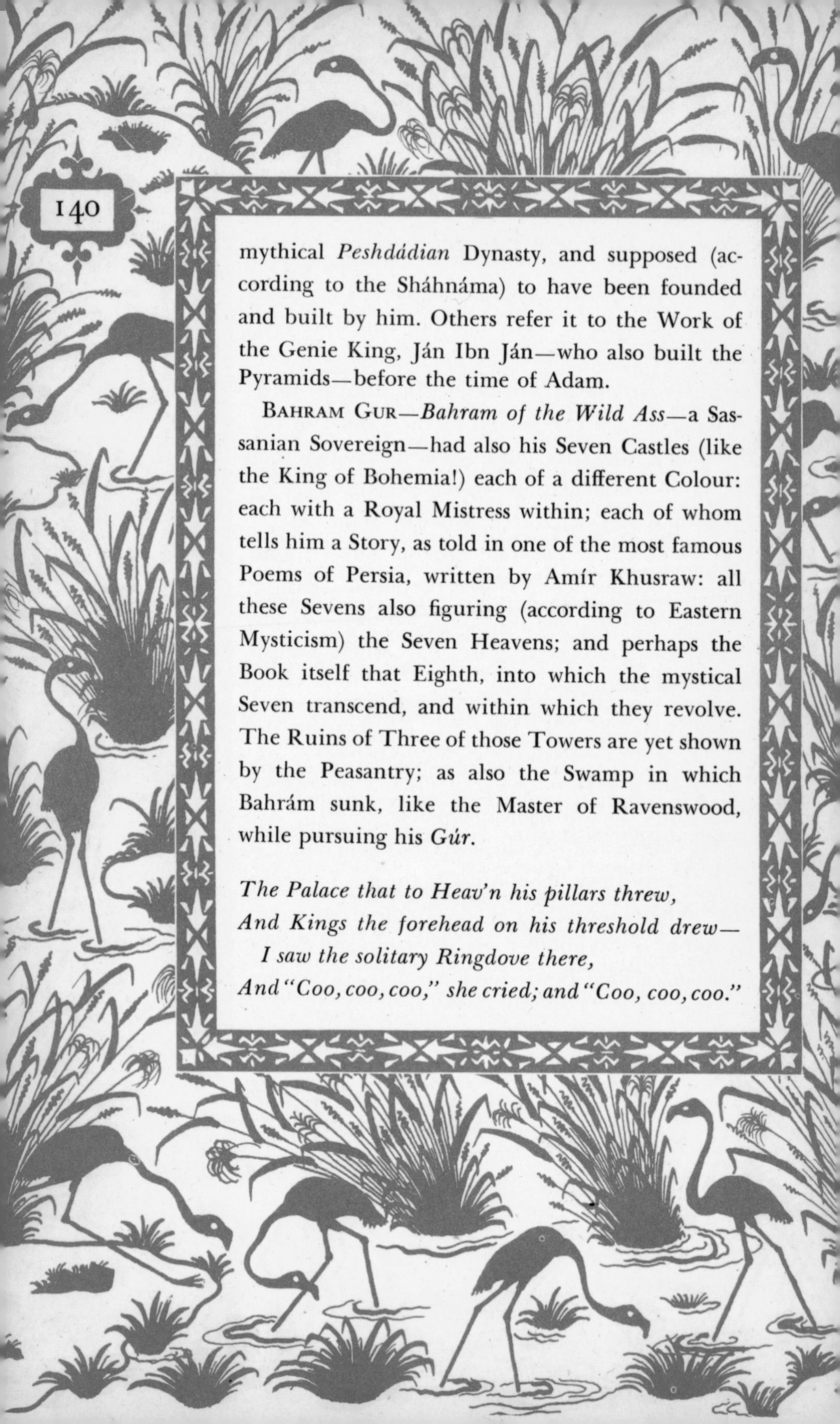

mythical *Peshdádian* Dynasty, and supposed (according to the Sháhnáma) to have been founded and built by him. Others refer it to the Work of the Genie King, Ján Ibn Ján—who also built the Pyramids—before the time of Adam.

BAHRAM GUR—*Bahram of the Wild Ass*—a Sassanian Sovereign—had also his Seven Castles (like the King of Bohemia!) each of a different Colour: each with a Royal Mistress within; each of whom tells him a Story, as told in one of the most famous Poems of Persia, written by Amír Khusraw: all these Sevens also figuring (according to Eastern Mysticism) the Seven Heavens; and perhaps the Book itself that Eighth, into which the mystical Seven transcend, and within which they revolve. The Ruins of Three of those Towers are yet shown by the Peasantry; as also the Swamp in which Bahrám sunk, like the Master of Ravenswood, while pursuing his *Gúr*.

The Palace that to Heav'n his pillars threw,
And Kings the forehead on his threshold drew—
I saw the solitary Ringdove there,
And "Coo, coo, coo," she cried; and "Coo, coo, coo."

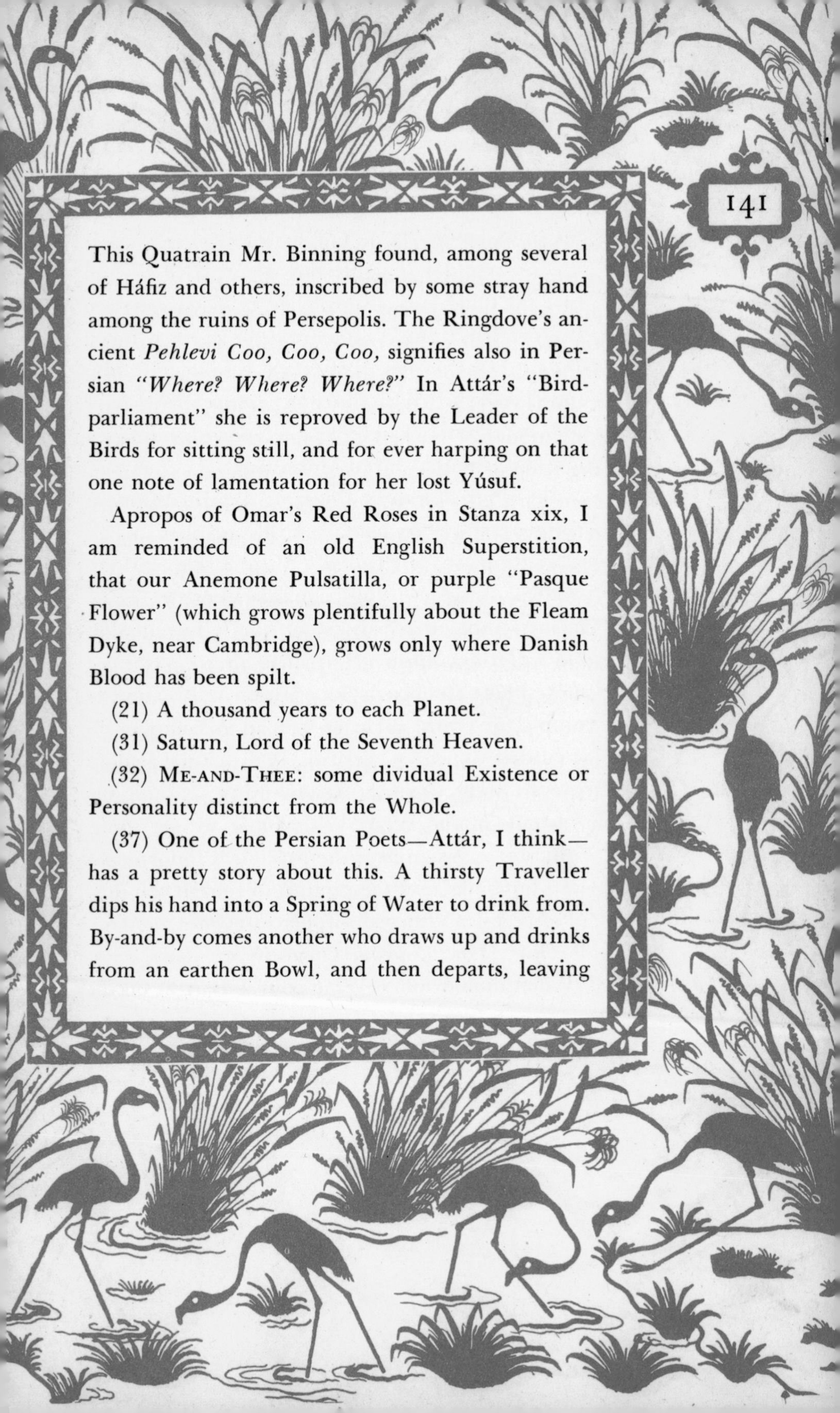

This Quatrain Mr. Binning found, among several of Háfiz and others, inscribed by some stray hand among the ruins of Persepolis. The Ringdove's ancient *Pehlevi Coo, Coo, Coo,* signifies also in Persian *"Where? Where? Where?"* In Attár's "Bird-parliament" she is reproved by the Leader of the Birds for sitting still, and for ever harping on that one note of lamentation for her lost Yúsuf.

Apropos of Omar's Red Roses in Stanza xix, I am reminded of an old English Superstition, that our Anemone Pulsatilla, or purple "Pasque Flower" (which grows plentifully about the Fleam Dyke, near Cambridge), grows only where Danish Blood has been spilt.

(21) A thousand years to each Planet.

(31) Saturn, Lord of the Seventh Heaven.

(32) ME-AND-THEE: some dividual Existence or Personality distinct from the Whole.

(37) One of the Persian Poets—Attár, I think—has a pretty story about this. A thirsty Traveller dips his hand into a Spring of Water to drink from. By-and-by comes another who draws up and drinks from an earthen Bowl, and then departs, leaving

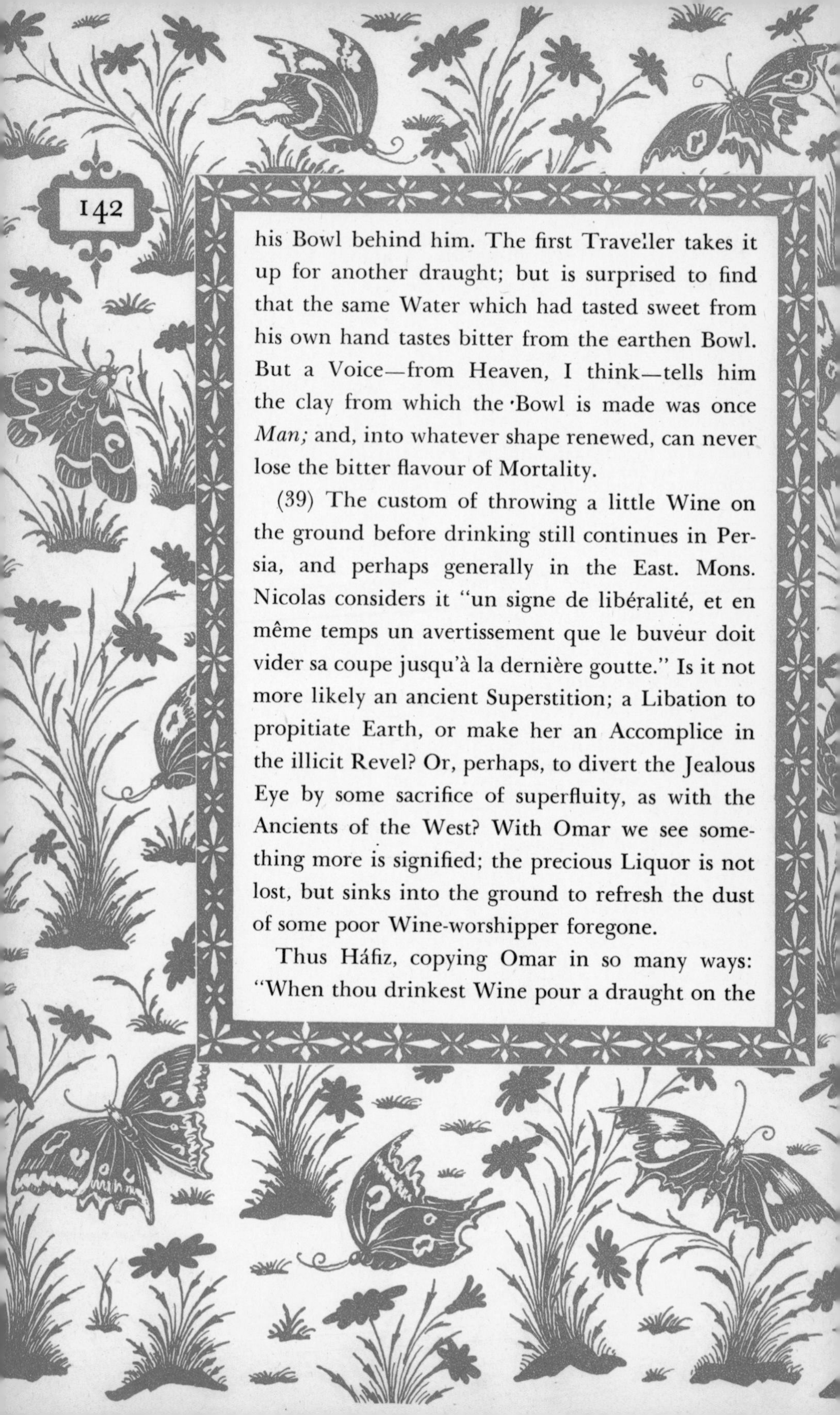

his Bowl behind him. The first Traveller takes it up for another draught; but is surprised to find that the same Water which had tasted sweet from his own hand tastes bitter from the earthen Bowl. But a Voice—from Heaven, I think—tells him the clay from which the Bowl is made was once *Man;* and, into whatever shape renewed, can never lose the bitter flavour of Mortality.

(39) The custom of throwing a little Wine on the ground before drinking still continues in Persia, and perhaps generally in the East. Mons. Nicolas considers it "un signe de libéralité, et en même temps un avertissement que le buveur doit vider sa coupe jusqu'à la dernière goutte." Is it not more likely an ancient Superstition; a Libation to propitiate Earth, or make her an Accomplice in the illicit Revel? Or, perhaps, to divert the Jealous Eye by some sacrifice of superfluity, as with the Ancients of the West? With Omar we see something more is signified; the precious Liquor is not lost, but sinks into the ground to refresh the dust of some poor Wine-worshipper foregone.

Thus Háfiz, copying Omar in so many ways: "When thou drinkest Wine pour a draught on the

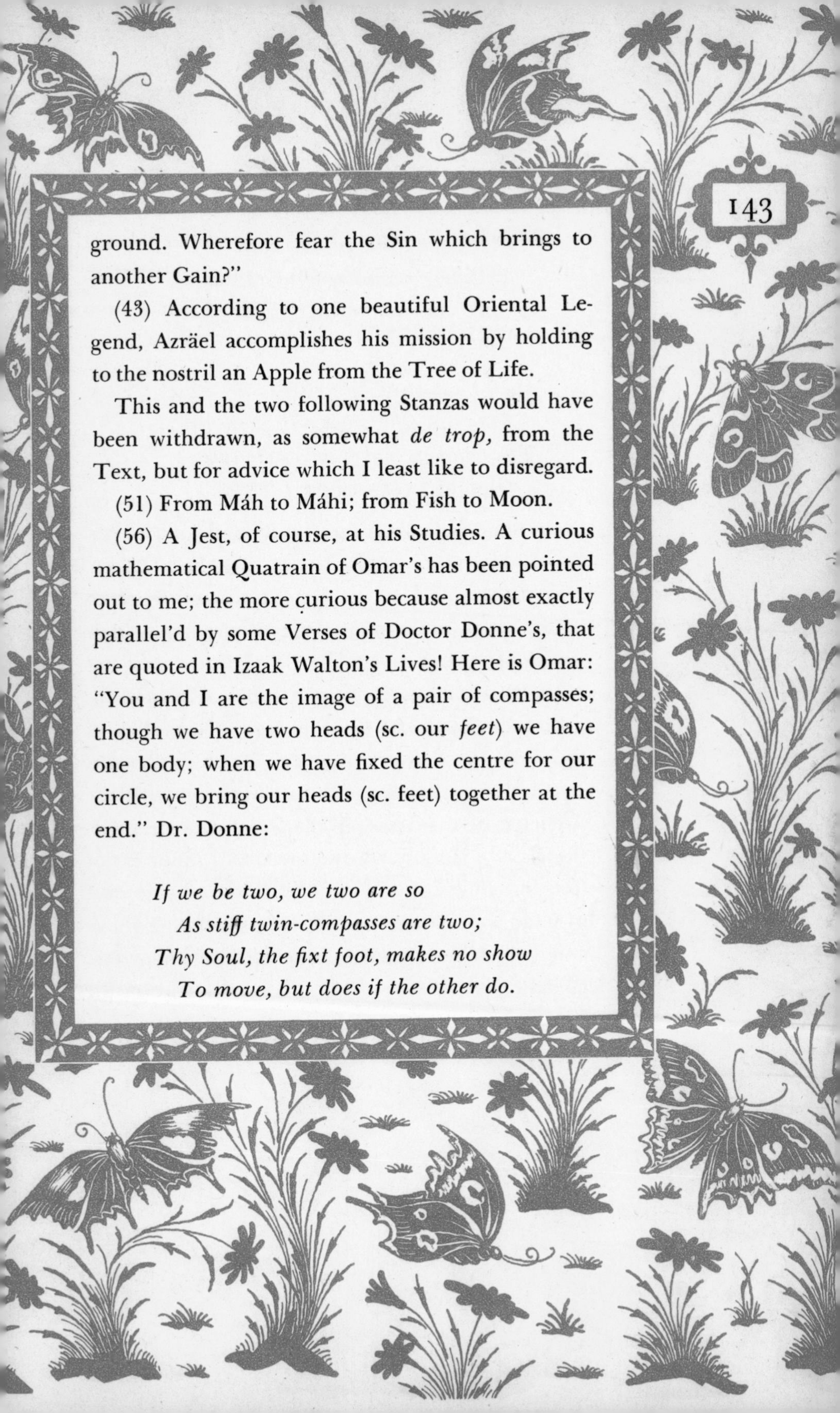

ground. Wherefore fear the Sin which brings to another Gain?"

(43) According to one beautiful Oriental Legend, Azräel accomplishes his mission by holding to the nostril an Apple from the Tree of Life.

This and the two following Stanzas would have been withdrawn, as somewhat *de trop,* from the Text, but for advice which I least like to disregard.

(51) From Máh to Máhi; from Fish to Moon.

(56) A Jest, of course, at his Studies. A curious mathematical Quatrain of Omar's has been pointed out to me; the more curious because almost exactly parallel'd by some Verses of Doctor Donne's, that are quoted in Izaak Walton's Lives! Here is Omar: "You and I are the image of a pair of compasses; though we have two heads (sc. our *feet*) we have one body; when we have fixed the centre for our circle, we bring our heads (sc. feet) together at the end." Dr. Donne:

If we be two, we two are so
As stiff twin-compasses are two;
Thy Soul, the fixt foot, makes no show
To move, but does if the other do.

And though thine in the centre sit,
Yet when my other far does roam,
Thine leans and hearkens after it,
And grows erect as mine comes home.

Such thou must be to me, who must
Like the other foot obliquely run;
Thy firmness makes my circle just,
And me to end where I begun.

(59) The Seventy-two Religions supposed to divide the World, *including* Islamism, as some think: but others not.

(60) Alluding to Sultan Mahmúd's Conquest of India and its dark people.

(68) *Fánúsi khiyál,* a Magic-lantern still used in India; the cylindrical Interior being painted with various Figures, and so lightly poised and ventilated as to revolve round the lighted Candle within.

(70) A very mysterious Line in the Original

O dánad O dánad O dánad O——

breaking off something like our Wood-pigeon's Note, which she is said to take up just where she left off.

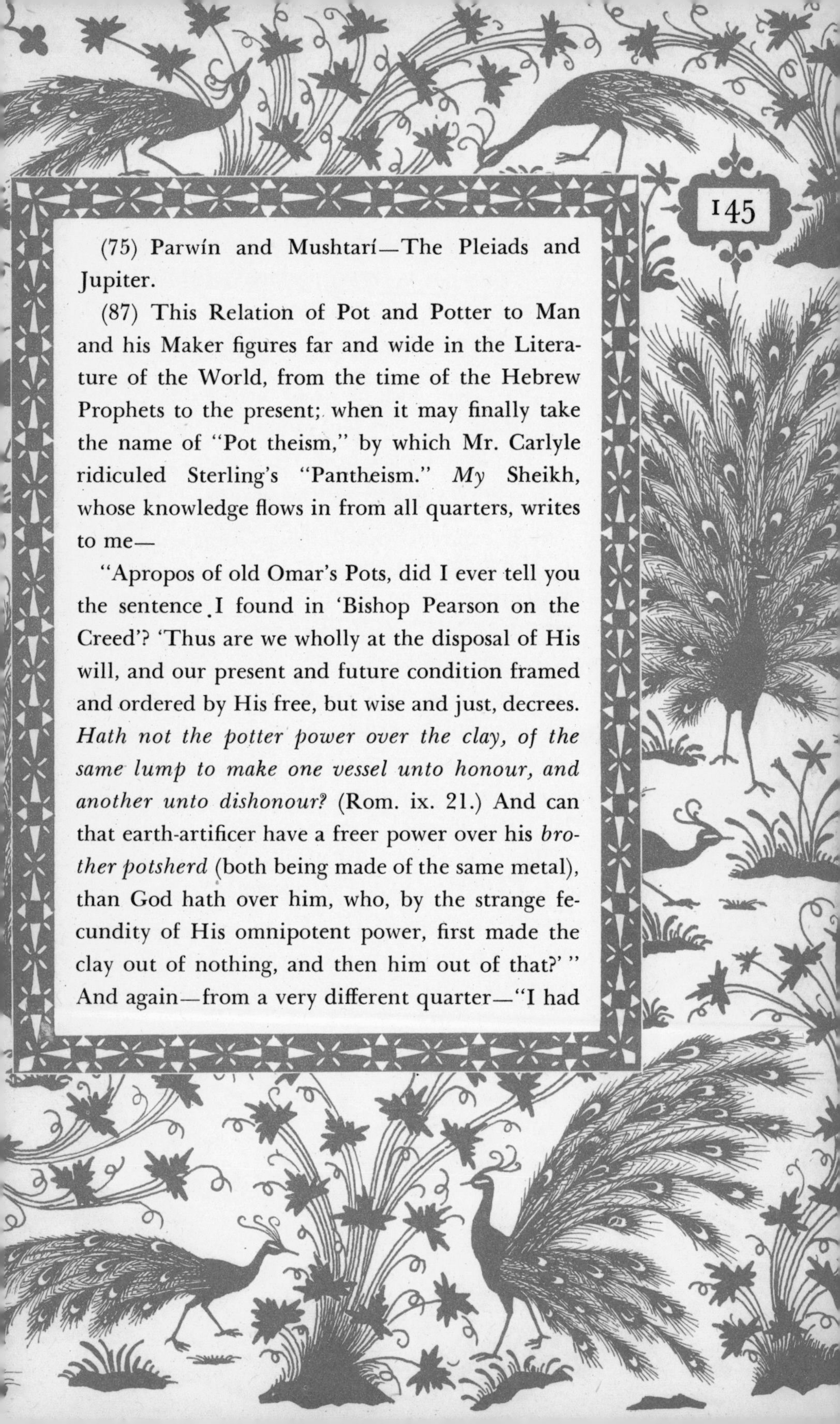

(75) Parwín and Mushtarí—The Pleiads and Jupiter.

(87) This Relation of Pot and Potter to Man and his Maker figures far and wide in the Literature of the World, from the time of the Hebrew Prophets to the present; when it may finally take the name of "Pot theism," by which Mr. Carlyle ridiculed Sterling's "Pantheism." *My* Sheikh, whose knowledge flows in from all quarters, writes to me—

"Apropos of old Omar's Pots, did I ever tell you the sentence I found in 'Bishop Pearson on the Creed'? 'Thus are we wholly at the disposal of His will, and our present and future condition framed and ordered by His free, but wise and just, decrees. *Hath not the potter power over the clay, of the same lump to make one vessel unto honour, and another unto dishonour?* (Rom. ix. 21.) And can that earth-artificer have a freer power over his *brother potsherd* (both being made of the same metal), than God hath over him, who, by the strange fecundity of His omnipotent power, first made the clay out of nothing, and then him out of that?' " And again—from a very different quarter—"I had

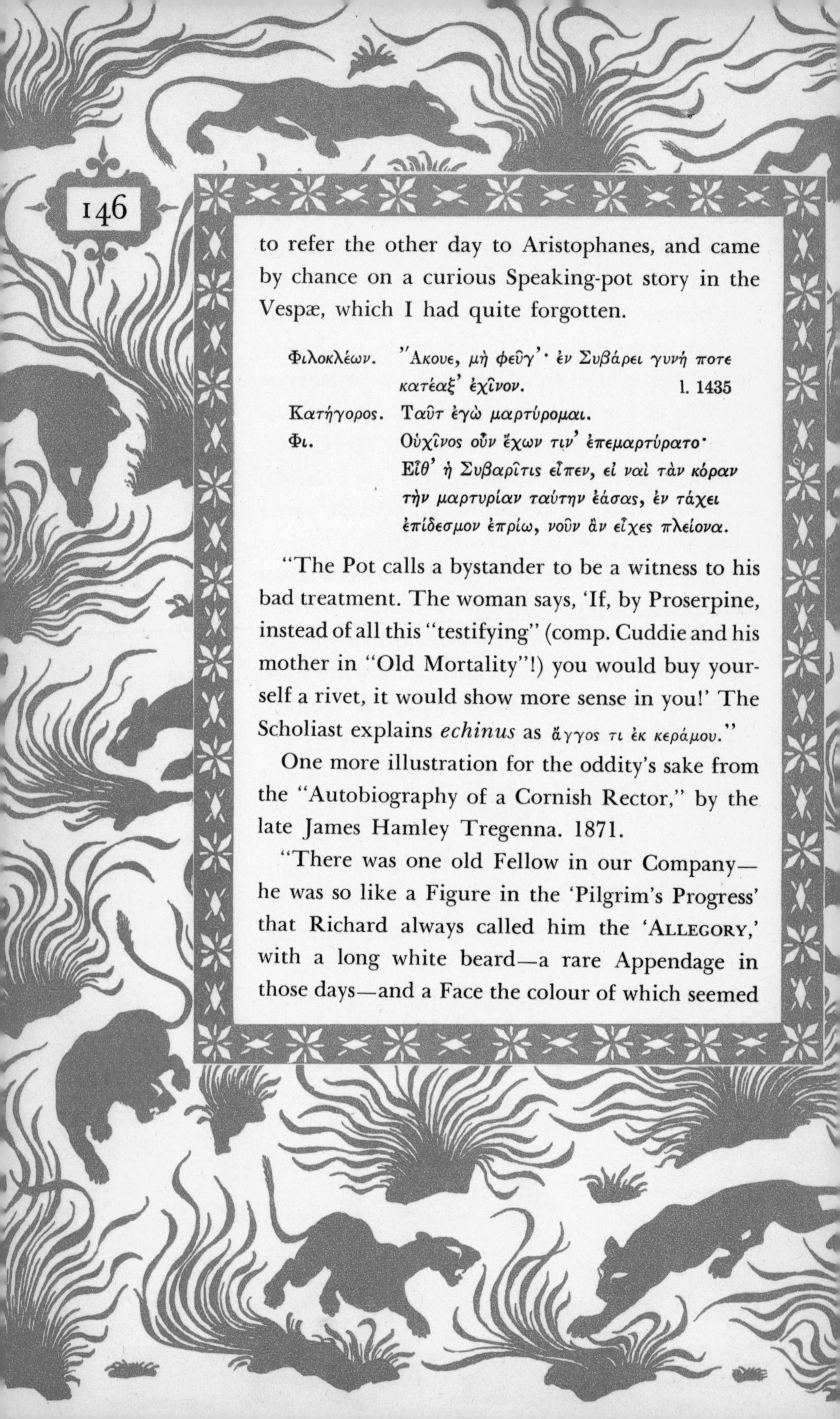

to refer the other day to Aristophanes, and came by chance on a curious Speaking-pot story in the Vespæ, which I had quite forgotten.

Φιλοκλέων. ῎Ακουε, μὴ φεῦγ᾽· ἐν Συβάρει γυνή ποτε
κατέαξ᾽ ἐχῖνον. l. 1435
Κατήγορος. Ταῦτ ἐγὼ μαρτύρομαι.
Φι. Οὐχῖνος οὖν ἔχων τιν᾽ ἐπεμαρτύρατο·
Εἶθ᾽ ἡ Συβαρῖτις εἶπεν, εἰ ναὶ τὰν κόραν
τὴν μαρτυρίαν ταύτην ἐάσας, ἐν τάχει
ἐπίδεσμον ἐπρίω, νοῦν ἂν εἶχες πλείονα.

"The Pot calls a bystander to be a witness to his bad treatment. The woman says, 'If, by Proserpine, instead of all this "testifying" (comp. Cuddie and his mother in "Old Mortality"!) you would buy yourself a rivet, it would show more sense in you!' The Scholiast explains *echinus* as ἄγγος τι ἐκ κεράμου."

One more illustration for the oddity's sake from the "Autobiography of a Cornish Rector," by the late James Hamley Tregenna. 1871.

"There was one old Fellow in our Company—he was so like a Figure in the 'Pilgrim's Progress' that Richard always called him the 'ALLEGORY,' with a long white beard—a rare Appendage in those days—and a Face the colour of which seemed

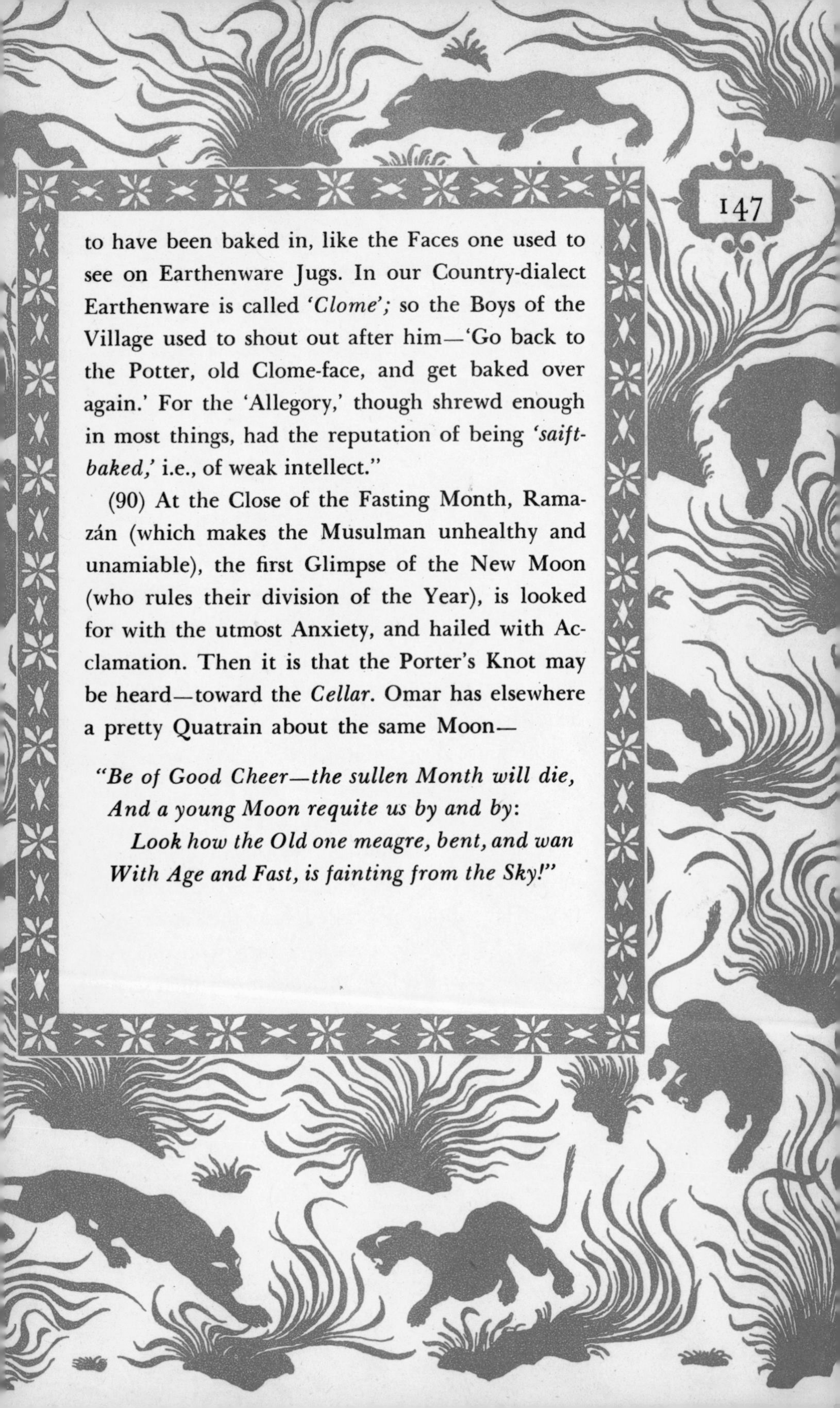

to have been baked in, like the Faces one used to see on Earthenware Jugs. In our Country-dialect Earthenware is called *'Clome'*; so the Boys of the Village used to shout out after him—'Go back to the Potter, old Clome-face, and get baked over again.' For the 'Allegory,' though shrewd enough in most things, had the reputation of being *'saift-baked,'* i.e., of weak intellect."

(90) At the Close of the Fasting Month, Ramazán (which makes the Musulman unhealthy and unamiable), the first Glimpse of the New Moon (who rules their division of the Year), is looked for with the utmost Anxiety, and hailed with Acclamation. Then it is that the Porter's Knot may be heard—toward the *Cellar*. Omar has elsewhere a pretty Quatrain about the same Moon—

"Be of Good Cheer—the sullen Month will die,
And a young Moon requite us by and by:
Look how the Old one meagre, bent, and wan
With Age and Fast, is fainting from the Sky!"

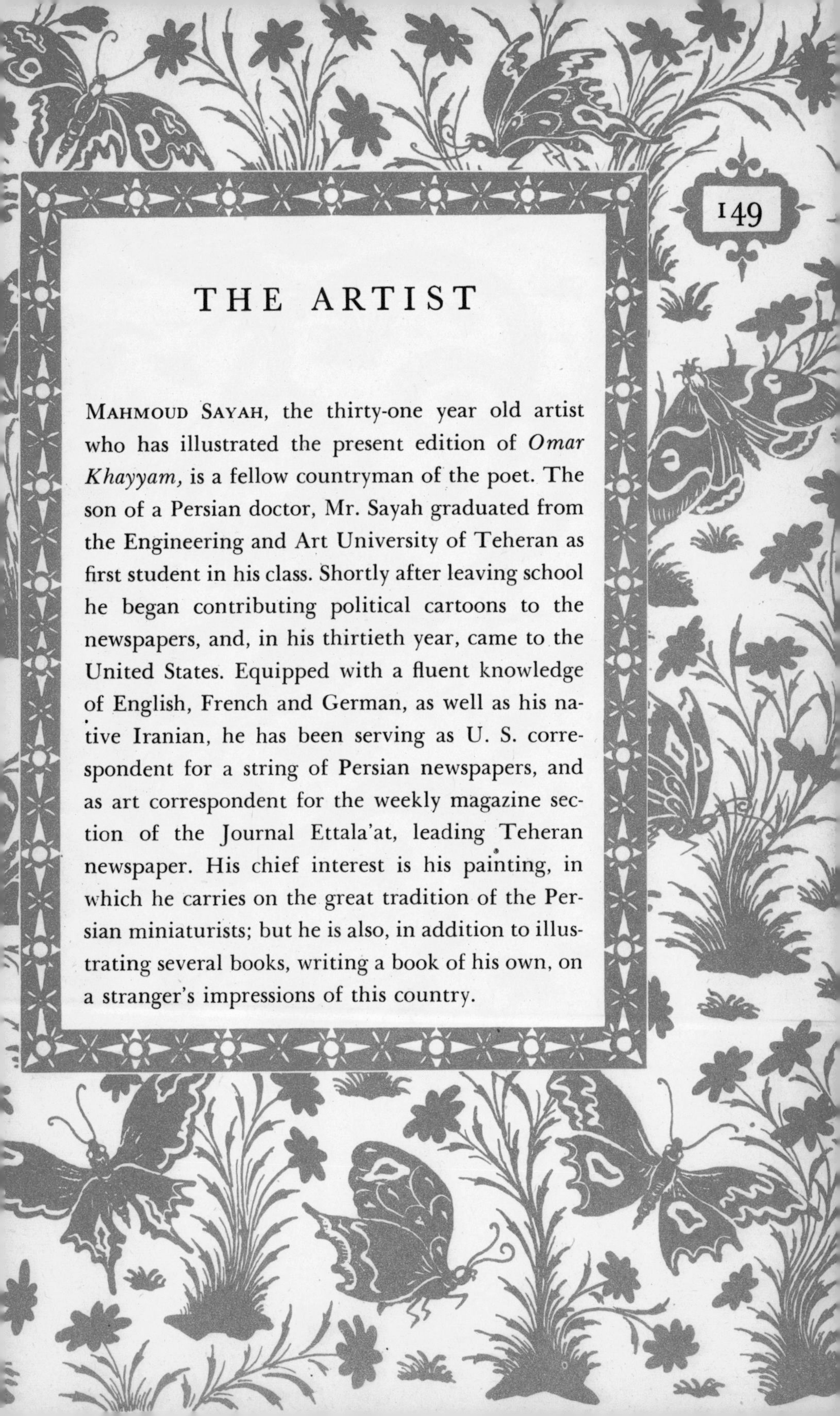

THE ARTIST

MAHMOUD SAYAH, the thirty-one year old artist who has illustrated the present edition of *Omar Khayyam,* is a fellow countryman of the poet. The son of a Persian doctor, Mr. Sayah graduated from the Engineering and Art University of Teheran as first student in his class. Shortly after leaving school he began contributing political cartoons to the newspapers, and, in his thirtieth year, came to the United States. Equipped with a fluent knowledge of English, French and German, as well as his native Iranian, he has been serving as U. S. correspondent for a string of Persian newspapers, and as art correspondent for the weekly magazine section of the Journal Ettala'at, leading Teheran newspaper. His chief interest is his painting, in which he carries on the great tradition of the Persian miniaturists; but he is also, in addition to illustrating several books, writing a book of his own, on a stranger's impressions of this country.